NO MAN IS AN ISLAND
NO MAN STANDS ALONE

Have you ever had the experience of déjà vu? The feeling that you have already been somewhere or seen something before?

Why do you feel compellingly drawn to certain people—even people you've only just met?

Do you feel a familiarity with distant locales or cultures such as the customs of ancient Greece or the rolling hills of bonny Ireland that you cannot explain?

Have you ever known that a particular outcome was inevitable, almost predestined?

This vivid trek through the mystical world of Edgar Cayce answers many questions about the evolution of the soul and about the loved ones who have been and continue to be our companions through time. At once an account of an astonishing life and a guide to fulfilling our spiritual potential, Intimates Through Time *proves that we are not in this life alone.*

INTIMATES THROUGH TIME

Edgar Cayce's Mysteries of Reincarnation

JESS STEARN

A SIGNET BOOK

SIGNET
Published by New American Library, a division of
Penguin Putnam Inc., 375 Hudson Street,
New York, New York 10014, U.S.A.
Penguin Books Ltd, 27 Wrights Lane,
London W8 5TZ, England
Penguin Books Australia Ltd, Ringwood,
Victoria, Australia
Penguin Books Canada Ltd, 10 Alcorn Avenue,
Toronto, Ontario, Canada M4V 3B2
Penguin Books (N.Z.) Ltd, 182–190 Wairau Road,
Auckland 10, New Zealand

Penguin Books Ltd, Registered Offices:
Harmondsworth, Middlesex, England

First published by Signet, an imprint of New American Library,
a division of Penguin Putnam Inc.

First Printing, March 1993
10 9 8 7 6 5 4 3 2 1

To Hugh Lynn Cayce,
who carried the torch
so that others would know the way—
and with gratitude to Tom Kay
for helping me along that way

Contents

Introduction

People have asked many times whether I knew Edgar Cayce, and I have always hesitated in replying. For though Cayce passed away some ten years before I ever heard his name, I do feel that I knew him very well and that his presence has been a big help to me in both my career and my personal life.

Whatever success I had with *Edgar Cayce—The Sleeping Prophet,* I attribute directly to Cayce. For in a very special way, from the other side, he not only gave me the title for the book but outlined the principal chapters, described how the book should be written, and predicted its eventual success.

At that time, some twenty years ago, I did not believe in life after death or the reality of reincarnation with its concept of an undying soul. I had looked at both but saw nothing I could consider proof, though I would have liked to do so, for it would have added an extra dimension to my life.

But something—call it destiny or synchronicity, the joining of people to activate a specific event—was to bring about a radical change in my outlook. I had just arrived in New York from California, where Jack O'Leary, a Doubleday executive, had suggested a book on Cayce. I was involved in another book but phoned my editor, Lee Barker, at Doubleday soon after I got in. He was on his way to an appointment, and before I could say hello, he said, "Drop by tomorrow, and we'll have lunch."

I was not too enthused about such a book, for there was very little interest in Cayce at the time. But as I put down the phone, the idea began to take hold of me. It was as though some invisible force were looking over my shoulder and directing my thinking. It was late, after eleven, but I started combing through some old files on Cayce, as though it were already settled that I would do the book.

The time seemed to fly, and just before one, fatigued by the plane trip, I decided to call it a night. At that precise moment the phone rang and a familiar voice boomed out. It was the spirit medium, Madam Bathsheba. And without the slightest preamble, she announced as casually as if she were introducing a friend, "Edgar Cayce just came to me. He wants you to know that he is very pleased that you will be doing a book on him."

A strange feeling came over me. I felt a sudden chill. Nobody in this world but Jack O'Leary and myself knew of the book. Moreover, I knew Bathsheba was not one to speak idly. Years before, at the Chicago World's Fair, she had warned Chicago's Mayor Anton Cermak not to get into the same automobile with a political figure greater than himself. Otherwise, he would pick up a bullet intended for the other and be mortally wounded. The mayor joked about it with reporters, some of whom remembered it later when an assassin, aiming for President-elect Franklin D. Roosevelt, fired a shot that struck and killed a fellow Democrat sitting next to him— Mayor Anton Cermak of Chicago.

So, although not much for spirits, I was instantly alerted by Madam Bathsheba's phone call. For, as I said, Madam Bathsheba was not one to speak lightly. Bathsheba had paused a moment, perhaps for dramatic effect. But I knew there had to be more, lots more, for her to call at such an hour. And there was.

"Cayce has a message for you," she said. "He wants you to listen very carefully."

I reached for pencil and paper. I had nothing to lose and possibly something to gain by taking down whatever came through. Who was I to say she was wrong, having no evidence to the contrary?

"He wants you to call the book *The Sleeping Prophet*," she said, "and this is what he wants you to put in it."

My pencil flew over the paper, for who could think of a better title for a book on Edgar Cayce?

"You are to describe the physical readings on people's health; his predictions of earth changes, toward the end

of the century, particularly; reincarnation and past lives—
very important; and his work with Doctor Ketchum, the
Yankee doctor."

I was writing so rapidly I didn't have time to think
about it.

"If you do as he tells you, the book will be an instant
best-seller, and you will finish it faster than any book
you have done before."

Thinking this was it, I had put my pencil to rest when
she added, with a little laugh, as though she had just
been told something amusing, "If you have trouble with
any chapter, just ask for help. Mister Cayce says he will
be looking over your shoulder until you finish."

I thanked Madam Bathsheba and told her to thank
Cayce for me. Looking back, I am not sure how much
of this influenced the book by instilling in me a feeling
of confidence. I did what Cayce had suggested, without
mentioning the incident to anybody at the time. After
months of research in Virginia Beach, I began writing
the book. It all went smoothly. I faltered over but one
chapter, that about Doctor Ketchum. Remembering
what Bathsheba had said, I meditated on it, visualizing
Edgar Cayce from his pictures and asking his help. Call
it what you like—the power of suggestion, the supernatural, imagination—but the writing block was removed,
and I finished the chapter in a couple of hours. I took
three weeks to write the book and had never approached
this writing time before nor have I since in some twenty-
five books. The advance sale of *The Sleeping Prophet*
to the stores was modest but satisfactory according to
Doubleday. And then something quite curious began to
happen. My editor, Lee Barker, phoned to say that reor-
ders were already coming in from the shops before publi-
cation, and nobody could understand why.

I could contain my secret no longer.

Barker laughed. "And you think Cayce is doing it?"

I laughed in return. "Well, he wrote it. And now he's
getting people to read it."

To date, the book has sold millions of copies all over
the world and helped generate dozens of Cayce books,
which sold millions more. Had I excluded Cayce there
would have been no book.

I don't believe I would have accepted any of this in

the beginning if it had not been for an earlier adventure into the psychic. It came at a time when my marriage had broken up, and I was considering another marriage. I had walked unannounced into a supper club on East 56th Street in New York City and, not seeing anybody I knew, had walked upstairs to the restrooms.

As I passed a small table, I noticed a dark, middle-aged woman spreading out some playing cards. She looked up with a smile.

"Would you like a reading?" she said.

I had absolutely no stomach for psychics and thought that anybody that went to one was a nut.

"What kind of reading?" I said with a frown.

"About your past, present, and future," she replied with a cheerful smile.

"Oh," I said turning away, "a fortune teller."

"I'm a sensitive," she said with a flash of anger. But she added in a more conciliatory tone, "I understand how you feel. You've just gone through a divorce. But you have two lovely children to show for it. Is that not true?"

I looked around the room suspiciously, wondering who had put her on. But there was nobody there. She smiled. "You shall be proud of your children one day. Your daughter shall be a healer, and your son will go into the law. Oh, not as a lawyer," she said hurriedly, as she read my face.

I still stood indecisively when she said casually, "You are thinking of getting married, but you will never meet with the girl again."

I immediately sat down, and she started fiddling with the cards.

What she saw seemed to surprise her, for her eyes opened wide.

"You are a newspaperman," she said, "but you won't be one long. You're going to write many books in my field." She looked up proudly, "And you will become widely known."

I restrained a laugh. For it did seem odd that anyone with my background would write about something that didn't even exist.

"What is your field?" I asked.

"The metaphysical," she said, almost impatiently. "You're going to write about me."

She returned to her cards. When she looked up her eyes had a distant look.

"Your third book will be a best-seller, and your eighth will spread around the world. You will write many bestsellers. In the latter part of your career you will write motion pictures and help direct them."

"And the girl," I said, "you don't see anything for us?"

"You will be married in seven or eight years to a beautiful blond girl, and you will alter her career. The other girl is gone, and it's just as well."

Maya Perez, who I got to know well over the years, had a pretty good batting average that evening. She was right, as it developed, in every detail.

I did leave the newspaper profession and turn to books. My third book, *The Sixth Man,* a study in male homosexuality, battered by the critics, did wind up on the *New York Times* best-seller list and stayed there for months. My eighth book was *The Sleeping Prophet.*

Twenty or twenty-five years later, my daughter was to become a physician and my son the head of an anticrime unit in the New York police department.

I wrote some twenty-five books, mostly on the metaphysical, and then turned to doing screenplays on two of my books: one on Edgar Cayce; the other, *The Search for the Girl with the Blue Eyes.*

Oh, I almost forgot. As for the girl, it was settled over the phone, and I never did get to meet with her again. I married a golden-haired beauty in eight years, as Maya said. She was a Radio City Rockette, in the front line center, so beautiful that with my encouragement she became a model and was an instant success.

I couldn't help thinking of what Maya had said that day of my eighth and upcoming book as I listened to Madam Bathsheba. But by this time, I knew enough about Cayce to think of him as a companion and friend. I had all the incentive I needed.

Quite often since I have felt Cayce's presence, and I would tell myself I was imagining it. But there was always a very real and tangible message. "You are to do three books on Edgar Cayce," a voice said, "and a motion picture."

Who else could it have been?

Hugh Lynn Cayce had already signed a movie contract with a Hollywood studio for a film on his father, and I had no intention of doing a second book on Cayce, not to mention a third. For what was there left to write?

As I shrugged to myself, the voice added, "That movie under contract will not be done."

Weeks later, Hugh Lynn phoned, saying he didn't like the movie script and had voided the agreement. "Would you write a book about a younger Edgar Cayce as the basis for a film?"

That became my second book on Cayce. It was called *The Prophet in His Own Country.* I followed this with a movie script. Though the movie has not yet been made, I have now completed the present book to round out the Cayce trilogy.

Edgar Cayce turned up in the strangest ways. On a trip to the West Coast to discuss the film, Hugh Lynn agreed to consult with a medium, with the proviso that the medium would be given no clue as to his identity. And, to his satisfaction, none was given.

As we drove into Hollywood for the session, Hugh Lynn mentioned that mediums were forever tuning into his father, once they knew that he, Hugh Lynn, was in the room. "That's why," he said, "I pay little attention to them."

As we walked into Maria Moreno's parlor, the medium gave Hugh Lynn a piercing look and immediately went into trance. She asked no questions. Speaking to him directly, she said, "You have been ill. You are still in pain."

I could see Hugh Lynn's start of surprise. He nodded. I had been expecting him three weeks earlier, but he had kept putting it off without giving a reason. And now I had the explanation.

As the sitting continued, Moreno reached over and touched Hugh Lynn's abdominal area. He winced, and I could see the shadow of pain cross his face.

"This is the problem," she went on. "But the spirit doctors shall fix it. The pain will disappear. You will be helped." Her eyes stared off into space. I could see that

Hugh Lynn was watching her intently, his skepticism on hold.

"There is somebody in the room that wants to talk to you," she said in a sepulchral voice. "His name is Eddie."

As much as I had written about Edgar Cayce, I had never heard him called Eddie. But I saw Hugh Lynn nodding, though still careful not to give anything away.

She closed her eyes, then kept repeating, "Eddie, Eddie, Eddie. He has a message for you."

And as Hugh Lynn's ears pricked up, her face lighted up with a radiant smile, and she cried, "Edgar Cayce is here. Edgar Cayce." She looked over at Hugh Lynn, her voice rising to a shrill crescendo as she exclaimed, "And you are his son. He's talking to you. He's saying he's glad you're here with Jess and that your movie will be made but to remember there will be some delay, till the time is right. It will be a big success."

I looked at Hugh Lynn. His face was expressionless. He had not moved a muscle. He would have made a great poker player. But he took Madam Moreno's hand after she came out of the trance and gave her a grateful smile. "Thank you," he said. "You are a gifted lady."

She shrugged. "I know nothing of what I say."

In the car, we looked at each other, and I could see that he was still impressed.

"Well," I said, "at least I know now why you were late."

He sighed. "I guess she said about what my dad would say if he came through."

I had no comment, for the experience was something that belonged to him.

"How about the pain?" I said. "Did she help you?"

He smiled. "It's gone."

There was little doubt in my mind that Hugh Lynn Cayce and I were the kind of companions his father had gathered around him so we could work out our left-over karma together. We often anticipated each other's thoughts, sought the same goals, and liked each other's company—all making for companionship.

Even God needed companionship, the great mystic said, and that was why he created the human soul and later cast it in his image, which is an image, Cayce added, that humanity had been trying to work up to ever since.

Universal law played no favorites. Everybody came back in groups, Cayce said, to be with the people they had shared a notable past with. There were no strangers in paradise.

"You are not alone," the mystic told the friends and travelers that came to his doorstep. "For you not only have the Lord as your companion but many you knew from the past who are with you in the present. Be not dependent on one another but go forward in a spirit of fellowship, as you are moved, to express yourself so that you may grow in love and valor."

Just as Cayce remembered them, so did his companions of old come to know him.

"With the rustling of a past-life memory," Cayce kept saying, "there is an emotional response as real and vivid as any real-life experience. What is déjà vu but thinking you have been someplace and known somebody before? Love at first sight is only an old love reborn and revived, waiting to be completed as it never was before."

In legendary Atlantis or on Main Street, Edgar Cayce concerned himself with the human need for love and companionship. "Without that feeling of being joined to another, of loving and being loved, there is a hollowness and aridity in life that inevitably diminishes the individual."

As I became familiar with what Edgar Cayce stood for, I began to better understand the relationships I found myself involved in.

When an elderly companion of Cayce's, who was nearing the century mark, looked me in the eye and said, "We all know you," I did not shrink back as I would have years before. Instead, I was able to take her hand and with a mist in my eye say, "Yes, and we are here to help each other in the same way today."

She smiled. For she understood, as I did, that some have a mission to spread the Cayce word, to kindle an energy that would bring hope to the heart of humanity, foreshadowing the universal peace that Cayce predicted, with Russia, transformed by a peaceful revolution, becoming "the hope of the world."

Cayce recorded lives in Egypt and in Troy, in the Holy

Land and in colonial America, and he shared all these lives with people he knew very well in this life. He was a wise man and a warrior, a healer and a wastrel—many things to many people. But above all he was a leader, a man to be reckoned with for his tremendous store of knowledge, which he shared with his old companions of then and now.

Some of his relationships were muddled, and some crystal clear. He had a lot to live up to and a lot to live down. He was a ladies' man and a great spiritual leader, known in antiquity as the man from Atlantis who had made Egypt the cradle of civilization on this speck of earth.

He was the great Ra, the Sun God who harnessed the Nile and built the Great Pyramids, and he remembered all this when he became Edgar Cayce, the twentieth-century mystic in America, the new cradle of civilization.

Some of the temptations of old, when he felt the normal lusts of a vigorous man, trickled into this life experience. But despite being confronted with mistresses and wives and sweethearts from the distant past, he mustered the will to keep his gift untainted for the first time in his various incarnations—and reaped the reward of a pure psychic gift, unparalleled since the Lord himself walked the earth two thousand years ago.

As I look back, I feel my own connection with Cayce was formed long before I ever heard of him. It had lain dormant in my consciousness, waiting to be triggered at a time when I was ready. And my readiness was reflected in the trust and companionship of the people who knew Cayce best. With this trust they had made me one of them, though as a reporter I had long stood outside their circle, content to look in from time to time and record their moving history.

My own karmic pattern explained the chance way—though there is no chance—that I heard of Cayce, my already having a psychic interest born of my earlier encounter with the psychic.

I was a typically skeptical reporter in New York City when I first heard Cayce's name. This was in 1956. I was doing an article on extrasensory perception (ESP) when I ran into David Kahn, a wealthy industrialist from Kentucky, who had made a fortune following Cayce's advice. He was almost frightening in his enthusiasm.

"You've got to write about Cayce," he said. "He's America's greatest mystic."

"Where do I find him?"

He pointed to the heavens.

"He passed on ten years ago, but his message lives on in Virginia Beach, where they've collected everything he ever said or did."

He smiled.

"Edgar Cayce always said that people meet for a reason, and I have a hunch we met so you would get to know about him."

As I recall, I was amused by his enthusiasm.

"And what is this message?" I asked.

"That all of us come into this life in groups, with companions we have known before, so that working with the same people we can learn and develop from the lessons of the past."

It was all new to me then, and I was somewhat incredulous. However, Kahn did appear to be what he was, a practical businessperson, a family man with a townhouse on New York's swank Park Avenue. He was obviously not a nut.

Five years later, on leaving newspaper work, I made my first visit to the Edgar Cayce Foundation in Virginia Beach.

I had no idea what I would find when I got there or what reception I would get. There was no reason for concern. Hugh Lynn Cayce, who headed up the foundation, welcomed me like a long-lost brother.

"I knew you would get here, sooner or later," he said, with a quiet smile.

The Cayce Foundation, housing the fifteen thousand Cayce metaphysical readings, had fewer than eight hundred life members, a ramshackle headquarters building with a small library, and no financial resources.

I had come down on a weekend, and the library was closed for lack of staff. But Hugh Lynn, delegated by his father to keep the work alive, pulled in a couple of volunteer workers to keep the library open and help me with whatever information I wanted.

Nobody could have been more generous of his time,

so solicitous that I mentioned it in wonder to a Cayce aficionado.

"I never met the man before, yet he acts like an old friend."

She laughed and said, "Who knows, he may well be."

The puzzle was soon cleared up. I was sitting at a library table that evening going through one of the folders stacked up on a table in front of me. I found it fascinating, for it was a Cayce reading on curing cancer, and I was totally absorbed when I was interrupted by Hugh Lynn.

"You might be interested in this Cayce work reading," he said, plucking a musty page from its folder. It was advice from Cayce, given in his sleep, on how to get the Cayce information before a broader audience. I scanned the reading; it was given in the Depression year 1931.

"It may surprise you," I heard Hugh Lynn saying, looking at me expectantly as my eye traveled down the page, stopping at a paragraph he had pointed out. It did surprise me. For if nothing else, it explained my reception.

"Be good to Stern," it said, giving a phonetic twist to my name, "when he comes down from New York City, for he will contribute much to the financial success of the organization."

I saw Hugh Lynn's eyes probing mine.

I was not impressed. There were many people by that name in New York. And, at the time, I had not the slightest idea of how I could help financially, had I wanted to.

Hugh Lynn showed me still another folder. The message was pretty much the same, that same year, when I was a boy, living some distance from New York. I shrugged and returned the folder, eager to get on with my reading. But Hugh Lynn was adamant. He brought forth still another folder.

I ran my eye over the page he indicated and stopped with a start. Butterflies fluttered in my stomach, and I was speechless for a moment. For in this Cayce reading, again in 1931, Cayce had suggested that Kahn, Dave Kahn, contact me and tell me about his work, with the usual injunction that I would then be helpful.

My mind flew back five years. At the time, 1956, Dave

Kahn had said we had met for a reason. And now Hugh Lynn was showing me that reason. I saw that he was watching me closely, observing my reaction, but I was not about to make a declaration, not before I thought it through. I had lived half a lifetime, questioning everything I saw and read, and I could not change overnight.

The next day I still hadn't mentioned the Kahn incident to Hugh Lynn. My reporter's mind kept thinking of ways the reading could have been improvised, even though there was no evidence of it. The page excerpted was of the same vintage as the others.

Now intrigued by Cayce, I decided to write a book about the metaphysical. It would include the work of many psychics, but principally the old master, Edgar Cayce. I had come for the weekend and stayed for months. Before I left I had recorded the many wonders performed by Cayce on the minds and bodies of the people who came to him for help. Every person receiving help not only felt a deep attachment to Cayce but considered him a special friend who had a strong influence on their life. "He was minister, doctor, and companion/counselor," explained sailing master Noah Miller, adding cryptically, "We felt we had always known him."

Cayce had made predictions that made the Kahn prophecy seem child's play. Long before Hitler's advent, he foresaw the Nazi dictator's rise, the start of World War II, the battle of Kursk that decided the war on the Russian front, and the end of the war in August 1945.

How could I question whether he had foreseen the arrival of a newspaper reporter? Not when he foresaw—long before Gorbachev—Russia's amazing turnabout. And glasnost.

The Door to the Future, published early in 1963, stirred considerable attention because it carried Jeanne Dixon's prediction of President Kennedy's assassination. As a popular book, it did bring the Cayce work to many people. But with *The Sleeping Prophet,* five years later, the life membership in Cayce's Association for Research and Enlightenment (A.R.E.) quickly jumped to more than 20,000. It kept mounting as the book fueled other books, until today there are nearly 100,000 members and a large new library that is the center for demonstrations and lectures on the metaphysical, serving visitors from all over the world.

Meanwhile, I became involved in Cayce books, Cayce films, Cayce lectures. It sometimes seemed that was what all my life was about—Edgar Cayce.

Though some questioned it, Dave Kahn had no doubt about my preexistence in the shadowy subconscious of his boon companion.

"You are the only one of that name I sent," he said, "and the only one I know who helped."

I got more credit than I deserved, without realizing how it must have minimized a son who had struggled all his life to keep his father's legacy alive.

Then one day, my doorbell rang in my beach house in California, and Hugh Lynn and his wife Sally stood outside my door.

Sally, with a sweet Southern smile, said in a determined drawl, "I have come to bring you boys together."

I laughed. "I didn't know we were apart." I turned to Hugh Lynn who had an amused smile on his face.

"If not for you, Hugh Lynn," I said, as Sally nodded, "there never would have been a me. For you held your father's torch aloft during all those lonely years when few would listen."

I saw the suspicion of a tear in his eye. And I knew there was one in mine.

Our connection was typical of the ties between the old companions who built their lives around the old master. There was a communication, beyond words, that appeared to keep us constantly in touch, almost as if we were on the same party line.

Sometime later, sensing Hugh Lynn was seriously ill, I had a sudden urge to see him. It was almost a compulsion. I booked a plane that very day and walked into his office the following morning.

He looked a little worn, but he still had a gritty smile and a hearty handshake.

"That was fast," he said. "I sent you a letter only yesterday saying I wanted to see you."

"I didn't get the letter," I said, "but I got the message."

We sat and looked at each other, as old friends will,

taking stock of all that had gone between them over the years.

"You've softened and grown gentler with the years," he decided.

"You've grown more tolerant," I said.

We both smiled.

He was not one to beat around the bush.

"I'll be leaving things in pretty good shape," he said. "My son Charles has already taken over many functions I once had. I'm sure he'll be fine."

As I made a move to demur at the obvious conclusion he had come to about himself, he waved me down with a chuckle.

"I know where I'm going. I've been there before. And I'll be back. But, meanwhile, I would like my old friends to rally around my son as they have me."

His piercing blue eyes looked resolutely into mine.

"You know I will," I said. "But . . ."

Again he held up a hand.

"Sing no sad songs for me. I go to join a merry company. And who knows but what I may see Dad again while we're biding our time wherever the good Lord wants us to be."

Two weeks later, with a smile, this gallant gentleman had moved on to a greater adventure, believing as his father did that the soul lives on into eternity.

Part I

EDGAR CAYCE THROUGH TIME

CHAPTER 1

The First Reincarnation

On this particular day Edgar Cayce went into trance, and when he awakened an hour later his whole world had changed.

For to Edgar Cayce, as to no other person in two thousand years, the meaning of death was made clear that day.

Looking at the incredulous faces around him as he came out of his subconscious state, he immediately sensed that something extraordinary had occurred.

"What did I say this time?" he said with a smile.

Arthur Lammers shook his head.

"All you told me," he said, "was that I had lived another life before and had been a monk in that life."

Lammers, too, looked around at the few friends who had witnessed the reading and saw they were as dumbfounded as he was. For all Lammers had asked was a simple question about his horoscope.

"If you are right, Cayce," the Ohio businessman went on with a bemused look, "there is no such thing as death. For if I lived before, so has everybody else."

Cayce looked at him with a troubled frown. "I don't know where it came from," he said, "for I know nothing about reincarnation. Nor as a Christian Fundamentalist do I believe in it."

Lammers appeared eager to go on to another reading. He was a successful printer, thirty-three years old, knowledgeable about metaphysical matters. He was interested in expanding his horizons.

"Don't you realize the significance of what you said? You not only made me a monk in Spain but said it was my third appearance on this plane."

Cayce's eyes were closed, and he appeared to be meditating. Always before he had counseled people, telling them what they needed to know. He would go to sleep and diagnose the illnesses of people he had never seen and prescribe the remedies that cured them, even sending them with prescriptions to doctors he didn't know.

Now it was something different, something he didn't believe in, and he didn't know what to do about it.

The reading had taken place in Lammers's hometown of Dayton, Ohio, on November 11, 1923. That year had been one of decision for Cayce in which he took on Gladys Davis as his assistant and made the move from his photographic studio in Selma, Alabama, to Virginia Beach. He was being told something, but it was contrary to anything he saw in Scripture. It was a week before he gave Lammers a second reading.

Again he got a past life, but this time it was coupled with a warning. In this reading he touched for the first time on karma, a debit and credit ledger of life that carries over from one life to the next and that must be dealt with if the individual is to develop. All this he said as he cautioned against vanity or ego in dwelling on past lives.

"In those laws of the Creator we see the plan of development of individuals set upon this plane [earth], to manifest the ability in the physical to enter again into the presence of the Creator and become a full part of that Creation. For that, this body [Lammers] was put upon this plane."

As I read it, Lammers was an instrument, chosen to bring out Cayce's first reading on reincarnation, just as Jesus healed the blind man so the world would know of his miracles. Lammers's life as a monk was of no great consequence.

By this time there was no stopping Lammers. "I want to know more about man's greater purpose in life," he cried.

He would have had life readings all day had Cayce agreed. Imagine, a monk in Spain! How intriguing! It beat printing. And what of the two other lives?

Lammers had six readings within two weeks. Two were lost—not at all unusual before Gladys Davis took over the transcribing of Cayce's remarks. As he read over the readings, Cayce's interest was developing, but he still didn't know what to make of it.

"Perhaps I was the catalyst," Lammers said. "The information was there; it just needed somebody sufficiently interested to bring it out."

Cayce looked at him doubtfully. "Why me?"

"Maybe this is what your gift is all about. Not to heal a few scattered people here and there, but to bring hope of eternal life to the multitudes."

Cayce sighed. "Lammers, I don't know even know what I'm saying."

"Your health readings are correct, so why shouldn't the life readings be correct?" Lammers smiled. "They all came out of the same bottle."

Lammers had received the first reading on a date with an exalted quality—number eleven, month and day. The number twenty-two had equal significance. So he asked for still another reading on November 22. This coupled the eleven and the twenty-two, when he felt Cayce's intuitive powers would be at a celestial high. Cayce, blissfully unaware of all this, agreed reluctantly to another life reading. It was not a lengthy reading. But when Cayce was told what he had said, he was as startled as he had been before. For in this reading Cayce not only spoke of Lammers's past lives but of somebody he knew even better than Lammers—himself.

As he went over the reading later, his eyes boggled. For he not only attributed a second life as a Trojan warrior to Lammers but he, too, became a Trojan warrior, a keeper of the gates when the Greeks were storming Troy three thousand years ago.

A Trojan warrior—this hardly suited Cayce's picture of himself. Looking into the mirror he saw a tall, spare figure with rounded shoulders and a chronic stoop, and he had to smile. He looked like anything but an ancient warrior.

"I'm more and more confused," he told Lammers.

Lammers was more and more excited.

"Don't you see, Cayce? We knew each other before. And that's why we've come together again. I'm more sure of it now than I ever was. It's the way reincarnation works. We were companions in arms once: now we're companions in spirit."

He looked at Cayce with a new light in his eye. "We have found our higher purpose."

Cayce scratched his head. "To what purpose?"

"Don't you see?" cried an enthusiastic Lammers. "To have the meaning of death made clear!"

Cayce looked away and pondered. He was still strangely troubled. Always before he had understood what he had said in trance, knowing that it was true. For there were people, with recognizable features, names, and addresses, who validated the readings by having been helped by them.

"You've given me something to think about, Lammers," he said. "And that's what I want to do now—think about it."

He really had something to think about. For he had given himself two more lives. By now he was properly confused. Here were lives in colonial Virginia and Troy, both so dissimilar, and a third at the time of Richelieu, the baleful cardinal of France in the uneasy reign of Louis XIII. It made no sense at all, not in his eyes. He decided there would be no more life readings until he had thought it through and had a better idea of what it all meant.

He was plagued by misgivings. He didn't know Lammers very well—not in this lifetime, anyway—and had even considered that Lammers might be pulling his leg.

He was caught between two rocks. If authentic, the Lammers readings posed a pressing moral problem, for they authenticated reincarnation. And there was no place in the fundamentalist Christian church, of which he was a devoted member, for heretical concepts such as reincarnation. He had nobody close to talk it over with. He had left his wife back in Selma, Alabama, with the children and Gladys Davis, the young aide who had become a part of the household.

He asked himself, Was it a sin to think of reincarnation in the same breath as Christ and God? Would he be forever damned if he did anything to accredit this discredited doctrine?

Lammers tried to put him at ease. "Reincarnation was a Judeo-Christian concept. And it's in the Bible, if you look for it. The pharisees believed in reincarnation. And some of it still remains in elements of Christianity." He shrugged. "If you consider Asia, most of the world population believes in it."

Cayce was not convinced. He was more concerned about what his Sunday school class would think about it.

Karma was a new and alien word. He looked it up in the dictionary, not finding it anywhere in his Bible. Webster had something to say about it. It was a form of Nirvana. But wasn't that a never-never land, a state of passive peace where nothing happened and nothing got done? He looked further, to another definition: Karma, the work a person does. "The force generated by a person's actions, held in Hinduism and Buddhism to be the motive power for the round of deaths and rebirths endured by him until he has achieved spiritual liberation and freed himself from the effects of that force."

One thing stuck out in his consciously logical mind. Why wasn't there some kind of remembrance—any kind—to provide some evidence of a questioned past?

"If we have past lives, why can't we remember them?" Cayce asked, as people have asked for centuries.

Lammers had studied what the Indian gurus had to say about a doctrine that was a crucial part of their faith.

"Then we would be burdened and influenced by the past and not have the free will to deal with conditions and problems formed in the past. We'd never learn anything. Without consciously knowing who we have been, we react to the way we handled our problems in our previous lives—love, finances, food, sex. That's where our aptitudes come from, carried over, often, from what we've been before."

Cayce had not gone beyond the fifth grade. But his perceptive mind saw an obvious inconsistency.

"So why did I remember?"

Lammers had a ready answer.

"The subconscious mind is a storehouse of all of our experiences and thoughts in all our incarnations. Nothing is forgotten or lost by the subconscious. You are speaking from something you knew in the past, with a subconscious that is rather unique."

Faced with what seemed an insoluble dilemma, Cayce was glad to get back to Selma and a wife he could talk things over with. She had always been good that way, as though she had always been there waiting to listen to him and comfort him.

Gertrude Cayce knew he was troubled, but as always,

she waited for him to speak, as if she knew instinctively the best way to draw him out of himself.

One evening, after the children were in bed, he finally sat down and told her what had transpired in Dayton.

"I always thought," he said, "that people's lives were influenced purely by the present. They were born in this world to love and work, beget children, and to die, facing the judgment of the Lord in death as in life. All that I find myself saying about past lives and reincarnation is alien to everything I've ever believed. And yet Lammers tells me I not only gave him three lives in the past but had three of my own, maybe more, one with him in ancient Troy, when he was Hector and I guarded the gate."

Gertrude looked at his solemn face and smiled.

"Could I have been Helen of Troy?"

He laughed. "Why not?"

She half-sighed, for it was not always easy to be married to a man who saw things nobody else did and heard voices no other person did.

"I see no reason why you shouldn't look into it," she said. "It is no stranger than healing people you have never seen, with remedies you never heard of."

She thought for a moment.

"Why not do some of these life readings on yourself?" She looked over with a smile at Gladys Davis, who had been listening. "And on Gladys and myself. Who knows what we were back in those olden times?" She smiled. "That would be more fun than sitting around wondering about it."

He nodded. "All right, looking at it that way. But first I've got some other reading to do." And he picked up the weathered Bible his grandfather had given him, the same grandfather who had showed the four-year-old Edgar how to douse for water and had predicted, "One day you will do much more."

His grandfather's prediction had puzzled him then, but he was always reminded of it as he went about his reading of the Bible each day.

Now he reread his Bible, trying to find allusions he may have overlooked before. For Lammers had told him that reincarnation was clearly mentioned in the Bible. "Some people read it in, and some read it out."

With a new perspective he read lines he had once passed over. He became excited as he pointed out these passages to Gertrude. from the Book of John he read aloud:

"I say unto thee, except a man be born again, he cannot see the kingdom of God."

And Nicodemus, the Pharisee leader, asked Jesus, "How can a man be born when he is old? Can he enter a second time into his mother's womb and be born?"

And Jesus replied, "Except a man be born of water and of the spirit, he cannot enter into the kingdom of God."

Cayce had puzzled over the next statement until its meaning burst on him like a bolt of lightning.

"No man," he quoted from John, "hath ascended up to heaven but he that came down from heaven, even the Son of man which is in heaven."

His excitement grew as he turned to Gertrude. "Can't you see what Jesus is saying? It never struck me before. Nobody leaves this earth plane without having first come down from heaven. So how did they get there unless they lived before and were reborn?"

Night after night the two of them pored over the Bible. Sometimes Gladys would join them. She seemed rather mature for her eighteen years, and she saw in reincarnation a possible reason for her easy familiarity with Edgar and Gertrude.

In the Book of John Cayce now recalled a familiar passage that posed a new meaning for him.

"And his disciples asked him, saying, 'Master, who did sin, this man or his parents, that he was born blind?' "

"I read that passage a dozen times," Cayce said, "and its significance escaped me. How could a newborn child have sinned? It was impossible unless he had a past life."

He turned to a passage in which Jesus had told a crowd of hecklers, "Before Abraham was I am."

They mocked him, saying, "How can that be, thou are not yet fifty years old, and thou has seen Abraham?"

And Jesus replied, "I know him. And if I say I know him not, I shall be a liar like unto you."

Cayce smiled as he looked at Gertrude and saw that her eyes were shining. He had thought to make her a devil's advocate, the role he took with Lammers, but instead she had become a believer.

He was still not convinced. For the rigid Fundamentalism of his early religious training clung to him like a wet shroud.

The Transfiguration had a strong effect on Cayce. He read it through again and again, especially where Christ, with Peter, James, and John, came down from the mountain after seeing a vision of Christ with Moses and Elijah. Christ charged his disciples to tell this vision to no one until he was risen again.

And his disciples asked, "Why then say the scribes that Elijah must first come?"

[Jesus answered], "I say unto you that Elijah is come already, and they knew him not but have done to him whatsoever they listed. Likewise shall the Son of man suffer of them."

Then the disciples understood that he spake unto them of John the Baptist.

As he finished the passage, Edgar looked at his wife, almost quizzically. "If they weren't talking about reincarnation, what were they talking about?"

But old doubts lingered on, and Cayce, as Gertrude had suggested, turnd to his own subconscious mind for reassurance and found it.

"The readings," he told a friend, "say that when the church leaders decided to carry the faith to all peoples, they decided to drop the idea of reincarnation. Thinking they'd have other chances, a lot of people stopped worrying about what they were doing. And some, losing their fear of authority on the strength of feeling immortal, thumbed their noses at the church and government.

"This was something the Holy Roman Empire would not long endure, and so they discouraged the notion of anybody getting a second chance, or even a third and fourth."

In his readings he discovered the soul, that intangible essence of a person that never died but continued to live on after the physical body expired. As Benjamin Franklin had said so picturesquely of his own immortal soul, it returned like a book with a new cover.

He had found a pathway to the soul in his own subconscious.

"In the subconscious," his subconscious reported, "there is a record of all the lives of the soul, not only on this planet or in this solar system, but in other areas of space, which could be a thought and energy form or any star or celestial body in an infinite universe."

And what of this subconscious mind of his? How could he rely on it with this new revelation that was as broad as the universe? He did a reading on the source of his information. And he was told that his particular subconscious was that of an old soul who had developed psychically over the ages until his subconscious, tuning into a universal subconscious, could tap the knowledge of any subconscious mind in any lifetime.

It was indeed a unique gift, exalted in this experience, as the need grew for humanity to heed the warning that "as a man soweth, so shall he reap."

The quest for the past drew the little family back to Dayton and a reading in which Edgar Cayce was asked about his present purpose and his past lives. Gladys Davis took the notes, while Gertrude and the Cayce son, Hugh Lynn, rounded out the circle.

The question was one of Cayce's own choosing, as he sought subconsciously to bring into context the associations that conditioned and influenced his life. The hypnotic suggestion was a model for the many hundreds of life readings to follow.

"You will give the relation of this entity [Cayce] and the universal forces, giving the conditions that are latent and exhibited in the present life. Also the former appearance on earth which built or retarded the development for the entity, giving the abilities of the present entity and to that which it may attain."

"Yes, we have the entity here," responded a sleeping Cayce. "In this sojourn, we find the entity has reached that plane where the mental and the environmental forces have set the conditions for the present sojourn, yet there are many urges to be satisfied in the earth's plane."

It seemed a little odd to expect an objective analysis

of character from the man whose character was the object of that analysis. But Cayce did seem quite objective—even critical—of himself in trance.

"One to many peoples very contradictory in thought, action, and deed. One little understood or comprehended by the greater mass of people. One given to be very eccentric in many ways. That finds very little capacity to be moderate, in one condition or another. This we find often brings the destructive elements to much that might be accomplished in a more moderate manner."

His listeners got more than they bargained for. As though a hangover from the past, he mentioned his constant struggle in this life to curb physical urges nagging him in his sojourns in other spheres.

"For in the flesh we find the mental, soul, and spirit become the subjugations to the wishes, the desires, of the carnal forces, and the urge then of the individual in the earth plane is governed by the direction in which these urges are guided."

He was almost painfully candid. "We find there are many [urges] in the present sphere not guided in the manner that the development has been to that point where it should be."

He didn't blame all these urges on the ethereal past, saying some were from sojourns in the earth as well—to be fought and conquered in this life.

"One who finds much in the scope or sphere of intrigue in secret love affairs. One given often to the conditions that have to do with the affairs of the heart and of those relations that have to do with sex."

But there was a better and redemptive side in which he triumphed over the vagaries of his past and, in his words, "found the greater strength in spiritual forces, developing to a point in this time where he would bring, through psychic forces, peace and quiet to the multitudes."

But it was not that easy, not for Cayce or any of his lifetime companions. It was a new concept for the West, not easy to follow when there was no proof to fall back on and public ridicule to deal with. But still, from what Cayce had to say, one could understand something more of the past and anticipate the future. He made it all seem so plausible. "Almost too plausible," his son Hugh Lynn once said with a smile.

At this stage, still at the crossroads of my search for life's greater meaning, I found Cayce provocative, opening up a whole new avenue of thought, indeed a whole new world.

To examine Cayce was to define reincarnation and immortality as well. The growing swell of interest in reincarnation in the West was due largely to the impact of his life readings. To learn what I could of the continuity of the soul, I thought it significant not only to scrutinize what he said and thought of his own past lives and their impact, but what so many of those he shared lives with in the present had to say about their past lives with him, and their influence on the present.

Examining Cayce's many lives, seeing him as his contemporaries saw him under hypnosis, it was easy to see his development into the unique figure he was to become, finally triumphing in this life experience, after a tumultuous inner struggle, over the carnal desires that plagued him through his seven exciting life experiences.

It became apparent as I examined the lives that jibed with his through the ages that a compulsive life pattern or karma drew the various people he dealt with into the life of the man who had many times been their leader. Some, not knowing at the time why they had been drawn, gave up homes elsewhere and came to Virginia Beach to be close to him and revel again in his wisdom. Some had been his soulmates down through time. And as he explained, love at first sight was an instant recognition of a love in the past, inexorable in its compulsive joining of men and women.

"Not all appearances [past lives] were given," as Cayce noted, "but those influencing or having a bearing in a greater manner on the individual.

"The expressions of a soul-entity [continuity of the soul] are influenced by what an entity [individual] has done regarding its ideal in a given experience. For the entity's development in the process of application of self makes for the varied effects. Hence, it is conditions rather than personalities that are to be met in relationships in varied experiences. These should not be confusing, yet to many who hold so much to personality they become so."

It was confusing to me. Yet I knew it was important that this point be fully understood. For in Cayce's own lives, one saw his personality on a constant roller coaster, up and down; now a high priest and virtual ruler of Egypt, then a humble warrior in Troy or a profligate ne'er-do-well scout in colonial America.

"What," I asked Jeanette Thomas, the administrator of the Cayce records, "did Cayce mean by conditions, not personalities?"

She had a ready answer, for she was familiar with the question.

"It means that if you're trying to understand how somebody that was Julius Ceasar had fallen to an estate where he was now a street cleaner, you'd have to get away from the personality image you had of Caesar and think of him as an ordinary man doing whatever he did to people to get where he did."

Not all life cycles had a part in molding the individual, as seen in a thumbnail sketch of Cayce's seven lives.

In Atlantis, long ago, he was the male half of a twin soul, and his name was Asule. He played an active role in the development of that legendary land known as the Lost Continent, where humanity was a thought-form—in the beginning—and the civilization more advanced than ours.

After that came a lifetime in Egypt, as the high priest Ra-Ta, a great metaphysician ostensibly forced into exile because of an affair with a lady belonging to another. "Again we find the entity falling in the way of the flesh, and fleshly carnal forces brought destructive elements to the entity."

Then in the city of the hills and plains in Persia, the life experience where, as the tribal chief Uhjltd, he further developed the psychic gift, starting up many healing centers. "From this plane we find the psychic forces related with the spiritual development which become accentuated at the present time."

In Troy as Xenon, the keeper of the gates, he allowed his mistress to persuade a curious people to haul in the wooden horse quartering Greek troops who put Troy to the torch and brought the fair Helen of Troy back to Sparta.

In Judea, at the time of Christ, he emerged as the disciple Lucius of Cyrene, mentioned in the Bible, again involved with women.

In France, and then colonial Virginia, he again indulged his sexual appetite and fathered an illegitimate child, between feats of heroism. And of course in this life, he disclosed a more complex and earthy character than is usually attributed to a spiritual nature.

In considering this plain, folksy philosopher, I had no idea he was ever assailed by the temptations plaguing the ordinary person. Yet while this was pertinent, it paled into insignificance before the burning question of how his life readings, tying in the past with the present, validated the continuity of life.

I had looked for instances outside Cayce's personal experience where there was a subconscious remembrance that independently established the continuity of the soul. I particularly noted the story of the young mother who asked Cayce for a life reading because of her unreasoning fear of the lions in a municipal zoo. She refrained from advising the mystic of the nature of the problem so as not to provoke some pat reply. Ordinarily, indulging her fear, she would have stayed away from the zoo. But she had two small boys who doted on the lion cage. They were almost violently alienated when their mother took them by the arm and dashed off with them when the lion so much as bared his teeth.

Cayce tuned in immediately.

The woman had lived before in Rome in the biblical period. And as a Christian, who would not put the emperor above her God, she was thrown into the arena. There, clawed by a lion, she had a terrible end.

How neat and tidy it was. While her conscious mind had forgotten, the subconscious remembered. No psychoanalyst could have been more helpful. With her fears explained in understandable terms, fear was banished. Something more than a domestic drama was resolved.

As he strove to keep the carnal thoughts he deplored out of his mind, Cayce's subconscious opened up, and he began to get impressions in the waking state of the soul that never died, reaffirming humanity's immortality to his satisfaction.

Quite often he speculated how he would let friends know of his survival once he had passed over. He had a friendly discussion about this with a close friend, Madison Byron Wyrick, the manager of the Western Union Telegraph Company in Chicago. "The question frequently arose between us," he recalled, "as to whether or not there was a survival of personality. It usually ended jokingly with one of us saying, 'Well, whichever one goes first will communicate with the other.' "

One day, some years later, he was notified of Wyrick's death. Intermittently, he thought about what they had discussed. And occasionally he would meditate about his friend, visualizing him as he had last seen him, with a smile on his face.

Wyrick had been out of Cayce's thoughts for a while when he was sitting alone in his living room in Virginia Beach, listening to the radio. The program was a popular one at the time in which Seth Parker appeared with a song group. Members of the group had decided they would sing songs their loved ones had been fond of during their lifetimes.

"One lady," Cayce recalled, "asked that they sing 'Sweet Hour of Prayer.' Another asked this lady which one of her husbands had liked that song. I remember that I was very much amused and leaned back in my chair, smiling to myself."

But not for long. Suddenly, he felt, with his heightened consciousness, that he was not alone.

"I felt as if there was a presence in the room. I was suddenly cold and felt there was something uncanny taking place, something I didn't quite comprehend. Meanwhile, the program was continuing, sharpening my reality of the difference between the obvious reality and what I was feeling. I was in a sort of twilight zone. For when I turned my eyes toward the radio, I saw my friend sitting in front of the radio as if listening to the program. He turned and smiled at me, saying, 'There is the survival of personality. I know that now. And a life of service and prayer is the only one to live.' "

For a moment Cayce thought he was dreaming. But his body and mind told him differently.

"I was shaking all over. I was that affected. But he said nothing more and seemed to disappear."

Cayce listened for a few moments until the program finished. He sat motionless for a while as if glued to his seat. Then he got up, after what seemed an eternity, and turned off the radio. But the chill remained, as though his body had been drained of its energy.

"It still appeared as if the room was full of some presence. As I switched off the light and climbed the stairs to my bedroom, I could still hear voices coming from the darkened room."

Jumping into his bed, still shivering from the cold, he awakened his wife. She drowsily asked why he hadn't turned off the radio, as he was still asking himself whether he was imagining it all.

"I assured her that I had turned off the radio. She opened the bedroom door and said, 'I hear it—I hear voices.' "

He was still too caught up in the experience to talk about it. But with his wife hearing the voices as well, he was sure now that his friend had chosen that moment to make his presence felt.

He leaned over his wife's shoulder and could hear the voices. "The words weren't distinct. But catching a word every now and then, I thought I heard somebody saying, 'Now you know.' But I could not be sure. I was never sure of the wording, not like I was of the message. There was no doubt in my mind that a friendly wager had been fulfilled."

CHAPTER 2

Cayce the Man

Edgar Cayce built his life around the people who came
to him for help. As they wandered into his studio, many
impelled without knowing why, he recognized some from
his own past, while others were made known in the life
readings themselves. Some of the men, like Kahn, had
been his aides in a past life in Egypt where he had been
a high priest with the power to heal. Among the women
were former wives, sweethearts, and mistresses who
brought into this life some of their earlier influence.

As he gleaned from his own past, he was not always
on the spiritual path, and so he made a heroic effort in
this experience to reach a spiritual peak not previously
achieved. It was not always easy.

These reunions had considerable significance. They
provided a coming together to continue the unfinished
labors and relationships of the past and gave him the
stimulation he needed to carry on. Ruth Burks, a one-
time magazine editor, was one of his guiding lights, even
though he saw her infrequently. As they had in biblical
times, their minds reached out and touched the other.
Like so many of these companion connections, it began
with a life reading. Coincidence seemed to play a part in
its onset, though Cayce himself never held with coincidence. It was all written out of the past, said he, to be
molded in the present, and foreshadowing the future. It
appeared to happen without plan. Ruth had been visiting
in Virginia Beach, not quite sure what had taken her
there, when she first heard Cayce's name and felt an
overpowering urge to meet him.

"I couldn't explain this impulse," she said, "but on
seeing him I felt I had always known him."

And so she had, according to her reading. For in this
shadowy world as Martha, a relative of Peter, she wove

the robe Christ wore to the cross and knew Cayce as
Lucius of Cyrene, a disciple of Paul, mentioned in the
Bible.

Although the reading took place nearly fifty years ago,
in August 1943, the then Ruth Buckwalter, married to
Leon Buckwalter, a successful businessman, remembered
every detail.

The communication between the seer and his subject
was almost instant. After that first reading, he had taken
her hand and thanked her for helping him. She was
puzzled.

"I don't see how I helped you," she said. "I didn't do
anything."

He explained that when he gave a reading he went out
into space on a beam of light to the source of universal
knowledge. On either side of the beam were obstructive
forces, but her presence, he told her, kept him on a
straight course.

She was drawn to his work, as she had been in the
storied past, and asked if she could help in any way.

Overburdened at this time with wartime readings for
worried parents, he needed whatever help he could get
from old friends.

"You can meditate when you get home," he said,
"whenever I am giving a reading." So on her return to
her home in Lancaster, Pennsylvania, given a time, she
would sit quietly by herself and concentrate on Cayce in
his Virginia Beach study.

She did this every day he gave a reading. But one
day, interrupted by a visitor, she had to break off her
meditation.

"Mister Cayce wrote the next day, saying, 'Where
were you yesterday? I couldn't finish the reading.' "

I had heard so much of her Cayce connection that I
had gone to Lancaster to see her. She was living in a
Mennonite retreat, and as before, she was performing
good works, reading to the blind, wheeling the crippled,
and generally looking after anybody with a problem. And
she was eighty-seven.

As we sat together, chatting, there were no restraints
between us. "You must have been around then, too,"
she said.

I smiled. "I guess we all were, if one was."

I kept thinking of what she had just told me.

For besides revealing their closeness, it spelled out a very powerful mind.

She laughed. "Well, I was the editor of *Mind Digest*."

When her husband died, she married Colonel Arthur Burks, a professional soldier and world traveler. But her attachment to Cayce remained strong. She went back for another reading. A year or so later, on his deathbed, Cayce sent word that he would like to see her. As she was getting ready to leave early that morning, she had a premonition of his death. She decided to wait till nine o'clock to call. "Just before nine, the family phoned and said he had passed away."

Before his death, they had corresponded from time to time, and she still treasures his letters. They are her most precious possession. She reads them from time to time. They are addressed to "My Precious One."

Their friendship did not go unnoticed. I told her the scandal-mongers had tried to make a scandal of their affection for each other. She laughed, and it was a jolly laugh that brightened her countenance. "They have nothing better to do," she said, "in the emptiness of their hearts."

She sighed, and then as she smiled, the years slipped away. "I feel we will meet again one day. For as Mister Cayce said, 'Death is only the other side of life.' And I never knew him to be wrong."

Cayce in many ways was unique. There was nobody like him in our lifetime. Just as there was only one Shakespeare, one Nostradamus, one Abraham Lincoln, there was only one Edgar Cayce. Any attempt to evaluate him by ordinary biographical standards would fall short of the man himself. For he was not only an unparalleled fountain of knowledge in trance, but a man of wisdom in the waking state, who could argue reincarnation with Thomas Edison and Woodrow Wilson.

As one looked into Cayce's life, it became obvious that a good deal of the information of his subconscious had trickled into his conscious awareness and given him a breadth and depth of mind irrelevant to his own sketchy education. He had never gone beyond grade school, and yet he could discourse meaningfully on life with the ease and facility of the greatest of philosophers.

"He would have been a great man," said his long-time associate Gladys Davis, "if he had never given a psychic reading."

He knew what it was to suffer the slings and arrows of misfortune, the withering scorn of neighbors, and the hostility of crowds, but it never soured him. He returned his critics' barbs with understanding and compassion. For he understood, like few people, that the negative vibrations of fear, resentment, and anger had a more disastrous effect on the person projecting those emotions than the objects of their scorn. Love was not an empty word, glibly rolling off his tongue, but a thought energy, translated by his efforts into the wordless happiness of little children, the gratitude of parents, and testimonials of hope from the ailing and troubled.

Not once did he help anybody with the thought of a reward.

"Helping," he said, "is its own reward. For we get to heaven on the arm of the man we're helping."

As a boy, impressed by the biblical healings of Christ, he had prayed for the power to one day help the sick. Had not Jesus told his followers that they could do what he did and more with the help of the Father?

Subsequently, while he was half-asleep, a lady in white appeared, saying that his prayers had been heard and that his wish would be granted.

At the time he thought it no more than a dream. For as a boy he was always hearing voices and seeing things nobody else saw. He was only four when his grandfather died, thrown and trampled by a frightened horse. His father, looking sadly at the boy's mother, said, "My Pa is dead, Carrie; he died trying to save the boy." And the boy, who had been riding with his grandfather, cried, "He isn't dead, Pa. He's been talking to me, telling me he's all right."

His mind was so confused by these distractions that he had no thought for his studies and became the laughing-stock of his school. Chided by his father because he couldn't spell, he turned his eyes heavenward and asked for help. And a voice told him that if he slept on the spelling book he would remember every word in it.

The next morning he confounded his father by his ability to spell every word in the book. However, having no bent for elementary studies, he dropped out of school at an early age to work on an uncle's farm.

In a small town such as Hopkinsville, Kentucky, where he was born and grew up, he was considered something of an oddity, tolerated only because he came from an old Southern family. His father was from a long line of pioneering farmers, and his mother, Carrie Major Cayce, was of similar stock. But the son found himself an alien in his own land. People looked the other way when they saw him coming, and the Catholic priest crossed himself and said three Hail Marys when he passed Cayce's house. Even when he started healing people, few took him seriously, except for the Yankee interloper, Doctor Wesley Ketchum, who saw in Cayce a means of getting an edge on the Southern doctors. Where else, said Ketchum, in what medical school, could one find somebody who, sleeping, could correctly diagnose a case and prescribe its cure?

Knowing how so many people felt about him, Cayce still was open and caring. For while every little facet of life stirred his curiosity as he was growing up, his greatest interest was people, sharing in their joys and tribulations, wanting to give of himself for the sake of giving, as he had done in the distant past.

An incident in his youth underscored the nature of this interest and how it affected him. He had taken a job in a local bookstore and was perched on a ladder, dusting off some books, when one of the two brothers who owned the shop cautioned, "Be careful, Edgar. You might fall and break *something*." A few moments later the second brother came by and said, "Be careful, Edgar. You might fall and hurt *yourself*."

This was something Cayce remembered all his life. He liked to talk about it. "Just a slight difference," he recalled, "but I saw what a difference it made in how I responded. I would have done anything for that second man because of his interest in me. I thought of him as my friend, and that he was. It made me realize that to have a friend, one must be a friend."

It was not hard for me to picture the living Cayce, even though I had never known him personally. He had a simplicity of spirit, a charisma reflected in his spontaneous charm and warmth, and a generosity that won over even his critics. He had a way with animals and flowers—and, above all, children. They seemed to gravitate to him, understanding with the simplicity of their natures, that he was a kindred spirit.

The twinkle in his eye bespoke a dry humor and an infectious geniality, sparked by bursts of temper that invariably made his point.

In forming friendships at sight, Cayce believed he had known the friend before. His belief in reincarnation, with its corollary of a karmic past, made him more tolerant of others and devoid of vanity. For he believed with the Preacher in Ecclesiastes that, in the vanity of vanities, all is vanity and that "the thing that hath been, it is that which shall be. And that which is done, is that which shall be done."

When a crate of the first book to be written of him—*There Is a River*, by Tom Sugrue—arrived from the publisher, he responded in a characteristic way. While the rest of the household excitedly thumbed through the book, he broke apart the wooden crate and fed it to the flames in the fireplace. There is no record that he ever read the book or anything else ever written about him. He was a product of his own thought: Think not of self.

"We all come together for a reason," he told Doctor Ketchum, "and when that purpose has been accomplished each moves on in his own way, to fulfill a still greater purpose."

Though often feeling apart from those closest to him, he saw in his wife the sword and buckler shielding him from his own self-doubts and fits of depression over his inability to adjust his spiritual nature to a material world.

In the terrible loneliness of a mind like no other, he cried out, "If God wanted me to heal people, why didn't he make me a doctor?"

And it was Gertrude who replied in a gentle and reassuring voice, "For then you would have been a doctor like any other doctor."

Once he was surprised in his study by a minister who had come to question his powers. As the minister walked in unnoticed, Cayce was murmuring with his head bowed, "Thank you, thank you, oh Lord, for another life." Only a few moments before a grateful mother had phoned to thank him for saving her baby.

Another minister, alarmed by Cayce's predictions of worldwide destruction toward the end of the century, called on him and asked, "Where would be a safe place for me and my family to live?"

Cayce replied, "Worry not so much where you live, Mister Minister, but how you live."

He tried to find time for everybody. Though his readings said he should read but twice a day or risk disintegration, he stretched this to seven or eight readings a day during World War II because of demands from parents like himself concerned about loved ones away at war. However he pushed himself, the mail piled up. Once, as his aides eyed a huge sack of mail, not knowing where to start, he said, "Take the telegram; there is a greater need there." Down near the bottom of the bag a telegrammed request for a reading had been mistakenly placed.

Cayce had the ordinary instincts. He liked the companionship of pretty women and that of intelligent men. He took a glass of wine occasionally, making his own wine. He considered the grape a food, and when any born-again Christian questioned this, he pointed out that Jesus himself had changed water into wine for the benefit of the celebrants at the wedding in Cana. He rarely fretted about his own health. At the dinner table one day an admirer noted with dismay that Cayce, tabooing pork in his readings, was consuming it with obvious relish. "But Mister Cayce," she said, "pork is bad for you."

Cayce smiled. "If I couldn't raise the vibration [quality] of this poor little hunk of meat, I sure wouldn't amount to much."

He had a volatile temperament in the early days, until he learned the self-control he advocated. Until this change took place he could be easily hurt or disturbed, but then a growing sense of balance would assert itself. Although he relied implicitly on the indispensable Gladys Davis, he would sometimes be annoyed, feeling she had assumed too much in interpreting a reading. He fired her a dozen times. But an hour or two later, he would look her up, smile, and give her an apologetic pat on the back. She would look up and return his smile, for she knew they would always be working together.

Gertrude was the partner who kept him on track when

he had the same misgivings about himself that a doubting world had. Gladys Davis was the outlet for the petty frustrations that plagued his day. As a man has no secrets from his valet, Cayce had none from his secretary. From the age of eighteen on, she lived in the house and went everywhere with him—and Gertrude—taking down virtually every reading for twenty-two years, until he died of a lung condition he himself had foreseen.

He had little interest in money for himself. Yet he went on an ill-starred oil search in Texas with Dave Kahn after World War I to finance a hospital for the incurably ill. There was oil where he said it was. But when a gusher couldn't be brought in, even though the oil slick welling up from the soil could be seen in puddles of rainwater, he got the feeling that he and materiality were never meant to join hands. His attitude toward money was almost childlike. A solid Christian, he felt the Lord would provide, though it was not unusual for his children to have patches in their clothes and him to have holes in his shoes. One harsh winter the family was without fuel. The children, huddled in their overcoats, looked up from a meager meal, to hear their father calmly asking the good Lord for firewood.

A couple hours later, there was a knock at the door. It was a road supervisor for the power and light company. His crew was ready to cut down an old light pole in front of the house. And for the necessary permission they were willing to saw the pole into firewood and stack it on the lawn.

When he was hunting oil, stories of his sorcery spread through central Texas, which was then experiencing a prolonged drought. One day he was approached by a cowboy in high boots, long spurs, chaps, and a Stetson, who challenged him with a gimlet eye.

"They tell me you can do anything," he said. "Well, it hasn't rained in these parts for four months. So tell me when it's going to rain."

Without thinking about it, Cayce looked up and said, "Next Friday afternoon at four o'clock."

At precisely four o'clock that Friday, there was a cloudburst. Nobody could remember when it had rained that hard, and it rained for a half-hour.

As the story spread, many Texans asked Cayce to locate water on their ranches and farms. In every case, water was located at the place and the depth given. Cayce became a sort of local hero because many of the settlers had been driving their stock to watering holes for years.

He didn't believe he had manifested the heavy rainfall. He hadn't given it that much thought. "It was only a prediction, which I didn't have much to do with."

However, he did sometimes visualize a desired end in emergencies. Once, he had been drawn into a ticklish situation where a Texan had become involved with another man's wife. When it looked as if there might be bloodshed, some of the family on both sides appealed to him to intervene. He talked to the various people, gave readings for the three principals, then prayed for a manifestation [a result] to show that he had been right in interceding. "If I never had any other manifestation, I certainly experienced one that night," he said. "For the couple remained true to their vows, and the families are good friends still."

In the Depression, the leaders of the Association for Research and Enlightenment (A.R.E.), which sponsored Cayce's readings, were dismayed that he read for people who couldn't pay for the readings. "We can't keep going without some payments," they said.

"The rain," he replied, "falls on all alike."

They backed off, defeated.

This was at a time when Hollywood executives, impressed by the accuracy of his readings, had offered him a stupendous sum to tell them what movie projects would be successful.

"I have found," he said, in rejecting the offer, "that whatever gift I have is not intended for my own advantage."

Without money for family necessities or to pay his secretary, he was asked to explain why he wasn't doing better. The question was put by his wife: "In consideration of the fact that Edgar Cayce is devoting his entire time to the work, give the reason for his not being able to obtain sufficient financial support for his family's material sustenance, and how may he, Edgar Cayce, correct this condition?"

Mrs. Cayce looked up expectantly as Edgar's lips

began to move. "Live closer to him who giveth all good and perfect gifts. Ask and ye shall receive; knock and it shall be opened unto you. Give and it shall be returned fourfold. There has never been the lack of necessities. Neither will there be, so long as adhering to the Lord's way is kept first and foremost."

In the Depression, the local grocery store cut the Cayce family off the credit list because of an unpaid bill for $87.50. The harried Gertrude asked her husband to think of raising the money somehow, for there were young mouths to feed.

"Don't worry about it, Mother," he said calmly, "the money will turn up." And he calmly went fishing.

That afternoon, the letter carrier arrived with a letter from Paris. Inside was a check from an old client for just enough to cover the bill. Gertrude heaved a grateful sigh. "Now take it to the grocery store, Edgar," she said.

"All right, Mother," he said good-naturedly.

An hour later he was back with a new fishing pole and an armful of tackle. Gertrude looked at him with despair in her heart. "Edgar," she said "you couldn't . . . ?"

"Don't worry about it," he said imperturbably. "The money will turn up somehow."

The seer's family would have been less than human had they not thrown up their arms. But, as the future was to show, Cayce was again prophetic. In every low spot a door opened, and the Lord provided.

Some called him a charlatan, and he had an early disillusioning experience with doctors who stuck pins in him to determine whether he was faking his trance state. He played down his boyhood vision, saying he may have been dreaming when the lady in white appeared to float out of the shadows and say, "Do not despair; your prayers have been heard." However, when he had a number of other visions that were prophetic in nature, he began to accept what he had been given.

The universality of his faith crossed all religious lines. He was equally at home with Catholic, Protestant, Jew, Hindu, Buddhist. He considered Jews to be the elders of Christianity. As Lucius of Cyrene, a disciple of Christ, in one of his lives, he had been of the Jewish faith himself, following in the footsteps of Paul.

Cayce was psychic while awake as well as while sleeping. He saw fields of light around people's heads—auras telling him about the state of their emotions and health. A woman, fresh from a quarrel with a neighbor, came marching into his study. He looked up mildly from his Bible. "I see a red aura around you," he said. "Come back next week when you're not angry anymore."

He was concerned about a woman who had no aura. Two days later she was dead.

Since he was so acutely sensitive to everything, he found it difficult to relax like an ordinary person. He had to make a continuous effort to close himself off. He liked to play cards, but once, without glancing at the deck, he correctly read off fifty-two cards in succession to demonstrate that any card game would be a sham—or a scam.

Like the mystic Lincoln, whom he had on a pedestal with Robert E. Lee, Cayce made friends easily and had the same homespun way of spinning out a story. But again, like Lincoln, there were corners of his mind he could share with nobody. Everybody became an outsider when terrible visions flooded in on him, as they often did. One sunny June day in 1936, he was hoeing in his garden when he heard a noise like the swarming of the bees. He looked up, startled, and there in the sky saw a chariot drawn by four white horses and heard a voice saying, "Look behind you." He turned and beheld a man with shield and a helmet who raised his hand in salute and said, "The chariot of the Lord and thy horseman thereof."

In this vision he saw the horseman of the Apocalypse, warning of war, and an America unarmed and a wide panorama of unprecedented death and destruction.

Shaken by this prophetic nightmare, Cayce dropped his hoe and rushed into the house. He brushed past his son, Hugh Lynn, and locked himself in his study. He emerged hours later, his composure somewhat restored, and explained he had seen the approaching World War II, with all its carnage and its millions of dead. And three of those dead, their faces clearly outlined as they hung from a barbed wire barricade, were young friends of his son.

Despite their close contact, Cayce always remained a hero to Gladys Davis. The work, as they called it, was her life. She didn't marry until after his death, yet she never considered it a sacrifice. Ever thoughtful, Cayce had allowed her to keep her small nephew in the house, treating him as family. Typically, he kept an eye out for the boy even when his own eyes were closed. One day, during a reading, Gladys looked out the study window and saw the boy teetering precariously at the edge of the small lake that came up to the backyard. Knowing the boy couldn't swim, she still didn't dream of leaving the reading. Cayce was on the couch, in trance, but suddenly, without blinking an eye, he said peremptorily, "Go out and get the child."

Gladys dropped her stenographer's pad and raced out to the water, just in the nick of time.

Early on, Gladys had a dramatic revelation of Cayce's remarkable gift. She had been with Cayce for about two months and was afflicted with dull, often agonizing, headaches, despite the glasses she wore to relieve the strain. Desperate, she asked for a reading—her first. The reading attributed the headaches to eyestrain resulting from faulty circulation and bad posture. Simple neck exercises were recommended—stretching the neck up and down and sidewise three or four times, then rolling the head slowly in each direction. This was a traditional Yoga exercise, though Cayce was not aware of it. He also advised ultraviolet-ray treatment three times a week and told her to discard her glasses. She didn't have another moment's discomfort. Only thirty years later did she finally go back to reading glasses when she couldn't find a number in the phone book.

Cayce was literally a dreamer, and he felt people could learn about themselves and the world around them by studying their dreams. "In sleep," he said, "the soul seeks the real diversion or the real activity of self." In one dream he saw himself climbing to a heavenly chapel to pray. A celestial custodian showed him a large room crammed with packages, beautifully wrapped and addressed to different people. They had not been delivered and the custodian sorrowfully explained, "These are gifts for which people have been praying, but they lost their faith just before the date of delivery."

These gifts were latent talents, so seldom drawn upon by the owners. Cayce took this as a message to get on with his work.

He had no quarrel with his detractors, including the scientists, who questioned his ability to diagnose the ailments of people at a distance and prescribe the remedy that would cure them. "I have questioned it myself a thousand times," he said. "Why shouldn't they?"

Yet he had no wish to participate in scientific experiments, any more than a Hemingway or a Steinbeck could write a novel with machines taped to their heads.

"What I do," he observed, "if it has any value at all, was not intended for the laboratory but to help people who needed help and who couldn't get it anywhere else."

Anytime he strayed from this motivation—to hunt oil in Texas or beat the market on Wall Street—the less effective he became. He would get headaches when materialistic questions were asked and he felt this, too, was a warning about the misuse of his gift.

As more and more positive results were noted by people, his self-confidence grew accordingly. But it was not until he saved his wife Gertrude, stricken with tuberculosis, that he became sure that this was to be his life work. Even so, it was only at the urging of his mother, who had been helped by his readings, that he found the courage to read for his wife.

"How can anyone understand," he related, "what it meant to take the life of one so dear to me in my hands, knowing that the force I had been so wishy-washy about for years must now be put to the crucial test?"

Only after she recovered through inhaling apple brandy fumes in a charred oaken keg as he had prescribed, did he resume the readings he had given up and turn away from the photography work that he liked because he could picture people as he saw them. But Gertrude encouraged his return to the work she regarded as his mission, even though it meant an insecure and uneasy existence for the family. The readings, she pointed out, had saved not only her but their son, Hugh Lynn, almost blinded for life when some flash powder blew up in his face while he was playing photographer. Cayce's reading, with Gertrude conducting, excluded surgery and recommended that the boy be kept in a darkened room for fifteen days, with dressings of strong tannic acid solution applied to his eyes.

The doctors looked at each other and shrugged. They

considered the sight irretrievably gone in one eye, and the other eye needing to be removed to save the boy's life. Yet, they still argued that the solution would irreparably damage the delicate tissues of the eye.

"Which eye," Cayce asked, "the eye beyond hope, or the one you want to take out?"

There was an awkward silence, and then one of the doctors set about preparing the prescribed application. Two weeks later the dressings came off. The boy's eyes were clear and bright. "I can see," he cried, touching his mother's face.

As he saw people getting well because of him, Cayce's interest grew not only in his work but in its source. There was only one person, his wife suggested, who could possibly tell him about that source. And that person was Edgar Cayce. So with good grace, he went to sleep and received the information that, as an old soul who had developed his psychic awareness in many lifetimes, he had a special link to the universal intelligence that knew about everything, past, present, and future. As it came to him in trance, so he explained it:

"In every individual lies a force which is a part of all the forces outside him. Not only I, but others, have this latent power to form a spiritual link with the universal mind which governs people with the same immutable laws with which it regulates the physical universe."

To draw on this infinite mind, which he thought of as a God force, he was told he had to lay aside his personality and his deepest desires and make himself the servant of those he would serve. "All people have greater powers than they realize, but they must detach themselves long enough to develop those powers."

It meant giving up one's identity. And not many were ready to do this, Cayce pointed out, any more than they were ready to join Christ two thousand years ago when he asked people to give up their worldly possessions and follow him.

Had Cayce, as his readings suggested, trod the bittersweet road with the Master, absorbing a message that influenced and made possible his own gift, as all gifts in his belief were made possible, with God's acquiescence?

Was his unique gift a steppingstone in the ultimate revelation of what life—and death—was all about? Were his miraculous healings manifested to bring credence to the broader spiritual truth of a purposeful and everlasting life? Did his subconscious, merging with the universal consciousness, come along at a time when a troubled world was ready, even eager, for some reassuring sign of its place in the universal plan?

All this he asked himself. For he knew there was nothing accidental, nothing left to chance in the Creator's grand design, or how else could the future be so accurately portrayed by his prophetic self? And so, believing this, Cayce pictured reincarnation as an instrument, not an end in itself, to harmonize our lives within the context of this design. "Each and every individual," he said, "follows out that line of development in the present earth plane as it has received from the preceding conditions, and each grain of thought or condition is a consequence of other conditions created by self."

It was difficult for me to conceive of a spirit with a volition of its own. How, I asked, did the spirit find its way to another body? Where did it rest and renew itself? Why did it keep coming back?

Others had asked as well: "Must each soul continue to be reincarnated in the earth until it reaches perfection, or are some souls lost?"

Cayce had a ready answer, for his sleeping mind, ironically, never slept. "The soul is not lost. The individuality of the soul that separates itself is lost. The reincarnation or the opportunities are continuous until the soul has of itself become an entity in its whole or has submerged itself."

"If a soul fails to improve itself, what becomes of it?"

Cayce's reply appeared rather enigmatic, but when studied, the implication became clear: "That's why the reincarnation, why it reincarnates; that it may have the opportunity presented. Can the will of man continue to defy its Maker?"

"Does every human being have a soul?"

He replied with a simplicity that advanced a provocative concept of not only humanity's relation with God but of God himself. "Every human being has a soul, that which makes it akin to the Creator, that which is given an individual that he may become a companion to the Creator. As we see in the forces all about us, nature herself desires companionship. So does God, who created it all. He gives us the opportunity to be his companion, by giving us a soul, which we may make a companion to him. But we have to do the making."

Psychic healing, telepathy, clairvoyance—all these Cayce saw as perfectly natural phenomena that almost anybody could invoke through meditating on the common connection with the universal intelligence.

"All healing," he said, "results from this internal power joined with an external force to bring about what we call a miracle. Miracles, in fact, are nothing more than a perfect understanding of the universal laws, an understanding which Jesus used to let people know who sent him."

Cayce pondered his Bible and the thousands of readings he had given and came to a realization that humanity was nothing without God. God, he decided, created humans in his image of perfection. The nearer humanity came to this image, the nearer it came to God. Otherwise, all striving was futile. For without a tie to the Creator, the Creation itself was negligible and purposeless, no more than the wind.

"If one sees God as a healer, the source of healing," said Cayce, "so will the healing occur. For as one meditates on this healing thought, the mind builds within the individual the energy force necessary for the healing. However, if one's God is merely fame and fortune or some frivolous pleasure, how can we expect that God will heal? Where is the perfect image? While many people believe they can buy anything whenever they want it, very little good can come of their efforts without the divine spark which links one to the all-powerful Creator."

His God was never very far from Cayce. He read his Bible daily, going through it at least once every year. It shaped not only his subconscious thinking but the way he expressed himself in the conscious state. He thought it presumptuous to say God was near him, seeing himself as ever striving to be near God.

I was to think of all this years after Cayce's death when I took my book The Sleeping Prophet on Johnny Carson's "Tonight" show. A skeptical Carson, as to be expected, was hardly a Cayce fan. There was an unmistakable look of satisfaction on his face as he asked, "Considering that

Cayce was an illiterate, a fifth-grade dropout, how could he have possibly described the human anatomy in such detail as you say and prescribe such complex remedies? Where did it all come from?"

I could sense the expectancy of the studio audience in the hushed silence. I had heard the question many times and had asked it myself.

"There is only one possible explanation," I said. "Everything else has been excluded. Edgar Cayce had the hand of God on him."

There was a moment of silence, then a thunderous burst of applause from the audience, and the program ended almost as though on cue.

The audience, like myself, was looking for some reassurance of God's interest in humanity. They found it that day in Edgar Cayce, a man chosen of the Lord.

CHAPTER 3

Atlantis Reborn

How could she be a princess in Atlantis, Eleanor Hoag asked herself, and a crippled child in this lifetime, a victim of polio at the age of two? She had always thought of a princess as being tall and straight and beautiful. She looked with disbelief at the man sleeping on the couch. But then as he continued, she became immersed in what he was saying, for he was telling her something that she had always agonized about—why she had been afflicted with this terrible burden, paralyzed from the waist down, barely able to get about with braces and crutches.

"The entity was in the Atlantean land, when there were those disturbances between the children of the Law of One [God] and the children of Belial [the devil].

"The entity was a princess then and brought disturbances to those that were just unfolding that made them weak in limb. Thus we find the entity meeting itself, in that which it has brought to others.

It was not all hopeless. She was only thirty years old then, back in 1942, and Cayce did recommend treatments with an electric appliance and massage, which, for a time, enabled her to move about at home, a few steps at a time, without the heavy braces.

But she would find her real healing, the mystic stressed, in the lessons she learned through patience and ministering to the needs of others, she would find peace and happiness that would make her at one with God.

At first she didn't know what to make of it. But even though she knew nothing about Atlantis, it helped to know there was a reason for her condition. And that having paid her karmic debt, she would return one day with the slate wiped clean, ready for a new life.

She was now seventy-seven, living in a Pittsburgh suburb, looking back on a life of service, happily married for twenty-seven years until her husband's death, finding peace in the belief that whatever happened to her had been part of God's plan.

I had never spoken to anybody who was more cheerful and upbeat. And yet when she was a child, one of a brood of four, her mother, embarrassed by her affliction, would hide her or ignore her. She was constantly made to feel she was a freak.

I was struck by what Cayce had said about her treatment of the less fortunate in Atlantis, reminding me, in a way, of what Cayce had subsequently said about the altering and improvment of the species in Egypt.

She had given it considerable thought herself. "As I got to know more about the Cayce readings," she told me, "I had an idea that I had not been sympathetic to the efforts to breed a stronger people in Atlantis, with well-developed arms and legs. And this was my lesson in that incarnation, as Cayce and others, in Atlantis, and then Egypt, led the movement to build a superior race."

Cayce had spoken of lives in Atlantis for some five hundred people. And many of these old companions were the first to help the young woman who had come to Virginia Beach from her native Pittsburgh area to work as a manicurist, without the slightest idea of the greater purpose behind her move.

"I had never heard of Cayce," she said, "until one of my clients came in with a patch on her eye, later removed, and said Cayce had restored her sight when nobody else had been able to help her. And so I got my first reading."

She didn't realize at the time that the client, Burlynn Davis, who operated a tavern in nearby Oceana, was one of the old Atlanteans who had returned to the Cayce fold. It was a wonderful feeling, Eleanor found, to be tended, encouraged, massaged—and loved—by these old companions of the Atlantean experience, led by Cayce himself, who helped so much with his practical advice, reaching into the mind as well as the body.

"To be sure the entity loses patience easily, but who knows it but self? While this is well, it is also well at times to give vent to one's feelings. As Christ gave, 'Be angry, but sin not; condemn no one. Put not a curse upon anything or anybody. Be with the Lord and he will be with thee.' "

There were other readings that placed her in the Persian and Judean period, the latter explaining to her satisfaction the friction between herself and her mother.

"What," she asked the sleeping Cayce, "has been the past association with my mother that has brought about the antagonistic and resentful attitudes? How should I meet this situation for our mutual development?"

"In the Promised Land you held to your faith, while your mother wished then for you to accede to the desires of your persecutors. You refused."

As she looked at it now, she realized that her mother, the same then, had been trying to save her. "I didn't understand then, and so resented her, with the resentment carrying over, just as hers did because I had left her frustrated and grief-stricken by my martyrdom."

Her marriage had been a good one; she had returned to her home area in Pennsylvania, entered business school, become a well-paid secretary, and had married Charles Van Horn, a skilled machinist with a congenital heart problem. They had dedicated their lives to good works, so that Cayce was able to say: "Those who come in contact with the entity in the present may count themselves fortunate, as they learn a lesson of patience, perseverance, endurance and kindness."

And so it was that Edgar Cayce made a reality, with real people, out of a legendary continent. For as Plato, the greatest scholar of antiquity, literally put Atlantis on our map, Edgar Cayce gave it flesh and bones and a history more fabulous than anything Hollywood could dream of.

But while a sleeping Cayce made a reality out of what had been myth, a waking Cayce didn't know anything about lost continents. And when his first mention in trance of Atlantis was called to his attention, he rubbed his eyes and said in that gentle way of his, "Now, I wonder where that came from and what there is to it."

As so many of Cayce's revelations, it came in answer to a simple question about something else. "Before this," said Cayce, "the entity was in the fair country of Alta, or Poseida proper; then this entity was in that force that brought the highest civilization and knowledge that has been known in the earth's plane. This, we find, was nearly ten thousand years before the Prince of Peace came."

Not since Plato, twenty-five hundred years earlier, had anyone spoken so realistically of the island empire beyond the Pillars of Hercules. And while Plato also mentioned the greater mass of land beyond Atlantis, unmistakably the continent of North America, Cayce was even more specific. After the last of three holocausts, in about 10,000 B.C., when Ra-Ta [Cayce] fled Atlantis to begin building a new culture in Egypt, waves of Atlanteans had dispersed in all directions, accounting for the superior and often familiar cultures in such diverse areas as Egypt, the Middle East, Peru, Mexico, Central America, and in our own New Mexico and Colorado.

Cayce, in a sense, had an advantage, for Plato was on the outside looking in, long after the fact, while Cayce was on the inside, as it were, recalling it all firsthand. He was there, too, at the beginning, fifty thousand years ago according to his readings, when the Atlanteans, not yet in the flesh, were thought-forms, disembodied energy, manifested into the physical by their faith in the Lord of Creation, who had no beginning nor end himself but always was and always will be.

In language worthy of any bard, Cayce saw his creation as a festive delight: "When the morning stars sang together and whispering winds brought the news of the coming of man's indwelling of the spirit of the Creator and he, man, became the living soul. And he, the entity, came into being with this multitude."

Again, I marveled over where it had all come from, as Cayce went on to describe the various people he had shared lives with down through the ages, beginning with the Atlantean age where the physical form was androgynous—of one sex—splitting off to male and female with the inevitable realization of the creative urge.

"When the forces in flesh came to dwell in the earth's plane, the entity [Cayce] was among the first to inhabit the earth in that form. . . . In this we find the larger development of the entity, for it was then able to contain in its Oneness the soul forces given to the sons of man and realize the fatherhood of the Creator."

I found Cayce's prose involved yet fascinating, but how could any of it be validated?

"How," I asked the custodian of the Cayce records, "do we know Cayce was on Atlantis or there was an Atlantis?"

Jeanette Thomas smiled.

"Oh, there's a great many things that give the Lost Continent some reality. You know, the Russians, who are always stirring things up, conducted all kinds of hydrographic soundings in the Atlantean perimeter from Bimini east to the Azores and one thousand miles north of that. They reported some evidence of mountain ranges, valleys, and sunken rivers on the floor of the ocean. Our own scientists turned up a sunken river, an extension of the Susquehanna River, which they feel disappeared with the great flood. And some land did rise in the Bahaman area in 1969, where Cayce said Atlantis would first show itself."

"All that may be true," I said, "but I still have difficulty visualizing thoughts becoming people."

"Hasn't it ever occurred to you," she said, "that thoughts have produced the world we live in—the tallest skyscrapers, the greatest works of art, the most divine poetry, and," her smile broadened, "the children we love so much?"

It took me a moment to digest what she had said. I still didn't have my answer. Still, I had thought from time to time, observing the infinite powers of the mind, that humans should be able to do whatever any product of our thinking was able to do.

"You mean," I said, "that thought-form humanity should be capable of sending a message without picking up the phone or taking a trip without booking a flight?"

She grinned. "Edgar Cayce did it all the time."

"There are not many Edgar Cayces," I said.

She nodded. "But there are Edisons and Einsteins and Marconis and the Shakespeares and the Keatses, who all add a new dimension to our world."

We were sitting in the same office in the A.R.E. headquarters in Virginia Beach where Gladys Davis had collected the Edgar Cayce readings with a loving hand and eye that had remained youthful until her death only two years before.

I saw Jeanette reach across her desk and glance

through the pages of a folder with an eye that knew what it was looking for.

"You know," she said, "Mister Cayce's meeting Gladys was no accident. Gladys had the job the moment she walked into his photographic studio in Selma, Alabama. She was only eighteen, with very little experience as a secretary. But he hired her without asking a question. He knew he had found the assistant he was looking for. As it developed, they had been together before, in Egypt and Persia, and, priorly, Atlantis. And there was a closeness time could never erase."

I smiled. "Do you mean that Gladys was also a thought-form?"

She passed the file over to me. "Take a look at Gladys and Mister Cayce's life together in Atlantis. And you will know that job was inevitable."

I glanced through the one page she showed me. The reading had been given in June 1924, a year or so after Gladys had become his secretary and a year after Cayce's reincarnation reading for Lammers in Dayton.

It was as interesting as anything Edgar Cayce had said about himself, for it detailed in no uncertain terms the evolvement of both Gladys and Cayce out of the mind into the flesh.

"In flesh form in the earth's plane we find the first in that of the Poseidan forces, when both were confined in the body of the female. For this being the stronger in the expressed or applied forces found manifestations for each in that [more adaptable female] form. Yet, with the experiences as have been brought in that plane and period, we find then the separation [male and female] of the body. These two [sexes] were the giving of the spiritual development in the land, and the giving of the uplift to the peoples of the day and age."

I looked up from the folder, incredulously.

"And Cayce recognized her from that?"

"Don't you see? His subconscious remembered. He knew they had been together before, just as he knew everybody on sight he had a life with before, not only on Atlantis, but in Egypt, Persia, colonial Virginia, or any of the other sojourns on this plane."

Thinking about it, one could easily fathom the close connection between the two. For it was almost axiomatic that the first woman in any man's life was the one he would never forget. And I supposed this was true in the reverse as well.

Cayce did not remain a thought-form long. He materialized in human form in keeping with the laws of Creation and evolution, which the Atlanteans did not find at all contradictory. God created humanity, said Cayce, then left the rest pretty much up to humans. They evolved, physically and mentally, according to their free will, particularly in response to challenges and the desire for self-improvement. So it was in ancient Egypt and Persia and is today in America, where humanity is breaking boundaries of time and space in its quest for the infinity Cayce so often dealt with.

The Atlantis that Cayce described was not unlike the fermenting world of today. Before it destructed, the Lost Continent developed a highly technical civilization that paralleled our own and, in some respects, exceeded it. In this period, Cayce, taking physical form, first manifested healing power and the wide-ranging knowledge of universal law that made him a spiritual leader in Egypt, Persia, and present-day America, the new Egypt among nations.

In Atlantis, he formed, as did Gladys Davis, the alliances with companions who were to be with him in various experiences, helping to shape his own life as their own was being shaped by him.

He sat with the mighty, urging peace and unity, while war and dissension darkened the horizon. There were constant challenges, developing the latent talents with which his ethereal nature had been gifted. As today, there were threats, internal and external, to the welfare of the state. Before nation turned on nation, giant dinosaurs roamed the five islands, threatening the human race with extinction. The islanders, briefly united, responded with ingenuity to muster the forces of nature against this formidable foe. But later the greater peril, that of nuclear weapons, foreseen by a prophetic Cayce, was unleashed by the warring nations of Atlantis to precipitate a succession of earthquakes and tidal waves that tumbled the mighty continent into the sea.

"It was a continuing battle for centuries," said Jeanette Thomas. "And in a way, necessity being the mother of invention, it showed how the Atlanteans evolved to survive this threat, developing the weapons as they needed them to stave off these enormous animals. When swords and stones became inadequate, they invented explosives, and when the thick-skinned mastodons shrugged off these charges, they moved on to electrical weapons and even considered death rays and nuclear energy."

I looked at her doubtfully. "Nuclear energy?"

"Oh, yes, they were an advanced civilization in some respects. But they made a destructive weapon of it and destroyed themselves."

"Atom bombs just to fight off some overgrown elephants and rhinoceroses?" It seemed preposterous.

She laughed. "History repeats itself. Why else did our scientists come to the nuclear breaking up of the atom but to win a life and death struggle with a deadlier adversary than dinosaurs?"

The atom, as it turned out, was not used on the giant predators. Instead fearing the fallout, the Atlanteans harnessed nature's cosmic rays to eliminate these creatures. And in disposing of the dinosaurs, which were larger than houses, the people somehow went unscathed.

This seemed to stretch things, even for Cayce.

Jeanette shrugged. "That's what the man said." She handed me still another paper from her bulging folder.

I read on, fascinated, for I had the feeling I was viewing a society caught up in a struggle for existence not dissimilar from our own today, except the predators among us were even more dangerous because they weren't classed as animals.

"Then," said Cayce, elaborating on the dinosaur peril, "with the changes that had come about, there were the invasions of that continent by those of the animal kingdoms that brought about that meeting of the nations of the globe to prepare a way of disposing of, or else be disposed of by these forces. There came then the first of the destructive forces as could be set and be meted out in force. Hence, the beginning of explosives that might be carried about, in a period when men first began to cope with those of the beast form that overran the earth in many places."

And then humans took to prayer, the danger so great they looked to the Creator who had presumably created them in his image and so should favor them over adversaries larger than any buildings humans had yet been able to make.

"Then with these destructive forces, we find the first turning of the altar fires into that of sacrifice of those that were taken in various ways [slaves] and human sacrifice began."

Many took refuge in flight even before the island of Poseida was destroyed by tide and flood. "With this came the first egress of the peoples to that of the Pyrenees first, and later we find that peoples who entered into the black or the mixed population, in what later became the Egyptian dynasty. We also find that entering into what later became the beginning of the Inca [in Peru] that builded the walls across the mountains in this period.

"But the multitude remained, and these brought about those destructive forces (that are known today) from the bowels of the earth itself—causing destruction to the land."

Jeanette saw Atlantis's loss as Egypt's gain.

"This explains Ra-Ta, for he said that the high priest came from a land highly evolved and was motivated to develop a Temple of Sacrifice and produce a race superior even to the Atlanteans."

Plato saw the Atlantean migration, after the last of three breakups, as part of a great invasion of the Mediterranean basin, repulsed by an Athenean military that could hardly have coped with a major power at that time. More plausibly, the Cayce version suggests the Greeks drove off a group of stragglers, just one of the many homeless, island-hopping contingents that moved on to Persia and then Egypt.

On both sides of the Atlantic, as Jeanette pointed out, there were almost identical calendars, more accurate than those developed in Europe for hundreds of years. "The accuracy of the mathematical calculations, in both the architecture and astronomy, was equally remarkable in both Egypt and the early Mayan civilizations."

In the Yucatan, in southern Mexico, and in Peru, as Cayce said, were landmarks of a culture that was old when the conquering Spaniards arrived. Pizarro and his men found two thousand miles of well-paved roads in Peru, along with the remains of many fine hostels.

There was an amazing similarity of place names, for example, the names of five cities in the Middle East about the time of Christ and five cities in the New World communities, named long before the first European explorers arrived in the sixteenth century:

Middle East	Central America
Chol	Chol-ula
Colua	Colua-can
Zuivana	Zuivan
Cholima	Colima
Zalissa	Xalisco

In a commentary on ancient civilizations in the Americas, the *New York Times* in 1962 quoted author William Luce:

> Thirty-two miles from Mexico City is an archeological site so old that even the Aztecs knew virtually nothing about it. This is Teothihuacan, the site of the Pyramid of the Sun. A ruin five hundred years before the arrival of Cortés, the pyramid has been reconstructed into a structure as tall as a twenty-story skyscraper.
>
> The ruins raise as many questions as they answer. Who the people were who built them, where they came from, why they built them and what happened to them?

Cayce didn't have any trouble with that. And the scientists were beginning to agree with him years after his death. In costumed movies about Atlantis, the Atlanteans were always white. But not with Cayce. He said they were red, like the American Indians, one of five races that had developed independently. The others were the black, yellow, brown, and white. How had Cayce known this, any more than he knew anything of the past? Yet in 1963, some forty years after Cayce spoke of the five races, Dr. Carlton Coon, professor of anthropology at the University of Pennsylvania Museum, created a storm of controversy with his book, *The Origin of the Races*. Summing up the book, for which Coon received Philadelphia's prestigious Atheneum Award, the *Philadelphia Bulletin* reported Coon's belief that humanity divided into five races or subspecies half a million years ago, perhaps longer, and that the five races then developed independently. According to Coon, *Homo erectus* (standing human) evolved into *homo sapiens* (thinking human) not once but five times as each subspecies passed the critical intelligence threshold.

And Coon, too, divided the races by color, as Cayce had done.

Cayce seemed to be winning the fight for credibility. Yet there were still the thought-forms to resolve and the invoking of cosmic rays he mentioned to eliminate the dinosaurs. There was something of the B-movie in the picture Cayce gave of the latter days of Atlantis—hovercraft skimming over the water with the speed of sound; machines crystalizing thoughts into words; fresh water that was self-purifying; rejuvenation centers for the deserving. Anything the movies had, Atlanteans had, including the adapting of solar energy to a point where they could muster deadly cosmic rays or nullify them at will.

In the harnessing of the sun, Cayce mentioned a ruby-like firestone with powers greater than a laser beam. By filtering the rays of the sun through the firestone, immense energy was generated. "The activity of the stone," said Cayce, "was received from the sun's rays. The concentration through the prisms or glass of the ruby acted upon the instruments that were connected with the various modes of travel, as remote control by radio waves in the present day.

"The firestone was housed in a dome-covered building with a sliding top. Its powerful rays could penetrate anywhere, either as a death ray or a constructive energy force. The influences of the radiation that arose in the form of the rays were invisible to the eye but acted upon the stones themselves as the motivating sources, whether aircraft lifted by gases or guiding pleasure vehicles that might pass close to the earth or the crafts on or under the water."

All over Atlantis, stations were set up to generate this cosmic power. The firestone was a calculated wonder. "It was a large cylindrical glass, cut with facets in such a manner that the capstone made for the centralizing of the power concentrated between the end of the cylinder and the capstone itself."

It worked in some ingenious way to eliminate the dinosaurs without affecting the Atlanteans who had devised this way of mastering nature in their battle of survival. So said Cayce.

I had come back a second time, and a third, to check what I could with the ever-obliging Jeanette.

"This time," I said, "it's the cosmic rays."

She smiled. "Thought-forms and cosmic rays. That's quite a package."

"How could these rays destroy the giant dinosaurs and still not harm humans?"

"Only if they were properly managed."

There was a twinkle in her eye.

"I've been saving something for you." She drew out of her desk drawer a copy of a newspaper clipping. I was looking at a heading that said, "Cosmic Rays Linked to Dinosaur Deaths."

I wondered what Hollywood genius had done the linking. But, no, the article was by David Dietz, Scripps-Howard science editor. The scientific credentials were of the highest. This possible cause of the "decline and disappearance of the mighty dinosaurs from the face of the earth," wrote Dietz, "was suggested by Professor Bruce Heezen and his colleagues of the Lamont Geological Observatory of Columbia University." The statement was made before no less than the Second International Oceanographic Congress of scientists meeting in Moscow under the auspices of UNESCO and the Soviet government.

The cosmic ray was tied in with a sudden reversal of the earth's magnetic field, transforming the north magnetic pole into a south pole, something happening every 700,000 or 800,000 years or so, according to the scientists. I remembered vaguely that Cayce had said something of the same sort in one of his readings.

"At least," I said, "they agree there were dinosaurs."

"And," chimed in Jeanette, "that there is a period when the earth's magnetic field reverses, and as it switches poles, the protective electromagnetic field around the earth disappears."

"Normally," I read on, "this field acts as a shield to screen out most of the cosmic rays from outer space.

When the shield disappears, the earth is subjected to the full fury of cosmic ray bombardment and of the sun, inducing skin cancer.

"It is a well-known fact that cosmic rays can cause genetic mutations which lead to the establishment of new species . . . by causing changes in the genes in the reproductive cells."

The article had more to say on this point: "Heezen thinks a sudden increase in cosmic rays could also lead to lethal changes that would trigger the extinction of some species."

Heezen meant some species of dinosaurs but not humans. There it was. Obviously, the Atlanteans had worked out some type of cosmic ray block, analogous to the sun block some use today.

I remembered then that Cayce had warned of a rotational tilt of the earth's axis, beginning in 1936, which could affect the earth's magnetic field and wreak havoc around the world, bringing destructive floods and earthquakes of a cataclysmic nature toward the end of the century.

Heezen apparently saw something similar happening. "The last reversal of the earth's magnetic field took place 700,000 years ago, and at the present time the field is decreasing in strength. If the field continues to decrease at its present rate, another reversal may occur in a thousand years or so."

I found myself suddenly distracted, thinking of Cayce's predictions of drastic earth changes in the late 1990s, destroying most of Los Angeles, San Francisco, New York, and other parts of this country and the world.

"When you're talking about 700,000 years," Jeanette said, "what's another thousand years or so? It could be tomorrow or next week, for all of that."

Cayce's readings on Atlantis, constantly presented as evidence of reincarnation, came long before the first atom bomb, before it was known that humans had the power to blast themselves back to the Dark Ages, turning the clock back to the Stone Age and life in a cave by a bleak campfire.

Just as it happened in Atlantis, warned Cayce, so could it happen with the planet earth if humans didn't mend their ways, thus bringing on another Sodom and Gomorrah with their abuse of God's commandments. And so it was with Atlantis when the aggressive misuse of solar energy, upsetting the atmosphere, brought about the final debacle.

"With the disregard of those laws applicable to the sons of God, man brought in those destructive forces that combined with those natural resources of the gases, of the electrical forces that made the eruptions from the depths of the slow-cooling earth, and that portion of Atlantis near the Sargasso Sea went into the depths."

"It doesn't look very promising, does it?" said Jeanette, "when you look around and see what is happening in Central America, Ireland, the Middle East, South Africa, other portions of Africa. As you know, Mister Cayce foresaw a world holocaust before the end of the century, if man doesn't mend his ways. But I think we'll be all right, for he is coming back in 1998, so he said, and I'm sure he'll be bringing a lot of help with him."

"In body or thought-form?" I said.

"I don't think it would make much difference; thought-forms were very real to him. There was a reading he gave for an associate in this life describing how thought-forms functioned in the flesh and out of it. 'In the beginning,' he said, 'there were more thought-forms than entities with personalities as seen in the present. And so it can be said that the psychic, the subconscious state, was the natural state of man in the beginning.' "

She looked up with a thoughtful expression.

"Mister Cayce loved children, and he would look at them sometimes, reading their minds as though gaining a wealth of knowledge. He felt babies were in the pure psychic state. For as he said, 'When a baby is born into the world, and it lies sleeping in its crib, what is it thinking of? Of what are its dreams? What it expects to be, or what it has been? Of what the thoughts? That which is to be, or that which was?' "

It was different with the adult mind, whether theologian or scientist, whose subconscious minds, the pipeline into the past, had long been blocked by the conscious schooling of life.

" 'The trained mind,' said Cayce, 'creates for itself mental pictures out of its own consciousness. But the baby, from whence comes its reasoning, from whence its dreams? A baby smiles, and we say it dreams of angels. And that may be true. But what molds that dream?' "

Cayce answered his own questions. The baby's dreams and thoughts came from what it had been fed in the past. There was no other contact. And this, he said, was as true of the Atlanteans who were the first to materialize into thought and out of it into body.

"From whence did they reason?" Cayce asked. "Obviously, from the creative forces, from which they received their impetus in becoming thought-forms. And from which brought a greater development of the psychic in the present time, for they were almost wholly psychic then, just as the baby."

And so the people of Atlantis, moving on to Egypt, were more inclined to remember than others. They had been in the psychic state longer, and so there was often a recurrence, as Cayce said, even today, of this subconscious ability to remember.

I saw it more clearly than I had, but the physical manifestation of the thought-form into humanity still baffled me.

"That is the easiest of all," said Jeanette, smiling at my bewilderment.

She picked up a Bible I hadn't seen before on her desk. And she read in Genesis, "So God created man in his own image, in the image of God created he him; male and female created he them."

I finally understood.

For what was it to the God who had created all heaven and earth in six days to have created humans any way he chose and with the same ease?

"I have no trouble with God as a thought-form," I said. "He has never been anything else."

CHAPTER 4

In the Steps
of the Ra

Ra-Ta intrigued me more than any of the other men that were Edgar Cayce. He was a mysterious figure who, like Shane in the movie of the same name, came out of the mist to change the lives of everybody he touched and then disappeared as quietly as he came.

He had the ancient culture of Atlantis in his veins, it was said, and he transposed the magic of that not-so-legendary island to an aboriginal Egypt whose natives still had the rudimentary vestiges of a primitive people. By the time he left Egypt, it had become the most civilized land in the world because of him. And his name, as a mark of his influence, had become sacred in his adopted land—for as he knew, he was the one and only Ra, the Sun God, to whom the Pharaohs themselves made obeisance.

It was difficult for me to imagine the tall, angular mystic of Virginia Beach, with stooped shoulders and a gentle eye, as the incarnation of that dynamic figure who had altered civilization by his presence. And yet, in a way, Edgar Cayce was indeed the astral descendant of the Ra that was. For in this life, as before, he had married the same woman, not caring what others thought. And, like Ra, as the patron saint of holistic medicine, had revolutionized the healing arts in a way only now beginning to manifest itself.

Like Ra, he had a single-minded purpose, the desire to improve the health and spirits of humanity, to help the sick and troubled regardless of race or creed. And like Ra, he was beset by carnal desires, which he resisted as he would the devil.

72

"When the devil can't get to a man," he said, "he sends a woman."

He had looked that devil in the eye and conquered it—at long last.

How many times must he have gone over his own readings and looked for a way to change the last act in this life, knowing that only he could change it with God's help.

Just as Cayce had searched into his own soul, I was about to look into it now. But how, I asked myself, did one come to understand and recognize anything as intangible as the human soul—Cayce's soul, in this case?

If there were anything to reincarnation, then the seven lives Cayce gave himself (exclusive of dreams) could develop some insight into the continuity of life. For as Voltaire said, "It is just as remarkable to have been born once as twice." And we were dealing with one life at a time.

As Cayce said, the only life that counts is the one we live now. In an ongoing saga, he stressed, we strive with old companions to deal with the karma from the past, behaving in such a way that we would start off better the next time around.

"Had it not been for the man that was Ra," an old companion told me, "I would have made the same mistake I made once before—in Egyptland. I was a nag then, as his reading pointed out, and a nag again in this experience, though I tried not to be. He told me to take a good look at myself, as if I were looking at a stranger, as there was danger of my repeating myself." She took that look and didn't like what she saw.

"As I thought about it, I realized I had always felt I knew better for my husbands than they knew for themselves," she smiled. "And what was worse I showed it."

She gave me a sheepish grin. "I didn't want my husband leaving me as Cayce said this one had in Egypt, when we were all happily together. I took a good look at myself, deep under the skin, and didn't like what I saw. He had always said, 'Forget self,' and I hadn't known what it meant until it was almost too late."

She stopped being so controlling, and her husband stayed the course. "I improved over Egypt," she said with a smile.

If Cayce lived before, as the Egyptian Ra, or any of the other personalities he mentioned, the first life reading with Lammers was obviously the forerunner of hundreds of others that helped establish the continuity of the soul.

I was in a quandary. How did I examine the reality of Cayce's lives? I needed something more, some eyewitnesses. Who could they possibly be?

"Why not," said Jeanette Thomas, "the people he shared those lives with in the past? Some of them are old now, in their eighties and nineties, but their minds are keen, and their memories sharp. I am sure many of them would allow you to regress them hypnotically in time, and there are others who remember consciously. They, too, are curious about how well they knew Cayce and how their lives were shaped by the past."

What possibilities they presented!

There was Ruth, the sister of Christ, and I didn't even know he had a sister. There was Luke the Apostle; Hector, the prince of Troy; Garcia, the woman who betrayed Troy; and dozens of others as inconspicuous in their past lives as they were in the present. And they all knew Edgar Cayce and he knew them all—the old ties so strong that they were drawn into his life in this experience.

Some were sure they had chosen their lives, just so they were near him again, feeling his gentle influence and guidance. "I chose my parents," said Anne Gray Holbein, "because they were friends of the Cayces in Selma, Alabama. The day after I was born he came into the hospital to see me, and he stayed with me all his life and thereafter."

Thereafter?

"The day my husband died, that was in 1969, I looked up and saw Edgar Cayce standing in front of me. He had a message for me. 'When one door closes, another opens,' he said. And he was right, for spiritually my life turned around from that moment."

I looked at her closely. She was obviously not a fanatic. Her cool gray eyes measured people with a glance. She was one of the first female optometrists in the state of Alabama and at seventy was still active, looking much younger than her years. I had met her at the 1987 Congress in Virginia Beach of Cayce study group leaders.

She had a curiosity about the past, knowing that it influenced the present and the future. She had no fear of death. She had lost two sons in the same year, ten years after her husband died, but believing, as Cayce did, in the continuity of the soul, she saw no finality in their passing.

She had past lives in Egypt, the Middle East, Troy, and colonial Virginia, but it was only recently, in 1984, forty years after Cayce's death, that she knew she shared any of these experiences with the man she was drawn to as though he were her father.

Without knowing of any past connection, she had called him "Daddy Cayce" from the first moment she could mouth the words. Until his death, she had leaned on his shoulder for guidance. He was the first to learn of her marriage and the first to know of its discord. She wrote him twice a month, and he always replied, even when he was so ill he had to be propped up in bed. When he was so fatigued from reading for people that he could hardly speak, he gave her the physical readings that saved her life when the doctors had given her up. And when his first grandson was born, she was the first he wrote with the glad tidings.

"I still have the feeling," she said, "that I need only reach out and Mister Cayce will be there."

The feeling had been mutual. Cayce made no secret of his paternal inclination. Her life reading, when she was eighteen, warned against marriage. But she was young and her sweetheart was going off to war. She disregarded the warning. "I wish with all my heart," she wrote, "that you were here to talk over what I am about to do. Possibly before the month is over, Fred [Holbein] and I will be married."

Cayce replied the day he got the letter, reminding her of her life reading. "Please read it again very carefully before making a final decision. But know I am with you and for you, whatever decision you make." No father could have been more concerned.

And so, she got married.

She smiled when I asked how well she had known Cayce.

"As a child, I thought of him all the time. There was a comfortable feeling of knowing him. Though I saw very little of him as I grew up, I had always considered him a second father without knowing why. And then, of course, after seeing my reading, which I got when I was eighteen, I knew why."

Though scientifically oriented by profession, Anne Holbein had a soul consciousness as vibrant as any I had ever met. Her subconscious mind, her soul mind, was so close to the surface that she was almost mediumistic. She looked like an ideal subject for a hypnotic regression into the past.

Wanting to know something of this past, I went through her life reading with Cayce. It told me what I needed to know. In one lifetime she had been Cayce's illegitimate daughter when he was a soldier of fortune in colonial Virginia; in another, his mistress in ancient Troy, when he was the keeper of the gate the Greeks were trying to batter down; in Persia, an older sister. And before that in Egypt, when he was Ra, she was an adoring subject, who as a child, with her family, had followed him into Egypt after the breakup of Atlantis.

It was no trick to hypnotize her, for her subconscious was ,always brimming very close to the surface, as all subconscious minds are when they draw on a timeless memory bank. She was a good subject, and quickly went under as I suggested in a normal voice: "Go back, way back, into the Egypt land, where there was an entity named Ra-Ta. Speak up with clarity knowing that what you describe is in your consciousness of that period in Egypt as you recall it."

I had reason to believe that whatever she said would be accurate, for in testing her memory, as I had tested others under hypnosis, I found that she had accurately described visits to her crib by her "Daddy Cayce" when she was just a few days old. There was a similar remembrance—and recognition—of her parents. The subconscious mind, as Einstein once pointed out, has powers the conscious mind doesn't even dream of. As I questioned her, I saw that she was completely relaxed, with her eyes closed, in the desired altered state. She answered in a barely audible voice, which became stronger as her mind seemed to piece together what she saw. As she spoke, simply and directly, I felt as if I had burst uninvited into an entirely new world. I had the feeling of an ancient mystique, of the dreams of a small girl and her family on the long trek in the footsteps of the leader they adored, and of the new life they found at the end of the rainbow.

"He left us back by the sea, and he went south and west to the land where there is a river [the Nile] that overflows and makes for wonderful crops. After he was gone, others decided to follow him. My family gathered us together. I was walking, but I wasn't very old. My parents were concerned about how we children would stand the trip. There were long spaces where they would carry us. The trip was hard on them, too. I was a middle child. There were two in front of me and two behind me. The two younger had to be carried all the way or rode on the pack. We used donkeys, small beasts that carried all our possessions. The baby's cradle was strapped on the side.

"Sometimes we would stay in a camp for days, then push on until we reached that beautiful river where the banks were so green, looking up at huge granite cliffs. And there we found our people who had gone before, led by that one known as Ra-Ta. He was such a handsome man, so beautiful with a royal presence. Even as a child I thought he was the most beautiful man I'd ever met.

"He knew—they knew—the people in the palace knew that we would do anything he asked us, that we would obey him in all things because he was that leader that we would give our lives for.

"He was Ra then. He shortened his name to one syllable. It gave him greater power, for it mated his energy to the sun. He had great authority, and he established schools. He was constantly trying to improve the teaching. Some of the people we found there were backward. They weren't even shaped the way we were. They were dumpy-looking. They had feathers like birds and short tails. They were like animals in a way. And yet they walked upright. They walked as we did, we who came from the north and the east of the land known as Egypt. Ra had decided to help these people. They came up from the south, up the great river on large barges and rafts."

I listened and marveled, for all this streamed out of the mouth and mind of a woman who had been conversing casually with me for a few moments before on diseases of the eye and life on the Mississippi. She spoke now with such conviction in a strange voice without the semblance of a drawl, that I no longer thought of her as the genteel Southern lady from Mobile, Alabama, with deep roots in the South of Robert E. Lee and Jefferson Davis.

She had a new homeland now, and a new family, and a new direction, with old companions that were also new. I supposed hers was a typical family of that time and place, and hers a typical childhood, for thousands like her had taken the long trek. Her family was aspiring, like Ra himself. They came from a region near the Persian Gulf, not far from where the city of the hills and the plains later prospered. She had overheard tales as a child of an earlier journey, of her parents following Ra when the storied island beyond the Pillars of Hercules was destroyed.

Ra had become installed as the high priest, telling the Pharaohs he would make a great kingdom out of a poor land peopled by those who were stunted and disfigured in some way.

"He had such magnetism that none could doubt him when he spoke. He was special because he had come from a special place, where people were advanced and could make things happen with the power of their minds. It was said they had once been all mind, though this is hard to visualize. For there is then nothing to see. But then they say that one sees with his mind, as strange as that may seem."

As people were treated in the Temple Beautiful, and their appearance improved, Ra's fame spread throughout the land, and thousands came to have their bodies—and minds—improved.

"The people with appendages were ashamed of the way they looked. They were in a lower caste than the others, those like ourselves who were formed with a smooth skin and regular features. But Ra, being in tune with the universal force, knew something of the power of thought in not only healing people but in reshaping their bodies and minds. And when all else failed they would perform surgery, which improved the texture of the skin and the hair."

Listening to that voice, now droning on so casually, I found myself picturing an evolutionary process I had never seriously considered until I sat entranced in a small room in Virginia Beach under the spell of a stranger I had met only the day before.

Yet it all seemed so real, so true, as it came off her lips that I wondered for a moment whether I was the one in a hypnotic trance. And as she went on, I could almost feel the tension building up as Ra more and more extended his powers and the ruling class in Egypt began to look on this alien upstart as a threat to their position.

It all seemed to be flashing across her horizons as though she were not only there then but now. And where it came from only the past knew.

At first, all went well with Ra. "He had begun the Temple Beautiful and the Temple of Sacrifice, where the healings took place. But there were whisperings about him and the women, one woman in particular, who he took from another. He was building up support with an increasing number of people who had followed him as we did. The natives, too, liked him for he was kind and treated people alike, whatever their station. And so dissension arose in the land when a movement began in the palace to oust him from the land. Some complained about all the outlanders coming in. And so when there was a change in the rule, they were able to have him banished by the new king. Some left with him, including the woman. He urged others to stay and do their best, promising he would be back one day. My family was told to remain; the children were still young. I was thirteen, just coming of age. We knew he would be back, for he was the great Ra, and the people wanted him back.

"We kept in touch through the caravans coming through all the time with their wares. He had gone to a country to the west, to Nubia, a land of darker people, but we heard he visited other lands. He kept doing his healings, and his fame increased.

"We heard stories about his healings in Libya and India and in Persia, where we had all come from. There was a demand in these countries to keep him there, as he brought prosperity with him in the caravans that were drawn by stories of his accomplishments. Meanwhile, in Egypt the traffic into the country diminished, and the pinch was felt among the merchants and others. There was a grumbling in the land, with people saying, even the natives, how good the land had been when he was the high priest and how he should be even more influential."

Just knowing he would be back one day was enough to give her confidence in what he said she would one day do. So remembering what he had told her once about her atavistic ability to draw, she kept busy with her sketching. "I drew scenes along the Nile. I drew the boats with their many-colored sails and the people with their colorful headdresses. I was overwhelmed by the beauty of the land and tried to capture it with my drawing stick."

This sounded vaguely familiar, and I tried to remember what it was Cayce had said of her life experience in Egypt: "The entity was among the people that did not first journey to the Egyptian land, but with the establishing of the young king, with the banishment of the priest that was a relation of the entity. Later, with the return of the priest, the entity made the drawings that would now be termed the commercial, architectural drawing for much that had to do with the interior as well as exterior of the buildings."

The land was an artist's paradise.

"I loved the river. The nourishment came to the land through the river, but not on the banks. You couldn't build or grow anything on the banks before the floods would cover them. The city was on the stone cliffs. There were carvings on the cliffs, and I loved to copy them. Because of my sketches I had become part of the court, and I was in the palace. All the women's quarters are so beautiful. They had stuffed pillows so soft, beds of feathers, luxury I had never known."

I wondered at the marvelous detail that colored her descriptions of every aspect of Egyptian living. And I marveled even more where it came from, for whatever she was speaking of had long since faded away. She was ensconced in the palace, where the adversaries of her beloved Ra reigned, but she seemed to have discreetly adopted a posture of neutrality, for they had given her the opportunity to do the art work for which she had this innate ability.

"I copied old writings on animal skins that had been

scraped and oiled. I no longer had to use a burnt stick to draw with. They made a fluid from berries that I could dip the stick in and copy with that. I learned to make my own colors as well."

While Ra was away, she worked on the murals in an unfinished Temple Beautiful. "I thought how pleased he would be as I decorated the ceilings and walls that had gone up. I ground up colored stones, mixing them with fluids for some colors. I made a deep royal purple that was Ra's favorite from the beautiful snails that abounded in that area. I would grind the berries that grew on the edge of the desert to make the deep reds and crimsons that made the walls alive."

In the Ra's absence she had married an Egyptian, knowing the priest would one day bless the union since he was for joining the races as a way to end unsettling rivalries.

It had been a joyful wedding day but nothing to the joy she experienced the day Ra came back in triumph. She was among those who lined the streets. He had waved and smiled, greeting all the people with equal favor. In the entourage was the woman he had given up so much for and the others he favored. He made no attempt to hide them, and he never had, for he was the Ra, and in his return from exile, brought about by the public outcry, he found vindication and new prestige.

"He was now the prime minister to the king, the Pharaoh, and none but the ruler could challenge him. And he would be the last to do this, since he had brought him back to bring the people together and see prosperity once more in the land."

After a while, this youthful protégé of Ra had some difficulty with her husband, and for a respite went back into the temples to work as she had before. "I wanted to be near Ra, for I loved him as one loves his mentor. At least I could see him from a distance. My husband begged my forgiveness after Ra spoke to him and told me I could do as I wished as long as I came back to him."

She agreed, on that condition.

"So I helped with the finishing touches in the Temple Beautiful. I put the colors on the walls. I did not see Ra often. He would look in to see how the work was going, sometimes smile in approval, and then move on. For he was always busy greeting people. He saw everybody that came to be healed, though some were healed by others he trained. And when there were operations to be performed in the Temple Beautiful, he oversaw them as well. They say that he never slept. But he always had a wonderful glow about him, and he never appeared tired. It was no wonder that people worshiped him, though he never said he was a god.

"Though he had been around longer than anybody could remember, he looked ageless. He was like a man in his prime."

As she paused a moment to collect her thoughts, I felt I would like to know more about this Egyptian fountain of youth.

"How do you think he did it?" I asked, feeling there had to be more than facial creams or a face-lift to stay so young so long.

"It was described in the hieroglyphics, the pictures carved in the wall. They were images on scraped animal skin kept pliant with oils. I copied many things without understanding what they were.

"There was talk of it being done in a secret chamber, with the rejuvenating rays of a rare colored stone, as was done once in Atlantis. Not everybody could go into this chamber. It was for those with lives important to the state. It could only be repeated for so long. For then life became wearisome for those who lived two or three spans on this earth. I lived but one span. And that was very heavy at times."

I could see where women would be drawn to such a man as she described. He had a magnetic power, enhanced by a striking appearance. "He seemed to give off a golden aura, like the sun itself. In coloring he was not as dark as an Egyptian and by comparison quite fair. But he was not as fair as some of the visitors, for his skin had a reddish tinge. His eyes were almost black at times. And yet they were blue when you saw them in the light. He could read your thoughts, by just looking into your eyes. I did not look at him directly. It was like looking into the sun."

She said this in such a way that I asked, "Were you in love with him?"

"We all loved him."

"Were you in love with him?" I repeated.

"We all adored him." She would not be pinned down. "He was much too high for one like me. He had a royal look about him."

She had felt that he would go on forever, but of late he appeared a little weary. He didn't smile as often, and he seemed preoccupied, looking off into space.

"The temples were all built, and the pyramids were being completed. I had the feeling that his work was finished, and it was time for him to rest. It was not in anything he said, for he didn't say very much. The thought of death never bothered him; he never spoke of it. For he knew where he had come from, just as we all knew. And I am sure he knew where he was going. Whatever there was to know, he knew."

One day she looked around and he was gone. There were no farewells, no good-byes, no sentimental exchanges. He had disappeared just as mysteriously as he had arrived. "The older people said we were not to fret about it. His energy would always be with us. He had gone off to renew himself, and he would be back again one day. There was no funeral, no body to be eulogized. His soul had departed."

In the reality of her regression I had come to think of her as a subject of Ra. I was surprised at the equanimity with which she received his death, for it could have been nothing else.

"He was not only your priest but your leader. Wasn't there any kind of inquiry to learn what had happened to him?"

"Those of the leaders of our people, who had come with him into Egypt, knew where he had gone and assured us that there was no need for alarm, he had been with us when we needed him."

"He had not been put away?"

She seemed horrified at the thought.

"Oh, no. It was his time to leave. He had accomplished what he came for."

I marveled again at the authority of the subconscious mind. For here I was—an experienced reporter, schooled in the hard-core reporting of who, what, where, and when—sitting on the edge of my seat as I asked of a woman in trance, "And what had he come for?"

The answer rolled off her lips, as though Ra himself were speaking.

"To bring about a unity of minds, to establish a oneness, to have all races know they were one and the same. For to that land he built there came people from all over to study with one who knew the secrets of the universe. I was of a lower order. Yet I was able to work in the temple because of his belief that people should be allowed to express themselves and live up to whatever their abilities were. Some could not draw a straight line and wondered at the pictures I drew. Yet they could play the flute, the pipes, and I could not beat in time with them. He wanted everyone to develop their inner capacities, for as the individual grew, so did the nation. No leader in Egypt had thought like that before."

He was little different in this respect from the Edgar Cayce his old companions from Egypt knew in this life. For, in this land, too, he had a revolutionary impact on the social order, for example, integrating Sunday school classes in the South never before integrated. As Ra, he had brought a revolution. And that may have been why he was exiled, not for one woman, or a half a dozen women, but for threatening an establishment that had made a slave state of Egypt. Always before the blame had been put on that one woman taken by Ra out of the arms of another man. But since Ra came out of exile with that woman, that clearly was never the sole issue.

When he came back after nine years he brought great plans, great expectations. And he started building: pyramids, temples, housing centers. He was always on the scene looking after things. "He was able to move the great stones of the pyramids as if they were made of cork," she said.

For centuries humankind had wondered how the Egyptians had moved the huge stones of the pyramids into place. Nobody knew, except perhaps the people who were there.

"Was it by air pressure or winches, some hydraulic force?" I asked.

"He talked to the stones. He would point and say, 'I

want you there,' and the stone moved there. It was as simple as that."

Simple? Unbelievable, was more like it. "Did he wave at the stone or create any pressure under it?"

"He didn't touch the stone."

Perhaps it was in the pitch of his voice. In some way, if Anne Holbein was accurate, this wonder from Atlantis may have changed the gravity field, floating the massive stones pretty much as the astronauts floated in space. I reminded myself what Cayce had said about not allowing our limitations to limit nature.

Ra had an equally miraculous healing gift. His protégé's right hand had been crushed by a stone. For weeks she had been unable to move it. She cried over her loss until Ra said one day, "What are you crying about? You have another hand, haven't you?"

She looked at him in wonder.

"Another what?"

"Another hand. Use it."

He stroked her hand a few times. It didn't seem to help, not at the time. "But I learned to do all the things I had done with my right hand with my left hand. Then, as if by a miracle, my right hand became useful again. Not as adept, as cunning as it had been before, but I could use it. Ra made it possible. He was so far and above all of us that he was like a god."

She had no idea what gravitational law he had evoked to lift the giant stones. But Christ had done more: changing water to wine, calming the waves, raising the dead, disappearing at will in a throng. Hadn't Christ told his people they could do what he did and more with the help of the Father? What was a miracle but that which ordinary people didn't understand—the first lighting of a match, the first gunpowder, the first plane to fly?

But the healing was something she should know about, since she had been the object of it.

"Did you feel any sensation when he stroked your hand? Did he say, 'I am going to heal this hand'?"

"His lips moved, but no sound came, and his touch was like that of fire!"

Why, if she so trusted in Ra, had she not allowed him to heal as soon as she hurt herself?

"I did not want him to know how clumsy I was. I had

thought it would heal in time. It was my fault. The stone was overbalanced and slipped off another stone."

"Had they been building the pyramids?"

"They were finishing the Temple Beautiful. He was anxious to finish the temple so we could accommodate all those from other lands who wanted to be healed. He felt it was a way of creating goodwill and bringing peace to our land. People were coming from many lands to study at his feet, returning to their homelands to heal their own people.

"In many countries during his exile he saw hardships and hunger. He did what he could to help the needy and homeless as they arrived. He helped them to get established in the soil, for ours was the most fertile spot in this part of the world.

"He made Egypt the center of civilization. People came from the Far East, the land of the yellow people, from the north wearing heavy skins. They were uncomfortable in our hot sun. We introduced them to the cotton cloth that protected us from the sun. They came from all countries to hear his wisdom and to learn to live with one another."

It seemed to me that Egypt was an ancient land much like America and that Edgar Cayce was like Ra in telling people, "Forget self and serve your neighbor."

Anne Holbein agreed.

"Ra taught that man had to share, to know that other men had some talent, some skill, some way of benefiting him without killing each other. And he carried this message with caravans to the east and west. And the people in the caravan would talk of this great man. And the leaders of these countries, the priests, the teachers, would come back with the caravans and sit at Ra's feet."

It was indeed a wonderful story. But as a reporter looking back twelve thousand years, I had an uneasy feeling that something was missing. There had to be something more than we knew to hasten Ra's exile, for he was a man of parts, of great service to those who ruled the land.

"What other reason was there?" I asked Jeanette Thomas, treating what seemed reality as reality. "It could have precipitated a revolution."

"I think you have a good hunch there," said Jeanette,

IN THE STEPS OF THE RA

pulling out a report by Hugh Lynn Cayce, the seer's son, which was simply titled "Egypt."

"How would Hugh Lynn know about it?" I said.

She smiled. "Oh, he had his pipeline."

I thumbed through the pages, and one paragraph caught my eye.

"On his return to the Temple of Sacrifice, which was being extended all the time, Ra-Ta saw there was an aggrandizing of the lusts of the body, rather than the activities that were to be carried on by the sacrificial priests. One ruling faction held that the sexual activity of the upper classes should be encouraged in the temple, to the exclusion of the progenerating priests, as it would produce the ultimate in perfect bodies instead of going to the effort of perfecting them after their arrival.

"The Ra resisted, angering the ruling class by charging they were tampering the laws of reproduction for their own sexual gratification. And they, with Machiavellian delight, plotted to hoist this upstart on his own petard, singling out a temptress so beautiful of face and form that he would not be able to resist.

"Among a certain priest's daughters was one of the king's favorites who made entertainment for the king and his council. She was a dancer more beautiful than any and was induced to gain the high priest's favor so as to cause some fault to be found in him.

"The activities in the Temple of Sacrifice brought Ra and Isis into closer relationship. Then came the decree that Isis had been chosen to be the channel through which there might be such a perfect body, and Ra-Ta went along with it. He was of those who trusted all, and the gods laughed at his weakness."

And when the perfect child was born, then came the charges that Ra had broken the very laws that he had established when he ordered the removal of sexual activity from the temples.

"Hence there came many divisions and the first uprising between church and state, until there was the trial of Ra and Isis, and they were banished into the Nubian land."

Through it all, Ra remained as mysterious as ever. In exile and out of it, he was untouchable, moving about, influencing people and nations, trying to improve the race by hastening the cause of evolution, and not hesitating himself to partake what he thought best for the state and himself. His obvious psychic powers, rooted in Atlantis, grew in magnitude as he used them. He was an elitist, and it was apparent that no one woman could long hold him. Yet he remained loyal to the lady Isis even as he participated in his own program to produce a race that was to dominate the known world's culture for thousands of years. He was a man of parts.

As well as I had known Hugh Lynn, I had never understood the connection he felt with an Egyptian sun god. It was as if he were tremendously in his debt, constantly obligated to mention the name Ra with reverence, and at times almost doing penance. Yet I had always sensed that here was a man who was secretly driven. At a time when the very mention of Edgar Cayce invoked laughter and scorn, the son had made a life's work of getting America's greatest mystic the recognition he deserved. At great sacrifice to himself and his growing family, he roamed the country speaking about his father's gift to anyone who would listen.

I remember calling his home in Virginia Beach one evening and asking his wife, Sally, how I could reach her husband.

"He's speaking in New York tonight," she said. "But I'm not sure where he'll be tomorrow. If the collection plate is generous, he'll move on to some other city to speak about Edgar Cayce. And if it isn't, I just don't know how the poor man is going to get home."

Handicapped by a nervous stammer, he had made an eloquent speaker of himself, rehearsing his talks endlessly before mirrors and the scout troop of which he was scoutmaster. "When I got them listening," he would laugh, "I knew I was ready for any audience."

Well educated, sophisticated, with a quick mind, he could have succeeded in any business or profession. But he saw his wife teaching part-time in a Virginia Beach school and his children go without comforts, in his dedication to a cause that for years didn't appear to be getting anywhere. Not once did I see him discouraged. But I knew there were moments when he must have sat down and wept at the poverty and humiliation he had imposed on himself and his family.

He heard his father, the epitome of Christian virtue, denounced as an Antichrist by some of the leading ministers of the day. And as a boy, he was taunted and shunned by other children. But none of this bothered him, for he knew his father was a great man. Had his father not saved Hugh Lynn's eyesight when the doctors said he would be blind for life?

Not knowing of any connection Hugh Lynn had with Ra, for he seldom discussed past lives with me, I was rather surprised that he should be considered an authority on that particular period.

I could see the twinkle in Jeanette's eye at my perplexity.

"You mean you didn't know who he was?"

I shrugged. "But why would he know what Edgar Cayce would know?"

"Because he didn't have to look very far."

"And he shared a life with Cayce?"

"Very much so."

"But why would he know about the plot?"

"Because," she smiled, "he was the Pharaoh who banished Ra. And he spent this lifetime making up for it."

CHAPTER 5

Persia

Anne Holbein had never known a time when she didn't want to be an eye doctor. Long before she had a reading with Edgar Cayce, she dreamed of being an ophthalmologist. But that meant four years of undergraduate study, four more of medical school, and three years' residence in hospitals, learning about the diseases of the eye and how to treat them.

It was the Depression, and all these years of training were out of her reach, financially. It was difficult, indeed, to manage four years of college, without all that graduate work. She persevered and went into optometry, which demanded an equal facility in the refraction of the eyes and the detection of disease. In becoming one of the first female optometrists in Alabama, she was saluted by colleagues and patients alike for her skill and dexterity.

She was still practicing her profession and would continue as long as she was able. For it was something she had excelled at as a pioneer in an art developed thousands of years ago in a land where the unforgiving nature of the hot sun on the desert sand resulted in a host of visual disorders and blindness.

The man she called "Daddy Cayce" had wanted to start her off in this life with a reading that "may be helpful to the entity in the present experience, as to conditions or surroundings. Then the why of things may be gathered from the experiences through which the entity has passed."

This was something that Cayce stressed, seeing so much of the present in the distant past. For remembrance was never wholly extinguished by the conscious mind, which controlled the activities of the average person.

"The soul mind manifests itself," said Cayce, "in what we do and what we like, what we want and what we reject."

And Anne was soon to find out why she opted for the eyes. The interest came down through the centuries, six thousand years before Christ, Cayce said, when she was an older sister of the tribal chief Uhjltd [Cayce] and studied with him in the Persian city of the hills and plains, where he reigned in an enlightened way.

"With the establishing of that city where the healing arts came, the entity was among those of that leader's people who eventually aided much in the healing activities during that sojourn.

"The entity aided those blinded by the sands and the glare. She was among the first in that environ to make for the protecting of the eyesight by the shades, by glass imported from the Egyptian and Indian experience.

"Hence in this material activity may the entity aid in bringing help even as then. Yes, as a teacher, a director in that field, may much of this world's good come into that experience."

Anne had been so responsive in previous regressions I had no doubt that as the sister of Uhjltd she would provide a good perspective on what was going on in the land where Cayce once trod.

I had long ago concluded, from regressions with novelist Taylor Caldwell and others, that time regressions, like dreams, had their roots in some reality—call it imagination or fantasy or whatever one liked.

"Dismissing it as imagination," a wise man had said, "neither explains it nor dismisses it. For imagination, like any thought-form, comes out of something."

As the regression validated a life experience, explaining an individual's activity that had no other explanation, it was something to think about, particularly with Anne, a marvelous subject who had shared so much with Cayce in the past.

In the few moments it took to regress her, Anne was sleeping like a baby. And babies, as Cayce said, were closest to their past, since very little in their present clouded that past.

She had no more trouble traveling back to Persia than she had with Egypt or colonial Virginia. She pronounced her name, Ujilda, as "Yelda," just as Cayce's name Uhjltd, was pronounced "Yuelt." She seemed to enjoy talking about him, basking in his fame and accomplishments, and looked at him with something of an older sister's sufferance.

Her voice had changed, and there was almost a whine in it, totally out of character. For Anne Holbein was anything but a whiner. She had made her way through life by taking the bull by the horns and giving it a good shove. She was more like the Egyptian girl who made a mission of her art work in the temples of Ra.

She had learned to sublimate her life in the life of her brother, as she had done more or less under the influence of Ra.

"He was only twenty-one," she was saying of Uhjltd, "when he was sent off to Egypt to be exposed to a sophisticated and metaphysical culture so he would rule our people with wisdom. He was drawn to Egypt, and I had wondered whether he would come back, he was so stimulated by that ancient environment."

She objected to a system that kept her as a woman from exercising the leadership due her station, but she did nothing to put herself forward. She offered advice that nobody listened to, and when she said "I told you so," nobody cared. The counselors who ran the country, with the father dead and Uhjltd away, had nothing to fear from her. She was a paper tiger, needing to be reborn, to one day express herself in a courageous way.

Still, she was proud of her brother. It showed in the way she talked about his achievements. For when he came back he took the land out of tribal squabbles into the first rank of nations, rivaling even mighty Egypt where his past as Ra had made him in this new lifetime an apt pupil.

"The land was in conflict, and there were constant raids by our neighbors. But when Uhjltd took hold, great changes started to take place. He was very handsome, with a charismatic look, and he took naturally to leadership. The people loved him. He had the widsom of an older man and set up many healing centers. One was a receiving center, adapted from a center in Egypt where he was so much at home. He brought back many herbs, which we planted on the mountain side. These herbs

were used in the healing. They were familiar to him. He
had used them all before. One plant was parsley, used
as a purifier. The herbs were used for respiratory ailments. To improve the vision, olives would be crushed
and the soothing oil used to remove crusts from the eyes
of the natives overexposed to the desert sun.

"The healings were a centerpiece of Uhjltd's adminis-
tration. With these miracles, like Jesus, he attracted followers, capturing the interest of the people. Not since
the great Ra, who was almost a living legend, had there
been anyone like him. He was a prophet with honor in
his own land.

"He had sent for two Egyptian healers to help train
his people. And they had brought others to lighten the
load. The two Egyptians, using the word *Ra* to invoke
their healings, were told by Uhjltd to remove that name
from their prayers. He told them that no mortal should
be worshiped. When he was asked if he had any relationship to Ra, he would only smile. He rarely got angry. I
saw him lose his temper only once, when he discovered
that one of the Egyptian healers was pressing a patient
for payment. Uhjltd asked no money. People gave what
they could, as they felt helped.

"He was furious when he found the healer—named
Tarah—had demanded the sick man turn over his young
daughter to him for the price of being made well. In a
rage he drove the Egyptian off, saying one rotten apple
could spoil a whole barrel."

It was a sad reflection on my experience as a reporter
that whenever I heard of anything unsavory, I felt I was
dealing with reality. However, in Uhjltd's attitude about
money for healing, I saw a reassuring influence on
Cayce's idealism in this lifetime.

"Not everybody was helped. Not all were healed, and
yet the dying in a way were very much a part of the
healing process. Some, beyond help in the physical,
needed a release from this life. We cared for them and
made their lives comfortable. We got families to take
them in. But they would go back home to die. Uhjltd
prepared them for death. He would take them by the
hand and look into their eyes and tell them that the great
spirit, the creator of all, needed them somewhere else
and that he would make it as peaceful as possible for

them to return to their creator. And he used seeds from a beautiful rose-colored flower to ease their pain. He had this huge bowl he had brought from Egypt, and he would grind the grasses and the seeds and some of the plants, mashing them into a powder. He had some extend their tongue, and he would place the powder on the very back of the tongue and give them a little sip of water. All this he learned in Egypt."

There was more about natural healing, which both Ra and Uhjltd appeared to espouse in similar fashion, as became the karmic forbears of Edgar Cayce.

"He trained some of our people to pray, to meditate, and to fast; to cleanse themselves in such a way that creative forces would come through them. They were vegetarians, free of the fermented juices that some people used. When it was their turn to serve in a hospital, they would do without food for three days to purify themselves. They would serve for the life of a moon, a month at a time. There were sometimes twenty-five workers in the centers. Uhjltd was there all the time."

I had not led the regression, instead letting her roam wherever her subconscious took her, so that what was important or significant would come out naturally. She had broken off her discourse about the eyes just as I thought we were about to get into the aptitude carryover Cayce had mentioned. But if a regression wasn't spontaneous, it was hardly validating in itself. She had a way of edging into things that was a peculiarity of her own subconscious. It may have been a reflection not on Anne Holbein's character but of Ujilda, who seemed to be a person not very sure of her situation.

She eventually got back to the eyes, as I felt she would. For she had left that significant chapter of her experience unfinished. Unfinished, it would not be that significant. For it was her subconscious that determined what was important. As though recalling what had gone unsaid, she now said, "After we removed the crusts from the eyes, this set up the patients for the healings. Then my brother would touch them and restore their sight."

There were also preventive measures, so that the glaucoma and other eye ailments endemic to that region would be curtailed. These measures could very well have spawned the first dark glasses, long before they were popularized by Hollywood.

"There was a stone so clear," she said, "that it could be scaled into thin transparent flakes and used to keep the glaring sand from hurting the eyes of people working in the sun. The glass was set into strips or thongs of leather and tied around the head to hold the glass in place before the eyes. Later, we learned to use metal and let the metal extend back over the ears."

They had learned to grind together the thin crystallike flakes with the colored stones and the sand to get the first tinted eyeglasses.

"Sometimes," she said, "we would use another powder dug up from the earth, a deep red powder, to remove scratches on the glass that a desert storm would leave. We called it rouge. It was a nonabrasive polish."

She did general work as well in the treatment center, applying color therapy with various-colored stones in cases of arthritis and other rheumatic disorders. "We saw a hundred people a day in the main receiving room. Uhjltd meditated over the sick people as a group. He would touch a patient and call on the divine force to guide him. But often there were other things that had to be done, and Uhjltd would know by his touch exactly what had to be used, such as herbs or healing waters."

The thought struck me that Edgar Cayce had not healed people in the same way. He would often send them to healers—osteopaths, chiropractors, medical doctors—who would effect the healing using diagnoses and remedies he prescribed. But he had never felt any inclination to heal by a laying on of hands. Yet by and large, the healings were a similar psychic process, with herbs, diet, and healing waters very much a part of the Cayce horn of plenty.

Large, bulging tumors would respond to Uhjltd's touch, the fluid pouring out like a fountain. As often as not he would treat people with the healing waters from the wells in that area, sometimes by dissolving powders into the water and having people drink it. "He would do it with diet, taking people off meat and giving them a large purple fruit like an eggplant, leeks, and parsley and the Jerusalem artichoke, which was good for the sweet sickness [diabetes]."

Help was given to whoever turned up, regardless of race or religion. Just as I was thinking how generous this was, and how appreciative the people must be, Ujilda thoroughly disillusioned me by saying, "The ruling people in the neighboring lands resented all this. They thought we were getting too influential. Too many of their people stayed on because of the caring and compassion they couldn't find elsewhere."

The world hadn't changed very much in eight thousand years.

In a period of months Uhjltd had brought peace to the cities and the countryside, organizing bands of youths to protect the caravans that came through their country. An end was put to rapacious raids, in which gold and young women had been the prize. The country prospered. However, there was a dissatisfied element, craving easy spoils. They turned the brasher young men against their leader, holding out the prospect of plunder in neighboring Lydia, the richest of all lands. This country was ruled by Croesus, the richest of all kings, whose wealth made commonplace the saying "as rich as Croesus." With Uhjltd out of the country on a friendly mission, one Oujida, the commander of the palace guard, led a body of troops in a raid on Lydia's royal school and carried off the King's daughter, Elia, and some companions, holding them for a king's ransom. Oujida sent Elia's closest friend and schoolmate, Ilya, daughter of a cabinet minister, to the king with the ransom demands. Oujida's troops looked on their young, nubile captives with hungry eyes. Rather than submit, Elia and the other hostages killed themselves, and the news of this honor spread quickly through the land of Lydia.

Returning from his mission, Uhjltd was dismayed by word of Oujida's actions. As news came of the Lydians arming, the bedouin leader debated his course. He could form a loyal army, quickly punish Oujida, then do battle with the Lydians before they could mobilize fully.

He chose a bolder course; he decided to ride off alone to the Lydian capital, demonstrating his good faith, and humbly offer whatever reparations the Lydians demanded. On the way his horse became disabled, and he had to proceed over the hot sands on foot.

Anne appeared to be caught up in her story, which

was one that she could have heard about only after the fact. But her voice was touched with admiration for her princely brother as she described his struggle through the desert against the elements. In the end she faltered, emotionally drained by an experience that for some reason she did not wish to continue.

Just as he had collected Edgar Cayce's account of the Egyptian excursion, Hugh Lynn Cayce had compiled one on the Persian experience, stringing together the loose ends until he had a moving narrative of one of the most momentous events in Edgar Cayce's past.

Picking up where Anne had become hazy, Hugh Lynn's account depicted a lone plainsman approaching a small oasis outside the gates of an outlying Lydian fort and, at a well beneath three palm trees, seeking a drink of water from a beautiful Lydian girl who appeared to be relaxing in the evening air.

"That girl was Ilya, mourning the fate of her companions, seeking the coolness and quiet of the oasis, away from the heat and squalor of the fort. And the lone plainsman was Uhjltd."

As they talked, strangely drawn to each other, Uhjltd identified himself and explained he was on a mission of peace. All the fruits of Oujida's freebooting assault were to be returned, he promised.

"And the girls," cried a bitter Ilya, "what of them?"

Uhjltd was taken prisoner by the commandant of the fort, exposed by a grieving Ilya. She later repented, finding herself believing him because of some unmistakable chord between them, and she helped him to escape. It was their destiny to help one another, now and in the future. But at this time, in retribution, the furious commander ordered Ilya turned out into the burning desert with two days' ration of food and water.

In a dream that night, Uhjltd saw the young woman struggling in the desert, without water or food. He retraced his steps and met up with a feeble Ilya, barely dragging herself along. With an iron will, parched and half-starved himself, he half pulled, half carried her over the hot sands, arriving finally at the foothills where fringes of grass indicated water nearby. He left Ilya in a small cave where she was protected from the sun and went foraging for food. Climbing into the hills, he fell off a ledge and broke an arm, fainting with the pain. After he came to, he limped his way back to the cave with a freshly killed hare he had found by an eagle's nest.

Over their food, a grateful Uhjltd said grace in a husky voice: "The Great One has answered our prayers. We have food and water, and we shall live. Let us offer our thanks."

As they murmured their prayers, they saw, as though in a mirage, a great array of white tents flung up in the desert sands, set off by clusters of palm trees and an expanse of cultivated land.

"This is a vision of the morrow," Uhjltd cried. "Here we shall teach the truths of the Great One." He held up his broken arm, and his eyes gleamed as he saluted the Creator. "My arm no longer pains me. He has healed me."

"The day came," wrote Hugh Lynn, "when men of many nations arrived in the city of the tents, seeking light and understanding. From Greece, India, Egypt, and even faraway China, seekers of truth came and sat at the feet of Uhjltd and then carried with them to their distant lands the teachings of this great leader. Thousands came to be healed, and many were the wondrous cures that were performed in the camp, both by Uhjltd and his students."

And Uhjltd took as his bride the fair Ilya. Before an assembly of his people he turned to the young woman who stood by his side with adoring eyes, and said:

"None among us has been more patient and loyal than our beautiful Ilya." He gave her a little bow. "Before you all I do now declare her to be my dear and accepted bride."

I now understood why Anne's voice had faltered and she had broken off the regression; she had seen herself being displaced not only in the healing center but in her brother's affections and she could not see any reason for going on. She had never married, and the special love between her and her brother was usurped now by another. They would meet again as he had promised, and it would be better then, she knew.

There was still Oujida to be dealt with, but Uhjltd seemed strangely reluctant to punish him, and the reason soon became clear. It all went back to the past they shared. There was a bond between the two men. In Egypt, Oujida had been a companion and rival of Ra. Coming from Atlantis like Ra, he restored a number of monuments for the old king and built that mystery of mysteries, the Sphinx.

"The entity [Pujida] was then in the name of Arsrha and the stone carver for the ruler. The entity gave the geometrical forces to the people, being then the mathematician and assistant to the astrologer and soothsayer of the day."

And in this lifetime, like so many from the past, the former Oujida took a well-worn path to the doorstep of his onetime leader.

"His name was Thomas B. Brown," said Jeanette Thomas, the keeper of the records, "and his career manifested the accomplishments of the past. He was an Ohio businessman and inventor, who provided Cayce with the radioactive appliance recommended for various disorders in many of the readings."

There was an attachment born of the ages between the two men. Brown, a hardline businessman, could not do enough for the man whose life he had entered for a third time.

"Even though the Depression was in the wind," recalled Jeanette, "Mister Brown raised large sums of money for an Edgar Cayce hospital and wrote a testimonial for the laying of the cornerstone: 'These words lie buried with this cornerstone, but not so our hopes for this institution and for what it stands. May its usefulness to humanity expand far beyond our present conception and for many generations light the way of mankind.'"

The hospital fell victim to the Depression a few years later. But the words lingered, along with the freely given help from this zealous companion out of the past.

My thoughts turned, meanwhile, to that wonderful pair, Ilya and Uhjltd, divisible only by death, whose love already appeared to have bound them for the ages.

I sighed a little as I considered how empty and transient life seemed without the perfect love that Cayce so often spoke of—the love of twin flames, of soulmates, the light of their love burning eternally into time. What a moving story theirs was.

I looked up at Jeanette and saw she had tears in her eyes.

"Isn't it wonderful," I said. "Uhjltd and Ilya, Edgar and Gertrude, working out their karma in Egypt, Persia, and now twentieth-century America?"

She gave me a strange look. "Ilya, you know, was not Gertrude."

"Not Gertrude? Then who was she?"

She laughed. "It was Gladys, Gladys Davis. She was Edgar's soulmate in Atlantis and again in Persia."

"No wonder she walked right into her job," I said, not surprised at anything by now.

"Yes," she said, "healing and helping people just as they did thousands of years ago."

CHAPTER 6

Beware of Greeks

As a boy I had been bedazzled by all those Greeks and Trojans killing each other for ten years over a woman. They said she was beautiful enough to launch a thousand ships, and I could well believe it as I thought of all the trouble she caused. Or was it Paris, the fair Helen's Trojan lover, who was at fault? But unlike Helen of Troy—mind you, not of Sparta or Greece, as you would have thought—he had not broken his marital vows to elope with another partner.

She was a woman whose fame had endured long after the dust of battle had blown over. And the men who had died for her, Xenon, the keeper of the Trojan gate, and the heroic Achilles, were mere pawns in the greater struggle for the straits commanding the Grecian seas.

Theirs, as a later poet wrote of another bloodbath, was not to reason why; theirs was but to do and die. And they did it very well, while Helen occasionally watched from the ramparts and looked into the unforgiving mirror for any new sign of a wrinkle. This was not the kind of company that Edgar Cayce would seem at home with. And yet in a life reading he became Xenon, that keeper of the gate in Troy when it was sacked by the Greeks after they duped the gullible Trojans by building a wooden horse outside the Trojan walls and faking their departure. Why the Trojans, despite the warnings of the prophetess Cassandra and plain common sense, dragged the horse through the gates that had withstood attack for ten long years was something I had never understood, not even as a schoolboy. And as we know, scores of Greek warriors, hidden in the giant horse, broke out of their hiding place as the city slept and opened the gates to thousands of comrades who had stolen back from their ships under cover of darkness.

How could Xenon, as a keeper of the gates, have permitted any such stratagem to succeed when the Greeks, particularly Ulysses, were known for their craftiness? Why did the Trojan people, under no restraint by their rulers, drag the horse within their walls after gallantly resisting for so long? However you looked at it, it didn't make sense.

It was hard to conceive of anybody like Cayce picking out a life as Xenon, when, if it was all imagination, he might just as easily have imagined himself Priam or Hector, both valid Trojan heroes, or one of the heroic Greeks, such as Achilles, Ajax, or Ulysses, whose fame endures to this day.

Who was this Xenon, whose eternal soul was that of Edgar Cayce's in that experience? Why was he Xenon, to what purpose? For wasn't this a fall for the man of influence in Atlantis, ancient Egypt, and the city of the plains in Persia-Arabia? Wasn't reincarnation an opportunity to learn from one life to another, to develop oneself for the common good?

I was curious about what Cayce had to say about the Trojan connection and intrigued, too, by a period of history glorified by the blind Homer in his *Iliad*. A sleeping Cayce had given Xenon life, and to that life reading I went. I soon found Xenon had been many things before being dragooned into service as a warrior in the defense of his homeland: "the student, chemist, the sculptor, and the artisan, as well as of the soldier and the defender in the last days."

These would hardly provide the qualities for a good fighting man, so it seemed odd that he did not have more military background to justify the position he gave himself in that distant time. But Cayce did not see Troy as a military power; in his eyes it was hardly a match for the Greeks who came seeking the beautiful Helen, abducted by a craven Paris from the palace of her husband, Menelaus, king of Sparta.

Troy, said Cayce, was a land given to the arts, explaining Xenon's preoccupation with a peaceable vocation. "As was manifest when the Trojan rule was in that fair country to whom the nations of the world have looked for beauty in culture, art, and refinement of a physical, mental, and material force. And we find again the soldier and the defender of the gate in this place where the destruction came to the body."

While hardly the background for spirituality, the life reading in that sphere did attribute to the Trojan Cayce "the love of the beautiful in any and every form, especially those that partake of the human form divine."

Conscripted, he did his duty without complaint. He didn't seem a bad sort, and he might have gone on to do things and improve himself spiritually if it had not been for war. But again I was struck by this attraction to women that seemed to dog him from one life to the next, in contrast to the image I had held of Cayce as virtually monastic in thought and deed.

In other books I had done on Cayce, I had not encountered this side of him. Somehow this made him vulnerable in my eyes. As he had said more than once as a warning against temptation, "Think first what the good Lord wants you to be."

Yet it also made him more human.

In the long struggle with the Greeks he not only joined in battle but was a trenchant observer as well. Not even the poetic Homer drew a more graphic picture of the historic conflict, some of which Cayce recognized in this life in a haunting dream:

"Again I was among those guarding the gates. I wore a garment that would be called a toga today. My trousers were of a cloth wrapped around me, gathered and pinned in the middle between my legs. Another square piece of cloth with a hole for my head dropped over my shoulders. I made armholes in this piece, so that my arms could come through and not have to throw the garment out of the way, which method afterward was adopted by most of the army (or the people, for I didn't recognize them as an army)."

I remembered fragments of Homer's *Iliad*, and what I did recall of his memorable duel between two heroic captains—Hector for Troy and Achilles for the Greeks—was no more haunting than Cayce's account of that mortal combat:

I saw the battle between Hector and Achilles. They were both beautiful of countenance. Both had matted black ringlets on their heads, which reminded me of

Medusa. The hair seemed to be their strength. I noticed that Achilles was very hairy, while Hector had
hair on his neck, which was a different color from the
hair on his face. I saw Hector dragged through the
gate, which I was guarding, into a large arena. He
was dragged around the arena several times. Although
he had lost quite a bit of blood, leaving the ground
and stones bloody as he was dragged along, I noticed
that he hadn't wholly lost consciousness. Eventually
the horses—in turning very swiftly, with Achilles driving—caused Hector's head to be dashed against the
pillar of the gate near me, and his brains ran out.
Before his life was gone or the last quiver of the mus-
cles and the nerves, I saw the carrion birds eat the
great portions of his brain.

At this point, though intrigued, I was confused. This
life as Xenon was so different from the spiritual growth
of the past that it appeared to deny the very concept of
karma and reincarnation. Others, knowing Cayce, shared
my confusion, for they asked him to explain this apparent
lapse in his spiritual development.

Cayce was fifty-eight when this reading was given in
Virginia Beach in 1936. It was conducted by his wife
Gertrude, with Gladys Davis taking notes and several
members of the Cayce study group present.

The question was put to the soul of Edgar Cayce, "especially that phase of its experience on earth known as
Xenon."

It got right to the heart of the matter.

"We ask that the Creative Forces present in this entity
review the activities of the experience of Xenon and tell
us how and why this entity failed or lost, when, according
to the information through these channels, this entity
Edgar Cayce as Uhjltd and Ra-Ta had manifested in a
marvelous man. Tell us in an understandable manner
how this entity may meet these failures now and attain
to the former estate as Uhjltd or Ra-Ta."

It was something I had wondered myself, yet recogniz-
ing that, in these two spiritually enlightened incarnations,
Cayce's soul was still trammeled by problems of the
flesh. The sleeping Cayce didn't equivocate.

"To understand the nature of Xenon and the failure

of its activity," he said, "they would have to know the conditions."

As he pointed out, the Trojan War took place a thousand years before Christ, a time fixed by historians. But Cayce, in citing the conditions, considered the larger period of Troy's rivalry as a city-state in Asia Minor with Sparta, Athens, and the rest of Greece.

"The period, as man would count time, was 1158 B.C. to 1012 B.C., at a time when many of those who had been in the Atlantis and Lemurian Age were entering in the affairs of man, in a cycle when there was the breeding of strife. So in that experience strife was bred among the Grecians and Trojans, both looking for an excuse that there might be a meeting of strength."

For some time the war had been brewing over which nation would control the area of the Mediterranean. Xenon was a victim of the power struggle. He was no more responsible for his soldiering than any GI in World War II. The extended rivalry, with its emphasis on militarism, upset his normal expectations.

"There is ever the combativeness between right and wrong or power and strength or the irresistible and immovable. They are ever constantly vying, one with the other. Into such an environ came (the soul of) Ra-Ta and Uhjltd for those experiences that would have brought— or were to bring—the strength, the power of resistance in the face of adversity, or that strength necessary in the face of the ups rather than the downs."

What about Xenon's free will? For it was the way people responded to events, not the events themselves that shaped their karma, as I understood Cayce. I looked for the chink in Xenon's armor, for karmically it had to be there.

Xenon had started off well enough and in modern parlance might have been voted the student most likely to succeed. In the tradition of Uhjltd and Ra-Ta, he was first a student of chemistry, mechanics, and other related matters. But he was "forced against his own will" into a conflict ostensibly over Helen, but predominantly, as Cayce suggested, for the control of the vital waterways governing the navigation between Europe and Asia.

In the end it was Xenon's ego that was his undoing, for, said Cayce, he took too much on himself, thinking he was a match for the cunning invaders. "There was little opportunity of the Grecian breakthrough, for the gates prepared against the invaders had withheld all the assaults, because of the power given the entity to guard the gate." But the Trojans, including Xenon, reckoned without the wiles of the crafty Ulysses and other Greek commanders, weary of a siege that had kept them from their homes for ten years.

"There rose conditions to weaken this power, through the subtlety not in the experience of the entity. These, by the misplacing of the trust in him, brought to the entity shame in the material sense, dishonor in the mental self. For he had come to depend rather upon the abilities of self, which is oft the undoing of the soul. In this manner then did the entity fail. And with the failure came the experience of being an outcast, as one dishonored, as one thought little of. At last losing self through self-destruction."

And so he had taken his life, but it was still not clear how and why. How had he failed the Greeks at the gate? And why was he covered with shame? He apparently had fought valiantly and been held in high regard by the royal Priam, the father of Hector and Paris.

"And this is the great barrier, the great experience which the entity must meet in the present, the one thing most needed, a regeneration from that experience."

This still tells nothing about why this failure had befallen him. But now we learn more on how Cayce, in this lifetime, could triumph over that past.

"In God put thy trust, not in the strength of thine own mind, nor of thine associations in a material world, nor of thine affiliations in this or that life experience, but rather in him.

"And as there was the failure then, so by the grace through him, there may be the spiritual awakening to man in this experience."

He had known many people in both life experiences, he said. But none had he failed above all others as in Troy: the man known as Lammers in this lifetime—and Hector in the other—slain so cruelly before the eyes of his people and never avenged; his father and brother slain; and his people massacred. The throne to which he was heir was lost, and his city wiped off the map.

The sleeping Cayce seemed to justify his Xenon self by what he had accomplished spiritually for others in the present. "For to many the power, the help, the aid which has come in their experience in the present has not only equaled but has surpassed any that was experienced in the period of either Ra-Ta or Uhjltd. For body-mind help has come to those in the present in no uncertain terms."

Had he not shown how the fallen Hector had lived on as Lammers to affirm there was no death? Yet, while he had helped the many in these two major experiences, he didn't fully address the question of why he had not applied these lessons from his past to the Xenon incarnation. How could he regenerate his physical person from experiences not only as Xenon but as the wastrel Bainbridge, in still another woeful incarnation?

"By the consecration of the mind, the soul, the body, by the simple method of living. And as the truth flows as a stream of life through the mind and purifies same, so will it purify and rejuvenate the body. For once this effacement urge or remorse is overcome, then may there begin the rejuvenation."

How could one blame Xenon for failing when all of Troy had failed—the invincible Hector, the self-indulgent Paris, and Priam himself? Only Cassandra, perpetuating the name of a prophet of doom for all time, and the prophet Laocoon had warned Trojans to beware of Greek trickery, and none had listened. So why blame Xenon above others higher in station?

I remembered now what Cayce had said about the devil sending a woman when all else failed.

That woman, it suddenly struck me, was Garcia, the mistress of Xenon, who had helped the Greeks, betraying the gatekeeper who trusted her. What woman of Troy would betray her own people? And that woman, Garcia, to compound the felony, was in this life the same Anne Gray Holbein who had been connected with Cayce when he was Uhjltd and Ra-Ta and who called him "Daddy Cayce."

Her betrayal didn't make sense, even looking back on Cayce's reading.

"We find the entity [Holbein] was in that land now known as the Trojan, or rather the Grecian and Trojan, during the periods when there were what are known as the Trojan Wars, during the activities between those over that entity Helen of Troy.

"During those activities the entity was the companion of the keeper of the gate to the city. And during the experience the drawings of the entity enabled those that were of the besieged to enter the city. Though little credit was given Garcia in the experience, yet such enabled the armies—or the individual active with Achilles—to succeed in bringing destruction to Hector's forces.

"And the entity saw those activities."

This was said with a finality that sent a shiver down my spine.

I turned to a wide-awake Anne Holbein.

"What is it you want to know?" she said. "I was such a poor thing as the sister of Uhjltd." She smiled and shook her head. "Poor Uhjltd."

"Poor Xenon," I said.

She gave me a blank look, and I could see the name didn't ring a bell. It had not been mentioned in her reading but in Cayce's.

She didn't mind being regressed again, and I got into the regression directly, letting her subconscious mind roam as it would. And it was not long before she was in Troy.

I asked her name.

She didn't hesitate. "My name," she said, "was Garcia. They called me Garcia."

"And this was in Troy?"

She nodded.

"And what did you do?"

"I lived with a Trojan who was one of the keepers of the gate."

"Do you remember his name?"

When she didn't reply, I wondered at it, just as I wondered why she had betrayed her own people.

"Why," I asked, "did you help the Greeks when they were engaged in a life-and-death struggle with your people?"

She shook her head. And then came the surprise, the key, if true, to the fall of Troy and the triumph of the Trojan horse.

She spoke most emphatically.

"The Trojans were not my people. I had been in Troy since they brought my mistress Helen there. Paris had brought her handmaidens with him because she insisted on it. There were four of us, and we had grown so tired of ten years of waiting for our Greeks to come and rescue us."

And so the riddle was solved. She had not betrayed her own people. She had betrayed the Trojans—and Xenon—out of her love for her homeland. The valiant Achilles was her hero. There were all kinds of wonderful tales about him, such as how his mother, Thetis, having been told at his birth that her son would be killed in battle, held him by the heel in the River Styx to make his body invulnerable to any weapon. But where her hand held the infant, there was no immunity, and a Trojan arrow, fired by the hateful Paris, found this Achilles' heel.

Garcia's faith in the Greeks persisted after this loss. For she knew that Menelaus would not yield his wife to a man who had betrayed him. Moreover, Menelaus's brother, Agamemnon, wed to Helen's sister Clytemnestra, was commander of the Greek forces and had vowed to his wife that the Greeks would not leave without Helen.

Anne, or Garcia, as I had come to think of her, was a remarkable eyewitness. I soon had the feeling I had an aisle seat on the center stage of history.

"What of Helen?" I said, asking her to describe the manner of her abduction and the face that had launched a thousand ships. It had always seemed odd to me that a solitary Paris could kidnap a king's wife from a palace crowded with his retainers.

She sighed, as though the remembrance was almost too much for her. "Helen was childlike. She was exquisite. Her eyes were the color of violets. I had never seen eyes like hers before. And her skin was transparent like alabaster. Her hair was like the color of straw, yet so fine and so beautiful.

"Paris had heard of her beauty, as had all Greece. He came as a friend when Menelaus had a journey planned. We lived up in the hills [of Sparta], the mountains there, and it was lonely sometimes. And with Menelaus gone, Paris persuaded Helen to come with him and bring her servants. He was the handsomest of men, almost as beautiful as she was. He had a ship ready, and we departed. We were gone before Menelaus got back. Helen knew that he would be gone some time."

Menelaus's lack of prudence startled me even more than Helen's fickleness.

"He went away and left this beautiful prince of Troy there with his wife?"

Menelaus may have been a mighty warrior, but I wondered about his intelligence. It seemed incredibly bad judgment.

"Paris," she said stiffly, "was a guest."

Her voice left no doubt of what she thought of Paris and his breach of ancient etiquette.

"And no sooner was Menelaus out of sight than Paris started courting her."

"She must have encouraged him?"

She made no reply. Her loyalty transcended every other condition.

Garcia was only sixteen when she was carried off, and now she was nearing thirty and tired of Troy and its dull people, so unlike her exotic Greeks.

"I dearly loved Helen, and I was so crushed that we were carried off like that, but it was good to be with her. After our people arrived to rescue her, the Trojans thought we maidens were plotting against them, so they turned us out of Priam's palace. They would have killed us, but Helen objected so much they finally sent us off to find companions among the keepers of the gates. And because we were Greeks and fairer than the women of Troy, we were taken in immediately."

"If they didn't trust you, why did they allow you to live at a gate where you might escape?"

"We all had a man watching over us. I was brought to the gate, and there was this man waiting for me. He was the man I was to be with. I had no choice. They had blindfolded me and taken me there. And when they removed the blindfold he was standing in front of me."

He had given her a warm greeting.

"He smiled and extended his hand, put both hands on my shoulders, and asked me if I would like to share his home."

Xenon had been an obliging partner, invariably trying

to please her. "There was only one thing he ever denied
me. He would do most anything else I asked. But he
would never take me where the other Greek girls were.
He had been told not to let me know where they were,
and I'm not sure he knew himself."

I had thought she was going to say the one thing denied her was marriage. But she didn't care about that.
She was Greek to the core, and he was of Troy, and
never the twain would meet—as a twain.

"I didn't want to marry him. I wanted to go home and
take the Greek maidens—and Helen—with me."

"You lived inside the gate?"

"In the gatehouse, inside. We could hear the noise of
the fighting, the clashing of the swords and the cries of
the people.

"We had no idea when it would end. It had been going
on for an eternity. We would hear Hector was winning
and driving the Greeks back, and then we would hear
that Achilles, our great leader, was victorious. We knew
that Achilles was blessed because our gods had blessed
him as a child. We thought one of the gods was his
father."

As the war wore on, in her desperation she tried to
escape.

"It was early in my banishment from the palace and
Helen. I had seen the Greek supply ships come and go,
and I had dreamed of going home on one of them. A
storm that night gave me a perfect chance. I didn't want
to leave a trail or make too much noise, so I crept out
of the gatehouse at ground level, made my way over to
a section of the wall that had been reinforced inside. I
was climbing up the inside wall when I was discovered
and ordered back under penalty of death. I went meekly
enough and took a tongue-lashing from Xenon with a
bowed head. I promised never to try this again. But I
didn't promise not to try to help the Greeks however I
could."

I recalled what Cayce had said about the drawings that
had aided the Greeks.

"I did make measurements and sketches of the city
and dropped them over the wall to let the Greeks know
what was on the other side of the city."

It took courage, for Xenon had threatened to kill her

if he found her helping the enemy in any way. "He said he would rather see me dead than betray his city."

Their relationship seemed one of convenience. She had lived with Xenon for nine years and had two children by him. As the battle intensified, the children had been sent into the interior where they would be safe. But she seemed curiously unaffected by the separation.

"They were Trojans like their father. I knew my life didn't belong with theirs. Xenon knew how I felt. We talked about the fighting, and he said it was to the death and that I should not think of myself as a Greek because I had been with him so long, that I was in fact a Trojan. I could not agree. But the children were definitely Trojan. I was afraid to tell them how desperately I wanted to go back to Greece. I was afraid that despite of Helen's influence with Paris and the others that I might be killed for my longing, especially when the battle was so fierce with so many dead."

What else had she and Xenon talked about all those years? They seemed to have so little in common. Yet Xenon was Cayce, and Cayce was Ra-Ta and Uhjltd, and she was of Egypt and Persia. There should have been a bond between them. It should not have been a complete washout.

"Did you know anything about what Xenon was like? He was a soldier, but wasn't he also a sculptor, a mathematician, an artist of some sort?"

I had struck a small chord.

"He listened to my stories of the glories of Greece and of the beautiful carvings and sculptures there. And he would reproduce things. He would copy some things from my descriptions, and he had his own ideas about a lot of things. He was a gifted person. But he was frustrated by a war that blocked his development."

"Did he have any mental or spiritual qualities, something that you cared about?"

"Little personal things, perhaps, but not in any expression of a personal philosophy. I cared, because he had protected me from the Trojans who would come by and shout things about the Grecian trollop staying in his gatehouse. And he would stand up and tell them quietly that I was his companion."

Their relationship didn't seem unusual. It reminded me

of all too many marriages I knew of in this life. Lives
of quiet desperation, experienced by one or both of the
partners, trapped by circumstances beyond their control.
The children didn't present a problem, not to Garcia.

I asked about them again. Would they go with her?

She stirred a moment, gave an audible sigh.

"I think not."

After Achilles' death, an irreparable loss, the re-
maining Greek commanders had felt the need to build
the wooden horse.

"Weakened by Achilles' death, they knew they had to
try a different approach. The Trojans had an advantage.
The Greeks had to depend on ships bringing in supplies,
while the Trojans had their supplies right there. They
could bring them in by land.

"There had been a lot of work done on the horse. We
could see from the top of the walls that they were making
something. Their ships would come in loaded with tim-
bers. And we could see them building this fantastic
horse. And then one day we looked out and there were
no Greeks to be seen. And we thought because of the
fierce fighting they had gone back to their ships to heal
themselves, and I was really grieved, though I knew they
would never leave, not even after Achilles was killed. I
knew the Greeks would never give up. The war had been
a long time coming, and it would not end without a
Greek victory. Spartans never gave up."

The Trojans had clearly left a potential spy in their
midst to plague them.

"If the Trojans were afraid of your loyalty, why did
they let you stay at the gate, of all places?"

"They thought I was under the influence of the man I
was living with. As long as I was separated from the
other Greeks, they felt they had little to worry about.
They didn't want to displease Helen, for she would have
taken it to Paris."

The drawings Cayce mentioned may have helped the
Greeks. But it was Xenon in the end that she worked
on, and she recalled his name now that he was no longer
a threat. Years of living together, sharing the two small
rooms of the gatehouse, knowing his kindnesses, all this
meant nothing against a Greek triumph and her freedom.

She kept telling Xenon and the other Trojans what a

great work the Greeks had created and how they must have regretted leaving it in their flight for home—knowing all the time that her compatriots, from the lights she saw at night, had retreated by sea only a few miles around a bend.

"I told Xenon it was such a marvelous thing the Greeks had built and that back in Greece there were many such artists who designed horses for sheer diversion. He disagreed. He said there was something about it he didn't like. And I said, no, there can't be anything wrong about it now that they were gone. It would be such an oddity here, I said, a trophy of the war.

"They won't be back, I told him. They are tired of war and want to get back to their wives."

The Greeks had staged their production well.

"The crafty Ulysses argued that since the Greeks could not take the city by storm, they should do it with guile. And so the wooden horse was built outside the walls, as the Trojans watched, beguiled. As part of Ulysses' scheme, the structure was made so large that it could not pass through the Trojan gates. He surmised that this would lull the suspicions of the Trojans, more than ready to believe after the years of siege that they had finally beaten off the Greeks.

"I circulated among the people, telling them this was a Greek peace offering to the Goddess Athena. And, of course, they believed what they wanted to believe. 'How could it be dangerous,' I said, 'when it cannot be taken into the city without breaching the walls next to the gates?'

"There were many who warned against Greek treachery. 'Do not trust them, for Ulysses still lives, the crafty one,' cried the wise old priest Laocoon, his cries echoed by his two sons. 'Whatever this horse may be,' he warned with anguish in his face, 'we must fear the Greeks bearing gifts.'

"Some jeered and some cheered, but the die was cast when two serpents came out of the sea and entwined themselves around the priest and his sons, crushing them to death. This was considered an omen.

"The wisest of the Trojans still held back, not quite convinced the war was so easily won after such arduous fighting. But when they tapped their weapons against the sides of the horse, a hollow sound came back, and their doubts dispersed. Little did they know that Ulysses, realizing they would do just that, had placed his platoon of men, led by Menelaus and himself, in an upper compartment of the horse, beyond the reach of the attackers. At the proper time, they could readily descend down a staircase designed for that purpose.

"During the night when the city slept, an ancient Greek warrior disguised as a shepherd, taken lightly by the Trojans because he was so old and decrepit, slid the bolts of the gates where the walls had been widened by curious Trojans to admit the horse. Then, undetected, he lit a small fire outside the walls, which had withstood the assaults of the Greeks. This was the signal for the ships bearing thousands of Greeks who had returned under cover of darkness to move into the unguarded harbor. As the gates were opened, the Greeks swarmed into the city, descending upon the sleeping inhabitants and putting the torch to the city. By morning the slaughter was over, and Troy was in ruins.

"Even though I longed for my home, I sorrowed that so many lives were spent, and I grieved for Xenon. For it was his gate that was first breached, and this was a disgrace he chose not to outlive. He was a good man and good to me, yet not one fit for war but pursuits of peace."

Had not Xenon, supposedly the reincarnation of two very psychic personalities in Egypt and in the city of the plains, had a premonition of Greek treachery?

Anne paused a moment, as I marveled anew at her graphic description of the fall of Troy.

"It could have been," she said finally. "He was disturbed that the people had pulled the horse in. He accused me of talking with the Trojans and convincing them the horse was harmless. He had issued orders against bringing in the horse, but later, thinking the horse harmless, he yielded to the public will. If they wouldn't listen to the prophetess Cassandra, who was the daughter of Priam and the sister of Hector, why would they listen to a gatekeeper?"

The Greek maiden Garcia had done her work well in the drawings of the strategic positions she had slipped over the wall. She had indeed earned her passport back to Sparta.

But how had she known there were troops in the horse, ready to leap out and open the gates to their comrades?

Even in her unconscious state her lips formed a smile.

"I didn't, but knowing the Greeks, knowing they were still in Trojan waters, I knew they must be up to something or they wouldn't have gone to all that trouble to build the horse."

"Why," I asked, "didn't the Trojans have the same idea?"

"The people believed what they wanted to believe. They were so tired of war that they found it uplifting to believe the Greeks wouldn't be back. But looking out from the top of the wall where I had gone, I could dimly see lights far down in the harbor, and I felt it was our friends coming back. This was the very day the horse had been wheeled into the city by the people. I had talked to many of them and told them that Xenon was letting his imagination run away with him. Nevertheless, he was sure he could handle whatever happened. So that helped." She laughed. "He thought he was as good as any Greek."

It was not a very good replica of a horse, for the Greeks had left it unfinished. "The body was sort of rough-looking, and the feet weren't finished, as though they had left it in a hurry before they could complete it. There had been a lot of fighting going on outside the gates, even as they were working on the horse, and the Greek forces had apparently been beaten back, but this was only to lull the Trojans to a sense of false security."

"But you couldn't have known of this then?"

"Why else would they have dimmed their lights and lingered in a cove around the bend?"

"Why couldn't the Trojans see the same lights you did?"

"They weren't looking for them."

She was proud of her fellow Greeks. "Our people were very smart. They argued philosophy a lot, but they were fantastic in mechanics."

All this time, she and Xenon were on opposite sides of the equine debate. And she, in speaking to people in the markets and the streets, kept building up the interest in the horse.

"Who finally made the decision?" I asked.

She laughed under her breath.

"As I said, the people demanded it. And Xenon finally gave the order. It was such a curiosity, and it looked fun to them, and there'd been so little fun for ten years. They wanted to see it up close. But they still had a lurking fear of a Greek ambush, so they thought to push it on its big wheels through the gates into the city."

How ironic, I thought, as she went on to describe the heaving and hauling, which, it occurred to me, was the first eyewitness account of the way the Trojan horse got through the gates of Troy.

"It took them the better part of the day because it was so tremendous and so heavy. They were so tired, so completely relaxed by the time they got the horse in, that they all went home and to bed."

The Trojans appeared to have a death wish, a desire to self-destruct, in thoughtlessly choosing the means of their own destruction.

"Didn't it occur to anybody that anything that difficult to push might have something in it—like armed men for instance?"

"They climbed up on ladders and tapped the sides of the horse, and, of course, it rang hollow, as I said, because the Greeks knew they would do this and had positioned themselves in the uppermost chamber of the horse."

Dusk came and nothing happened. She was disappointed. "I just knew that horse was the solution to our problems. I climbed to the top of the wall to look out toward Greece and a dream of maybe one day seeing those green hills with the beautiful flowers."

By this time, darkness had cast its cloak over the city, and in the stillness of the night she could hear the sound of the crickets and the whisper of the wind off the sea. And then there was a rumble from the horse, and she saw troops pouring out of the side at the same time she saw dark shadows moving down on the waterside.

And where was the keeper of the gates? Asleep at the watch, for he, too, had checked out the horse and found nothing amiss.

"He was still apprehensive. And I think the fact that I couldn't help smiling as much as I did made him suspicious."

She didn't have time to think about him. Her attention was riveted on the men pouring out of the horse.

"They dropped down from the belly and cautiously made their way over to the gate, removed the bar and swung the gate open. As I listened I could hear the hordes of soldiers come up from the ships. Fighting started immediately inside the gates but not on a large scale, as most of Troy was asleep."

Xenon, awakened from his slumber, had accosted her angrily, even as the fighting was going on.

"He accused me of talking with the Trojans and convincing them that the horse was harmless. He was beside himself. He grabbed me by the throat to choke the truth out of me. I swore I knew nothing. And actually this was the truth, because I had no idea beforehand of what the Greek soldiers were up to."

"Why," I asked, "didn't they listen to Cassandra?"

"They had willed the war to be over. They were in no mood to be warned about Greeks bearing gifts."

Her attitude about Xenon puzzled me, since she had mentioned how kind he had always been to her.

"Did you love him at all?"

"I cared for him."

"Didn't it occur to you that he might perish in the first Greek thrust through the gates?"

"I cared for him because he had cared for me. There was no deep love there. My love belonged to Greece. I knew I would find someone back there, though by this time I was almost thirty."

There had been a life shared in the Persian city of the plains and in Egypt. Didn't she feel any recognition or familiarity, any caring brought over from these experiences?

"I cared for him. I took care of his needs. I did as he bade. I wondered about him later." She was a woman who knew what she wanted.

I thought about reincarnation and how it presumably worked.

"If you believed in a continuous life, wouldn't you . . ."

She cut me off.

"At that time, I believed in my gods and my gods alone. Zeus and Athena and, of course, Apollo."

Of course. She was a creature of her own time and place, even as she lay there on the couch, recalling that past.

"In other words, the whole framework of your outlook was determined by your beliefs at the time? Did you believe in an afterlife at that time—or just for the gods and goddesses?"

"Only those that lived on Mount Olympus had eternal life. We were mortal, and only as they pleased did we become immortal."

I found this intriguing. For her beliefs were adjusted to the culture she had lived in and knew.

"In the Egyptian and Persian sojourns, they believed in reincarnation. So you believed in reincarnation? The Greeks didn't believe, and so you didn't believe in it then? You were a child of your own land, your own time, and your own beliefs?"

She shrugged. "I was a Greek."

She had been in the gatehouse while the fighting was going on. Xenon, meanwhile, had gone out to join in the fighting. It had gone on sporadically through the night. She could hear the sounds of battle clearly.

"It was still going on as the day broke, as Apollo the Sun God started his circuit. I could see the Greeks were winning, and I was so relieved that I slipped out of the house, and a Greek soldier grabbed my arm. I spoke to him in our language, and he clasped me to his breast and passed me on to another who led me out to the ships."

I could hardly believe she could care so little for a companion who had been her mentor in one experience and her brother in another.

"He was not the man he was before, and I was not the same. The conditions were different."

"And so what did you learn?"

"Self-denial. I gave up two children, knowing they would not be happy in Greece. I was not without feelings. I cried a little. He had been kind to me, and I knew he had perished along with so many of the others. He had told me once that if ever he did not return in a day's time that I was to lock the house and tell the other gatekeepers nearby that he had gone over and that one of them would take me in."

There was no need for that now, for she was returning to her beloved homeland, with the fair Helen and the other handmaidens, more than ten years after she had left.

She had lost two children in that lifetime, and she would lose two again in the present. But the gods of the Greeks had been kind to her and not so kind to the man who gave his life to an empty cause.

But one day, as we knew, he would redeem himself and all the mistakes and sins of the past with tried and true companions.

CHAPTER 7

Lucius of Cyrene

There were many lives in the psychic development of Edgar Cayce. But none was more gratifying to Cayce than that of Lucius of Cyrene, one of the seventy disciples of Christ and companion of the Apostle Paul.

Lucius's origin, of which little was hitherto known, was set forth in unusual detail by Cayce, fostering the belief by some that he was especially curious about his own biblical past. Drawn to the Bible even as a child, Cayce now understood why, as that child, he had given himself the task of reading the Bible through each year of his life. For as he believed, he was speaking about himself and people he cared about, then and now. Yet, it was somewhat mind-boggling to an inveterate Bible reader like himself to skim through his favorite book and find his Lucius self twice mentioned with Paul, in Rom. 16:21 and Acts 13:1.

"I would find it hard to believe," he said, "if I didn't know the Information was invariably correct."

Cayce's story of Lucius, which he was too modest to publicize at the time, gives us a picture of the early church and its growing pains as well as a candid portrait of Lucius as a wandering wastrel drawn to the church by his passion for a Master who seemed capable of accomplishing any wonder.

As in Cayce's previous lives, there were problems with women that at times seemed to complicate his survival as a high churchman. But the early church, with its standards still loosely ordered, was a lot more tolerant than many contemporary Christian sects.

Cayce had more detail on his early life as Lucius than on any other life he gave himself. He grew up in the city of Cyrene in Cyrenaica, where as Ra-Ta, the high priest, he had been befriended in exile by the Nubians and the

Libyans. His father, Phillip, as he tells it, moved the family to the Roman province of Phrygia in Asia Minor, and he received a Greek education. But at an early age, Lucius and his sister Nimmo, drawn by the wondrous tales carried by the caravans from the East, were among those flocking to the Holy Land to revel in the Master and his miracles. With some Jewish background of his own, Lucius felt, like so many of the time, that the Messiah—Jesus—had come to liberate the Jews from Rome by leading a great political uprising. Despite misjudging Christ's purpose, he was still moved by the message of everlasting life. With his magnetic personality and his devotion to Christ, he became one of that company of disciples who went everywhere Jesus himself went. After the Crucifixion, he was chosen by the Apostle John to be a bishop at Laodicea in Asia Minor and became a strong influence on his younger relative Luke, the dear and glorious physician of the Gospel.

The Lucius reading came late in Cayce's life. Any earlier, said Cayce, he would not have had the maturity to handle such a distinction. Cayce didn't always like what he said about himself. And he wasted many sighs over Lucius of Cyrene, a man who dearly loved women. For the readings transcribed not only the spiritual but the physical side of Cayce's nature in that lifetime, a side he resisted, not always successfully, through many incarnations.

Often reading for people in his past, Cayce was introduced to himself as Lucius of Cyrene in a reading for a New York divorcée. She was a member of his Bible class with an abiding interest in the early Christian era. The reading, late in 1938, some six years before his death, hit Cayce like a revelation out of the Gospel itself. For he not only became Lucius of Cyrene, who had walked with Christ, but he had picked out a young Judean wife who was a companion of the mother of the Lord and of Christ's dear friends, the sisters Martha and Mary. And the woman who was given the reading was that very wife. Her name was Mariarh, and she was considerably younger than the graying Lucius.

As he knew Lucius, so did Cayce seem to know Mariarh. She had lived as a young girl in Bethany, not visiting Jerusalem until she was fourteen, the age of accountabil-

ity, the marriageable age, to be polled for taxes by the
Romans. A frequent guest in the home of Mary and Martha and their brother Lazarus, whom Jesus raised from
the dead, she met many of the followers of Jesus who
were to later form his church.

"Then," said Cayce, "following the Resurrection, when
there was the selection of those to act in the capacity of
ministers, or deacons, when all their material belongings
had become as part of the disciples' or Apostles', the
entity Mariarh heard much of the activities of Philip and
Peter but became closer associated with one Lucius—a
kinsman of Luke."

Cayce didn't elaborate on this connection, but pausing
a moment, added slowly, as though apprehensive of what
he was about to say, "And Lucius is the entity, now
Edgar Cayce, through whom this information is being
given."

Gladys Davis, taking the notes, stopped short. Never
before, not in the fifteen years she was then his secretary,
had Cayce's subconscious plucked from the universal
consciousness a wife or mistress of the past outside his
immediate household.

Cayce continued for a time as though nothing had happened, discussing the burgeoning relationship of Lucius
and Mariarh in the matter-of-fact way he discussed everything in his sleep.

Although little more than a teenager, Mariarh joined
with Lucius in his work, establishing missions outside of
Palestine and eventually in Laodicea after their marriage.

"For it was there that the entity Mariarh went with
Lucius when there was the establishing of the church,
when Paul preached in Laodicea. These were a portion
of the kinsmen of the people from the Roman land. And
there Mariarh ministered as the helpmeet of Lucius for
those early peoples of the church. There the entity spent
the rest of her days, living to those periods when there
were the . . ."

Just then, Cayce sneezed, faltering in the middle of
the sentence. Whatever it was, the recollection was too
much for him. "We'll finish it in another reading later,"
he said. "There's enough to think about for the present.
Very startling information for us, too."

Today's Mariarh, a social secretary in reality, was as

startled as Cayce by the information. In one sense, she felt it accounted for her appreciation of Cayce not only as an individual but as a Bible teacher whose classes were the highlight of her week in Virginia Beach.

The reading was quite a jolt to Cayce's image of himself. For it would seem there were already enough complications in his personal life without bringing in more conditions from the past than he could reasonably handle. As it was, the matter was still unfinished, for what was there that had made him sneeze and break off?

Cayce had wondered, too, why it had taken him so many years to come on this most hallowed identity of all, as a companion of Christ and one who spread his word. But, as he reread the reading, he saw this was plainly stated.

"It may be questioned why such an outstanding experience of the entity now called Cayce should not have been given in the first. But as has been indicated, each entity, each individual grows or applies or is meeting self in the varied experience as the tenets of an individual experience are applied in this present sojourn or activity."

Knowing himself, he felt he would not have been ready, spiritually or emotionally, to handle such a distinction. "If this had been given in the first, there would have been a puffing up, as there was that unstableness throughout the experience until there were the lessons to be gained from the companion [namely Gertrude] for whom he had gone into exile and with whom he was now united after years of fighting his own secret desires.

"Then meeting the companion in the present experience brings about the humbleness that was gained, and still held."

The more Cayce thought about it, the more he realized that he could not just let things stand. His curiosity had to be appeased, and there was only one way this could be accomplished.

Recovered from his reading as Lucius, he sent a letter to the New York woman five days later, addressing her in a jocular vein as Mrs. S. but with a serious undertone.

"After the attempt for your activity in Palestine, I don't know whether that is just the way to address you or not. Guess you saw we were shut off before the Infor-

mation was finished, possibly too much for you to digest
at once."

This was in December, just before Christmas. Wishing
her a happy holiday, he suggested getting together for
another reading after the Yuletide to see what a sequel
would bring.

"Will have to see you to talk this over with you. Hope
you don't feel too horrified at some of the disclosures,
but study what we have gone over and let me know what
you think."

After Christmas she responded. She began her letter,
"Dear Mr. Cayce," then deploring the stiffness, "Yes,
this does sound strange."

She found the reading amazing but was far from horrified: "Just very humble and much surprised to think I
was of any help or a helpmeet to anyone of such importance, a prophet doing such important work."

And then she asked, "Did you know before this that
you were Lucius?"

His answer was a prompt no. For he was still amazed.
Meanwhile, she read and reread her reading, still failing
to grasp the reality of his biblical presence. But as she
thought about it, she realized that since her reading came
from a desire to know more of a Judean existence, there
must have been something of that past in her subconscious to justify the reading.

"I can hardly wait for the rest of the reading," she
wrote. "Don't you think it strange that you should sneeze
and bring the reading to a close. Has that ever happened
before? Waiting to hear further," she punned, "with
abated breath."

The day after he received her letter, Cayce, normally
a poor correspondent, wrote back that in all the readings
he had given himself over the years the connection with
Lucius had never been made.

She had received a Bible dictionary for Christmas.
And he, knowing of only two scanty references to Lucius
in the New Testament, asked if she "would be so kind
as to copy what your Bible dictionary has to say about
Lucius."

He mentioned resuming the reading as soon as he
caught up with a backlog of requests. "I imagine a good
bit may be said about you in that experience. Have never

had an experience like this before, where two lives seem to have been so close in their activities, reliant one on the other for the greater part of their activity in such an outstanding period."

He was sufficiently interested to give himself a reading on Lucius specifically. A wealth of detail poured out, charting an intimacy with another woman of that period with whom he had two children. And if that wasn't enough to contend with, they were apparently born during an interlude when he was separated from Mariarh.

What with Ra-Ta and now Lucius, and still others to come, it seemed to a mind like mine that Edgar Cayce had a lot to cope with out of the distant past. And nobody, as I had gathered from his own flagellation, suffered with this legacy more than himself.

It had not been easy for him as Lucius. He never really belonged to the old guard of the early church, though he moved about with them freely. For one thing, he didn't have a very good start. He was of Greek and Roman parentage, named Lucius Ceptulus. And though Paul testified that Lucius's mother was of the Judean tribe of Benjamin, the Jewish fathers of the church, led by Peter, thought of him as a Greek, due somewhat to his Greek-like passion for romantic attachments, which they considered a worldly triviality.

"As a developing youth and young man," said a sleeping Cayce, "Lucius was known rather as a ne'er-do-well, or one that wandered from pillar to post, and became, as would be termed in the present-day parlance, a soldier of fortune."

It was as such that he drew in, not only Mariarh, but a Roman woman, Vesta, with a distant connection with the Roman court and made her his mistress. They had two children, Pebilus and Susana, leading some to say scornfully that Lucius was indeed the father of the church.

There was nothing said about a complete break with Vesta. She appeared to grow tall as he did, separated but secure, becoming a deaconess in the church of Laodicea and a respected figure, having outlived and outgamed the gossip-mongers of the time.

Somewhat chastened, Cayce now had a better picture of Lucius as he made an appointment for the New York social secretary, a woman of forty-five or so, for the resumption of the cliff-hanger. Shortly after the New Year, he went into trance and, in a soft voice, began to visualize the totality of young Mariarh's life.

"Mariarh of the Samaritans—Judean hill country—triumphal entry of Jesus—associations with the women Elizabeth [mother of the Baptist] and Mary—affiliation with those during the Pentecost, wedded to Lucius of Cyrene."

The reading cast a new light on the growing pains within the hierarchy on the troublesome matter of bachelorhood and celibacy. The Apostle Paul, perfectly in character, demanded celibacy as a requisite for the activities of a bishop or a leader.

"With the activities in the ministry," said Cayce, "when the entity [Mariarh] was with her companion Lucius in Laodicea, when Lucius was made by Paul Barnabas bishop of the church there, there came some hardships to the entity, owing to the teachings of Paul concerning the interests of those who were as leaders of the churches."

Lucius stood by his wife, keeping her in Laodicea with him, with the support of Barnabas and Luke. "Only when there had been with Luke and Barnabas the greater and better understanding did there come to be a greater activity by Mariarh in these surroundings."

Meanwhile, life became easier for Mariarh when she gave birth to a son, Silvanus, who later "came to be reckoned by the leaders in Jerusalem—James, the brother of the Lord, Peter, and Andrew—as one chosen for service in the name of the Master."

Mariarh lived to a ripe old age, proud of the son serving as a helper with a mellowing Paul and with this revelation in this life was looking forward to learning more about her companions in Judaea.

The social secretary, as to be expected, was fascinated by her second reading. It opened up a whole new vista for self-expression in a Christian way.

"I don't think we are going to be able to look very far ahead," she wrote Cayce, "until we are able to look back."

She had plenty to look back on, as did the Virginia woman who was then Vesta. She was a thirty-three-year-

old homemaker who had become enamored of the Cayce
readings and had a sharp, inquiring mind with which she
pursued her past life and her present.

As with the New York woman, Cayce's appearance as
Lucius was incidental to this woman's appearance as
Vesta. For in her reading, similarly to Mariarh's, Cayce
turned up as a Palestine companion.

In the questions and answers following the extempora-
neous reading, she asked the sleeping Cayce, "Have I
met or been associated in the present with the father of
Pebilus, my son in Palestine? If so, in what association
and name?"

Without batting an eye, Cayce picked a name out of
that past.

"This," he said, "was Lucius."

The association was obvious.

I didn't know what to make of all this. I had no way
of gauging the truth, except for the usual argument that
if Cayce was right about everything that could be validated, why should he be wrong about that which could
only be validated by the measuring of events and charac-
teristics predictable from the past? The universe was lim-
itless, but humans were bound by their own limitations.
That was the rub. And there was another.

Why should all these biblical figures, so much at home
in the Holy Land, suddenly emerge incongruently in a
materialistic nation like ours? I recalled Cayce saying that
if a man knew the question, he already had the answer
deep in his own subconscious. And so, rummaging
around in my head, I realized I had made an improper
judgment. America was not materialistic in its deeper
nature. It was the heart of the world, generous and com-
passionate, holding the torch of liberty aloft while crying
out, "Give me your tired, your poor, your huddled
masses yearning to breathe free."

It was the hope of the free world, a spiritual bastion
for the survival of Western civilization, the home of the
New Age, of eternal promise, of which Edgar Cayce was
an everlasting symbol.

In the land of the New Age, the miraculous—and the
spiritual—was not unusual. "As they grow more spiritual," said Cayce, "so do people remember more of the
past, which they can relate to the present." In this life-

time, remembering some of her past, the Virginia Vesta, paired with Cayce in the past, became a valued aide in the present. The remembrance Cayce spoke of had brought her back, somehow, into the fold. Both felt the affiliation could be very helpful and mindful of the past in a tide of spiritual collaboration that overrode any other consideration.

"My dearest friend," the one-time Vesta wrote the one-time Lucius, "I have been thinking of little else this week than our talk Monday and have tried to bring myself to tell you what is in my mind and heart. I have attempted to think through all the things you taught me, what I have come to believe through my daily contact with you and your wonderful advice when I have been so confused by the problems that have confronted me. Without you, I would have surely failed. Is it any wonder then that I love you and would want always to be an aide to you?"

Was this a predictable echo from a distant past that could only be validated by the present consequence of that past?

"I have the feeling now that I must begin helping in whatever way I can, to teach younger children [as she had as Vesta] some of the many truths I have learned through you. It is something I have been thinking about for a year and have been putting off because I would much rather be at your side in whatever you are doing."

And then she wrote, as she may have once before in another land, "I know you can understand how I feel. Won't you give me your assurance and help in putting into practice the lessons I have learned through you? In our mutual oneness of purpose maybe I will someday be as wonderful a teacher as you are."

And as she prayed she would, so did she go into teaching, "emphasizing and directing my energies—sometimes, it seems, almost to the extreme."

Even today she was not unlike the Roman woman who had become a deaconess of the church after having known the good and the bad of life. For years later, a Los Angeles woman, listening to her discuss the Cayce readings, expressed the reaction of an enthused audience: "When she speaks I have a sort of glowing feeling, the way I feel when the Christmas trees are lit on Hollywood Boulevard."

As with most Cayce life readings, the burdens and joys of the past were carried over into the present. Just as there was a Lucius and a Mariarh and a Vesta, so was there a Pebilus, reborn as the spiritual son of Vesta, who with her teaching as a guide was preparing to become a minister in this life. Drawn to her as by a chord out of the past, he wrote to her frequently, sometimes as his spiritual mother and his teacher, in a lighthearted but contemplative vein.

"My dear little mother," began this student of divinity. "You are the kind of gift in your presence that a fellow could never express his thanks for, when you add up all the lovely things you did for me, for the kids, for our friends. For example, you did me a big favor in that last talk about my book and thesis. Having you with us was a very precious thing. God grant that it may not be too long before we take up again this strange but dear companionship that goes in such odd jumps."

No mother and son could have had a deeper communication. They not only expressed their love for each other, but the things that reflected on love, and they gave it the energy of two souls that remembered. How many mothers, I wondered, had known such a tribute as this that came from a son out of the past:

"In you the old ideals are planted deep and there is a river of love in you which can bring the ideals to fruition in all others. From you I have learned some of the deepest spiritual piloting I shall ever know, beginning with the phrase which always calls your face before me, 'What is your purpose?' "

With a saving grace, the Palestinian Pebilus recalled his reaction in his divinity class to the bits and pieces of church history, the gaps, the speculations, when something of the larger reality flowed through him from his own remembrance.

"I think of 'my mother' often in my New Testament classes," he said, "because she knows more about what went on in those days than my very learned professor. I like to picture her taking over this class for a day and throwing a few bombshells around. I think these Harvard guys would eat it up. The other day when the professor said he wished he knew who wrote Hebrews [New Testament] I had to sit on my hand to keep from raising it and saying, 'My friend Barnabas.'

"You can imagine how hard it is to study thousands of pages of guesses, and to memorize all these theories of Bible scholars, when inside you feel sure of just what was the situation between Jesus and the Essenes, while [they're] never dreaming that he was the one. It's the same in studying church history as the New Testament. You feel so silly memorizing little fragments which men have blindly saved in the thought that this is all they can know of the past. And as you study, the room is positively swimming in Akashic records revealing the whole wonderful story."

It was all he could do to restrain himself one day when the professor announced, "We know practically nothing about the church at Laodicea."

How well he knew somebody who could have told them all about it. As the visions of Vesta and Lucius, Barnabas and Paul and Silas rolled out of his head he wanted to shout out, "The hell you say," and stomp out of class.

Fortunately, he restrained himself, or the modern church might have lost a gifted theologian.

I had wondered myself, of course, how Cayce reacted to some of these past-life situations he found himself in. Here he was with a Mariarh and a Vesta, both now in this life, both close to him, both looking to him for wisdom and inspiration and for the love, which, even of an innocent turn, could help them emotionally.

I had asked Jeanette Thomas about this and wondered at her smile.

"I have something here that may help," she said, plucking the inevitable folder out of a vault as well guarded as the Akashic records.

As I read I felt an involuntary smile coming to my face. For no Hollywood director could have conceived a scene more dramatic than that perceived by a prankish Edgar Cayce.

Conceived by Cayce, the event was reported by the present-day Vesta years later, when she was able to look back on the incident with a certain amount of equanimity. Showing another side of himself, the sometimes impish Cayce decided to test the past. So he invited the Virginia woman cast as his former mistress to meet the wife who had displaced her in Lucius's affections—without informing that wife, Mariarh, of his little plot.

"After I had my life reading," the one-time Vesta recalled, "Mister Cayce told me that Mrs. S. was coming to Virginia Beach from New York and that he would be most interested in seeing us meet. He told me she had been his wife in Palestine also, always assuming that we were ever married. In any case, we had a family of children, so one might assume we had at least gone through the 'Roman marriage rites.' He told me that he had not told her about me, at least he had not identified me, and that when I met her, I would know, but she would not know about me. He seemed interested in what her reaction would be to me."

For a moment the thought crossed her mind that Vesta was again being downgraded for the wife that Lucius had finally settled on.

"It interested me," she said, "that he did not seem concerned about how I might react to her."

However, she didn't mind, for she had her own idea of how she would handle the situation this time. The tables of history were turned, for she was now the younger woman, and the more knowledgeable, in this case.

The plot thickened as Cayce, with Gertrude and Gladys and the former Vesta in the car, picked up the New York Mariarh at her Virginia Beach hotel to take her to Cayce's Tuesday night Bible meeting—a biblical setting that pleased Cayce's ironic sense of humor.

Our Vesta was on top of the situation. "Actually," she related, "I do not know what I expected to feel, but I was very surprised to find that I felt very sure of my position, as related to Mister Cayce and as the wife of Lucius."

In the car, responding to the challenge of the past, she playfully chatted with Cayce, as though it were old times, while Gertrude and Gladys were cheerfully chatting together and Mariarh was beginning to sulk. The fallout was more than Vesta could have ever hoped for.

Mariarh had planned to stay in Virginia Beach for two weeks, attending classes and visiting friends. Instead, annoyed beyond reason, she checked out of her hotel the next day and went back to New York.

"Without realizing why," our Vesta related later, "she had been so upset by my presence she just had to turn around and go home."

"That," I told Jeanette, as I returned the file, "was no way for a deaconess to act."

She agreed with a smile.

"But you know how women are. They never forget."

CHAPTER 8

Soldier of Fortune

As so many others, I had always thought of Edgar Cayce as the ideal Christian gentleman. I had the impression from people who knew him that while he loved light entertainment, such as a movie or a concert, he was as straitlaced as one would expect of a man who read the Bible every day.

So, naturally, I was surprised when I visited the Cayce Foundation years ago to find that my impression of incorruptible morality was not shared by some of the women who roomed at the foundation headquarters and knew him very well.

Indeed, two or three of them, even then weathered with age, winked slyly at my observation that he was an admirable man who lived as he preached, by the word of God.

"Oh, Mister Cayce had his moments," said one of the women, a perennial flapper. "He was quite a hand with the ladies, you know."

Two others nodded and looked wise. "Oh, yes," they chorused, "Mister Cayce liked the ladies."

I was thoroughly mystified, not only by what they were telling me, but by an apparent lack of loyalty for a departed leader at whose feet they had worshiped for so many years.

"I don't get it," I said to Gladys Davis, the loyal secretary who had been with Cayce for more than twenty years and had been the beneficiary with his two sons of all the Cayce readings.

My confusion grew as she started to laugh.

"That's John Bainbridge they're talking about," she said with a twinkling eye. "And I don't blame you for being confused."

I was even more confused now. "But we were talking about Edgar Cayce."

"But he was John Bainbridge in one of his seven lives, and John Bainbridge was a very naughty man, taking his pleasure where he found it."

"But these ladies seemed to know him."

"Yes, they did. And some were old-time favorites of his."

My head was spinning. "And they really believe this?"

She waved her arms eloquently. "That's why they were drawn here, subconsciously at least, to be rejoined to him." She smiled. "On a more spiritual level, of course."

"They were talking as if he were very much alive."

She laughed again. "He is alive for them. That's the wonderful part of it. None of us ever dies around here. We just float on and bide our time. Somebody once said that people are like books. After they wear out, they get a new cover and come back into circulation. John Bainbridge is just as real to his old friends as Edgar Cayce the twentieth-century mystic."

It still bothered me. "How can they be so sure?"

"They've had readings from Mister Cayce explaining to their satisfaction the connection to him."

I couldn't picture Edgar Cayce as a womanizer. He had taught fidelity and the sacredness of one's vows, preaching of a high morality that would one day make a person a companion of God. How could such a man be a lecher? I recalled his advising married people not to respond to any extramarital temptation, even if they felt a compelling urge for somebody else.

"The Mister Cayce we saw," explained Gladys, "was not the Mister Cayce of the past. He grew into his role as a spiritual leader. Like most of us, he was not born perfect.

"He mentioned this failing many times in his readings for himself—in Egypt, the Middle East, and in Troy, and earlier in this life as well.

"He felt this was one of the reasons he came back in this lifetime to triumph over the temptations of the past and perfect his psychic gift in the process."

Speaking of himself in a reading, Cayce had painted himself even more critically, not as the adventurer Bainbridge, but as the high priest in Egypt, an experience that seemed to cast a baleful influence on his colonial life and even the present.

"Again we find the entity falling in the way of the flesh, for 'the sons of God looked upon the daughters of men and they were fair and good to look upon.' "

It was the Bainbridge experience, though, consummating in a total dissoluteness, that charged his soul with a new and greater resolve to liberate himself from the frailties of the flesh that had plagued his past.

"And the fleshly carnal forces brought destructive elements to the entity [Cayce]. And in the present plane we still find the same urge to be overcome in the entity. For there is that innate call and desire in the flesh for those fleshpots again as recalled of Egypt, and the entity needs to keep the forces of mental and spiritual development ever alive to press onward to the higher forces."

This reading was given in 1925, when Cayce was a middle-aged forty-eight, and the battle was won long before his death twenty years later.

Gladys knew of this triumph of the spirit. For as she said, she had known from the time he engaged her as his secretary that they had been drawn together out of the past.

My eyebrows raised the least bit at this. "When he was Bainbridge?"

Gladys's eyes twinkled. "I missed that one."

She brought out a folder on the Bainbridge reading. I soon saw why the ladies of the A.R.E. had smiled so knowingly. For one had been the loving companion of Bainbridge, traveling among the Indian tribes with him, and was with him when he lost his life, fleeing from hostile Indians.

"This entity," as Cayce noted, "was a companion with Bainbridge at the crossing of the Ohio River, though the entity succeeded in escaping through the efforts of Bainbridge, who lost his life there."

Gladys chuckled to herself as she retrieved the folder.

"What is so funny?"

"Mister Cayce was consistent. The woman he traveled with through the Indian country was with him in biblical times when he was Lucius of Cyrene. They were still drawn together, still trying to work things out." She shook her head. "There may have been some poetic justice, but it was most likely karma."

I rummaged through my head trying to place the woman. There had been Vesta, and there was Mariarh. So there must have been a third woman as well.

"Not so," said Gladys. "It was Vesta. Lucius as Bainbridge finally made his amends. He laid down his life for the woman he hadn't done right by."

Bainbridge was a ne'er-do-well, a gambler, a soldier of fortune who had become very fond of the lady. The affection was returned. "Thus we find the entity, with the companion, at the age of seventeen years entered into that life as an entertainer and as one who aided in inducing individuals to spend money, as travelers who sought the gaming table, as well as the drinking that was a portion of the companion's activity."

"There were many lives, in Egypt, the Middle East, and in Troy," said Gladys, "where he had experiences with women, but none as openly as when he was a scout in colonial Virginia." She gave a little sigh. "I think the ladies you mentioned were thinking of his affair with the Indian princess he loved and then deserted, taking some of her possessions with him and leaving her with a great distrust of the white race.

"This depredation did have a strong influence on Mister Cayce's life. He always felt that his poverty in this lifetime, his trouble in obtaining and holding onto money, resulted from his improper use of money as John Bainbridge."

As a reporter, primarily, I found it difficult to accept anything I couldn't check out tangibly. Reincarnation was at the top of the list, for to my practical bent at that time it clearly appeared the product of wishful thinking—people wanting to believe there was more to life than a brief span on this plane, almost over before we knew it. My skepticism didn't bother Hugh Lynn Cayce, the mystic's son, then in charge of the A.R.E. He posted a notice on the A.R.E. bulletin board advising the resident women to stop trying to convert me to their belief.

"He will come to it in his own time," he said.

I had my doubts—this was many years ago—but I was intrigued by a frontier character so alien to everything the mystic Cayce embodied.

Gladys Davis was familiar with the Bainbridge story, for she saw it, as I did, as an anomaly in the lifetimes of a man whose life reflected a devotion to the Christian ethic.

In the subconscious, at least, Cayce had no qualms about examining the flaws in the Bainbridge character. "The body [Bainbridge] was known under two names [John and Bainbridge] and was never wed during that sojourn upon the earth plane, though as John Bainbridge he was in many escapades that have to do with the relations with the opposite sex."

Originally, Cayce's John Bainbridge came from England as a British soldier, drifting down from Canada to Virginia where he became a wanderer in the land, so much the adventurer that, as Cayce noted, "many peoples suffered in his wake." He settled for a time in Virginia, trapping for furs with the Indians. Carried off in an Indian raid, he escaped to become a scout in the English struggle to dominate the new land. He eventually made his way to a fort on the Great Lakes and again had trouble with Indians. Though he left a trail of broken hearts around the frontier country, he seemed capable of great kindness and courage. He led a crossing of the Ohio River at Shelby, Kentucky, with Indians in hot pursuit, sharing his last scrap of food with a hungry boy before the Indians finally caught up with his riverboat.

Gladys had smiled at my look of surprise.

"Mister Cayce never knew himself what to make of Bainbridge's burst of generosity. It seemed so out of character. But one day he was in a Virginia Beach barbershop, having his hair cut, when the barber's three-year-old son caught his eye. The boy was playing around on the floor, holding a piece of cake in his hand, nibbling at it every once in a while. Suddenly, he looked up at Mister Cayce with a smile of recognition. 'I know you,' he said, standing up and handing him the cake.

"The father was annoyed. 'You don't know Mister Cayce,' he reprimanded his son. 'You've never seen him before.'

" 'Oh, yes, I have,' the boy replied. 'We were together on the river, in a boat, and we were both hungry then.' "

It seemed a bit precocious for his age, but as Gladys

observed with a smile, the experience could have aged him fast.

The boy, as he grew up, later recalled his parents talking about this incident with Cayce. The family had moved from Akron, Ohio, not far from the Ohio River, but, of course, geographic proximity was not a paramount connection from one life to another. He could just as easily have been reborn in Egypt, Gladys noted, if it served his opportunity for growth.

The boy later joined a Boy Scout troop led by Hugh Lynn Cayce, the mystic's son. For Edgar Cayce it was an amusing affirmation of Bainbridge's reading, this Cayce connection. He had one regret: not pursuing a reading on the boy that could have enlarged the experience.

At the time, 1930, this gentle, unobtrusive man lamented, "I would certainly love to get a life reading on the boy, but I don't know how to approach the parents on it."

As a rule, Gladys reminded me, Cayce gave his readings only on request, occasionally excepting a close friend or member of his family.

While not in itself proof of reincarnation, this little story, verified by the boy, did make one wonder whether coincidence alone had brought the boy's family from Ohio to Virginia Beach for this affirmation of reincarnation.

The Bainbridge sojourn puzzled me. What could Cayce have gotten out of this experience except a lively reputation among the women of his study groups? He had backslid from his glory days in Atlantis, Egypt, the Middle East, even Troy. Failing to exclude the carnal in those lifetimes had festered the Bainbridge experience to such an extent that it became self-purging, as Cayce himself explained.

"One," he said of his past, "who finds much in the scope or sphere of intrigue in secret love affairs. One given often to the conditions that have to do with the affairs of the heart, and of those relations that have to do with sex.

"One [moving on] that finds the greater strength in spiritual forces, and developing those forces. One given to make manifest in the present plane the power of psychic and occult forces. One that will bring through such manifestations joy, peace, and quiet to the masses and multitudes through individual efforts."

During his latter years, his self-doubts left him, along with the sexual confusion. Because Cayce gave John Bainbridge "two names" some thought there were two Bainbridges, living a century apart in colonial America. But as both Gladys Davis and her successor, Jeanette Thomas, observed, Cayce made this point only because he had one name in his previous lives—Asule in Atlantis, Uhjltd in Persia-Arabia, Xenon in Troy, Ra-Ta in Egypt. There were other discrepancies that put him astride two different centuries, namely, the seventeenth and eighteenth. But he made it clear, analyzing a dream in October 1925, that his only arrival in America was in 1625, near Jamestown, Virginia.

"We find there are just three hundred years to the day and hour, in which time and space, as known in the earth's plane, have passed since the entity landed in this place."

All in all, there wasn't that much about Bainbridge in the A.R.E. files. He was hardly the kind of man you would invite home to meet your mother. As so often before, Anne Holbein was the missing ingredient, synchronistically available to fill out the Bainbridge portrait. As a reporter, I had always looked for one strong contact, somebody independent but knowledgeable, knowing the subject intimately but still on the sidelines. That was Anne's position in this life—someone who knew enough of Cayce's past to throw some light on how that past had shaped the present.

In her regressions, she had been clear and lucid, sticking to a narrative sometimes more compelling than anything I read elsewhere in fact or fiction. I thought her just the woman I was looking for. Yes, woman. For I had found women more sensitive, more intuitive, more likely to heed that special sixth sense without caring what anybody thought.

I had found a few things in her life reading that had gone unexplained. For instance, the name Mary Bainbridge was assigned to her by Cayce in her colonial experience, without any indication of how she had come by it.

"I thought it strange," said Anne, as she agreed to still

another regression, "that Mister Cayce never mentioned my then parents in my reading and yet said I would be close to some of the grandest families in Virginia, the Custises, the Lees, the Randolphs, and so on."

It did seem an incongruity, but all of it was incongruous, I told myself, unless it added up to something rational, connecting cause and effect. There had been that other apparent inconsistency, in the Trojan experience, where she presumably betrayed her own people. But as we learned, there was no inconsistency—for she was not a Trojan.

Though there were other lives with Cayce, it was the Bainbridge past that seemed to shade the present. From the time in childhood that she started thinking of him as "Daddy Cayce," he had dominated her thoughts. It was to him she turned, not her own parents or husband, in times of crisis. He was the first to know of her impending marriage when she sought his blessing. And a physical reading, advising the use of apple brandy fumes, saved her life when her lungs were hemorrhaging shortly after her marriage.

She was eager to know more of this paternal connection. Under hypnosis, she slid into the Bainbridge experience without difficulty. She was aware of her surroundings and what she was saying, yet at the same time she was deep into her own subconscious, the storehouse of memories as durable as the instinctual drives of humans dredged out of their primitive past.

"I don't want you to think your answers out or interpret them in any way," I told her as she lay on a couch in my Virginia Beach house, the oneness of her soul linking up to its remembered past.

It was not long before she became the child Mary Bainbridge. Her voice was low and halting, almost as though she were afraid of making herself known. She was in Virginia, in the seventeenth century, and the English ruled the land. She was born out of wedlock to a woman of easy virtue who died soon after her child was born but not before giving her the name Mary.

Without friends or family, Mary Bainbridge became a bond child of the Crown and an indentured servant as soon as she was old enough to work—at eight years of age. At thirteen, she was delivered from her bondage by an unseen hand, which made the payment the Crown required to liberate her. This same hand soon thereafter found her a job as a waitress at a tavern in Jamestown, Virginia, where the ladies of the evening applied themselves in the rooms overhead.

"The sly looks and winks of the customers soon told me who had arranged for my being there." He was a hawk-faced man of forty or so with the same name as hers: John Bainbridge, a soldier of fortune. Even before she met him she heard lurid stories about him, but somehow she sensed he was her protector. People in the tavern showed her unaccustomed respect. "I was given a room in the back of the tavern and never went upstairs. But the ladies frequented the tavern, drinking with the men who came in. They were kind to me, and I soon learned that my mother had been one of them. Nobody spoke of my father, almost as if they were afraid to mention his name."

"Did you have any idea who your father was?"

"I wasn't sure. Because there were a lot of Bainbridges in the area."

I imagined there were. "Did you wonder about it?"

"Some, but I was too busy working and learning to read from the cook to think of much else."

Her manner was so natural, the narrative so intriguing, that I soon found myself looking forward to each new disclosure.

"There was the one man I noticed because the others gave him a wide berth. He would sit in a corner and watch me, and he made sure that nobody took liberties with me. After a while he took to speaking to me. He told me I was not to mingle with the ladies who worked upstairs. He seemed to know them very well. Some of the men who came into the tavern would tease him about the number of Bainbridges in that area. He'd laugh and tell them they were welcome to try it. But it was the kind of a laugh that cut them short."

"To try it?" I didn't know what that meant.

"Just because he was better than they were was no reason to put him down. But they didn't press it; he was quick to anger, and he wouldn't take anything from anybody. He had a reputation as a backwoodsman, and they knew better than to go too far."

She spoke clearly, without hesitation, as if it were all passing in review, but there was an indefinable sadness in her voice that spoke of a lonely and cheerless heart.

"Didn't you wonder that he might be a relative since you were bearing the same name?"

"Not at the time. There were so many Bainbridges about my age. Aside from the ladies upstairs, everyone told me I had no mother, no father."

Was he, like Ra, the father of many?

Anne could only shrug her shoulders.

"I didn't want to know."

"How often did he talk to you?"

"Only when we were apart from others. And then he would say that I should tell him if anybody mistreated me or flirted with me. Sometimes he would bring me wood carvings by Indians from his trips, and gold coins, like on my birthday, which he knew about. He would ask me if I had any problems."

"What did you tell him?"

I could see her shrug her shoulders.

"I just worked and ate and slept. There wasn't any more to my life. I didn't expect any more."

She was fourteen when the tavern burned down. And he turned up to take her into a new home near Williamsburg, Virginia.

"He had friends that he thought I could work for, that would not put me in the public like I had been. He didn't want me back in the tavern because of what might happen."

"What do you mean, might happen?"

"That I would join the ladies upstairs. So he took me to these friends that had a lovely home in Williamsburg, and they were able to give me a job. I was supposed to be the upstairs maid in charge of the bedrooms, but whenever there was a crowd and they needed more serving people downstairs I would come and help. He said they would be kind to me, and they were, in a fashion, though they didn't pay very much attention to a serving girl."

"What was their name?"

"Randolph."

That was a famous name in Virginia—and Williamsburg.

"He had pretty good connections," I said.

"He knew a lot of people, and they seemed to respect him, and yet at the same time they apparently didn't want to be seen with him."

I understood the Randolphs and Thomas Jefferson were related.

"I don't remember any Jeffersons, but there were some people with a funny name like Custis."

The Custises, as I recalled, were related in some way to George Washington. Bainbridge must have done something right.

"He was not one of them," she said, "and he didn't come very often, only to drop by and see me a while. He arrived and left mysteriously." She had heard that he was close to the Indians and had some influence in keeping them off the warpath.

"You think these aristocrats may have used him to get things done?"

"Or he used them."

Anne Holbein was a woman of some sophistication, not easily impressed by the rich and the famous in this life. And so I was amused now by this star-struck reaction to the swells she served in that plantation-style home, providing a glimpse of a society already planning the revolution against the mother country.

"I would hear them talking about how the colonies were growing, and they would talk about the king and what he was doing to them. They used a lot of words that I didn't understand, but it was very thrilling to hear them so excited about conditions that they would pound the table and shout about the way things were being managed."

Aside from this minor diversion, her life was so unspeakably dull that it was a poignant contradiction of the charge that wishful thinking made grandees of everybody with a past life. Not Mary Bainbridge. For soon, poor child, she was to develop a bad cough that was to be the death of her.

"What made you sick, do you recall?"

"I started coughing; I couldn't get over the cough."

"Were you out in the rain or the cold?"

"I worked in the vegetable cellar sometimes when they didn't have anyone else to go down there. That's where they stored the vegetables to keep them fresh."

"And it was damp there?"

She shivered slightly, as though looking back some three hundred years into that dank chamber.

"Yes, it was damp," she said simply, with no tone of reproach.

"Did you work there for long periods of time?"

"Sometimes it would be all morning if there were a lot of people. I fixed the vegetables, so the cook could take care of them." Her brow furrowed in a frown, as if she did not want to mislead me in a most important matter.

"This wasn't the same cook that had taken care of me before at the tavern. This was the cook at the Randolphs. Her name was Agnes or Agatha. I don't know which. They called her Aggie. She was kind to me."

"How long were you ill with this coughing?"

"I guess about two years."

I had a picture of a thin, frail, unwanted girl hacking her lungs out, without anybody much caring except the cook. She was too weak to work and was confined to her bed.

"Did they call a doctor?"

She shook her head.

"They called John Bainbridge to come. I was so glad to see him. He squeezed my hand and told me that everything would be all right, that they would take care of me, and that I would be blessed." She sighed, a desolate sigh. She seemed to be reliving the experience, clearing her throat. "It hurt so when I coughed. They said it was my lungs."

He didn't stay long, but she remembered what he said about her being blessed. She knew then that she would never get well. She had another visitor, a glum-looking man with a black bag. He came only once and shook his head and told the servants who looked in on her from time to time, "Just make her comfortable. That's all you can do."

She knew then that she was dying. But she didn't care. She was so weak she couldn't sit up even with pillows propped behind her.

"My arms and legs looked like naked bones. My skin was as white as snow, no color in my nails or lips, no color anywhere."

It was all so real and vivid that I had the feeling that

I was not listening to Anne Holbein, but poor little Mary Bainbridge, an unwanted child, with only one tie to the world she would soon be leaving—a wastrel named John Bainbridge.

"Were you afraid of dying?"

"Not really. Life had been so hard for me. It had been a struggle from the time I could remember. And Mister Bainbridge had told me that death was not something to be feared, that it was a gentle passing to another life. I looked forward to another life."

A look of peace and composure came over the face of the woman I had regressed. I thought of what she had said about struggling, and I could see from her face, even with her eyes closed, that the struggle was over. But the soul had not died with the body. It had moved off but hovered somewhere about, for she remembered her own funeral.

"The cook started crying over me and saying, 'She's dead; she's gone.' I tried to comfort her because I was still there. I was standing for the first time in months, but she couldn't see me. And then they brought in a box they had built at the plantation. They couldn't see me, but I was still there, watching."

The reality of her death was such that I found myself asking, "Did they wash and bathe you?"

Her voice appeared to have a new strength, as though she had shed her frail, useless body and was gathering strength for the brighter world of the morrow.

"They wiped me down, yes," she said. "They brought in warm water, and I thought that rather strange since I knew that what water was left was growing colder and colder. And then they put a white robelike nightgown on me and laid me in the box. They had some of the servants come in from the farm, from the plantation. And they dug a hole in the ground and put the box there."

There were services of a sort.

"Someone I never saw before said something about Jesus and God. He wore his collar backward." She gave a little laugh. "It was funny to see him like that, and he said something about 'Dust thou art to dust returneth.' I didn't know what he meant but there was a brilliant light which I turned to and suddenly I had left them all behind."

I didn't know what to make of it. Yet there was no doubt that the personality of Anne Holbein, a seventy-year-old matron, was completely submerged, and I was listening to an unhappy girlchild who had found an adventure in death.

"Weren't you surprised," I asked, "to know what was going on at your own funeral?"

"I kept trying to tell them that what they saw was just a shell and that I had crawled out of there, but they didn't hear me."

Nobody had ever listened to her, so this was no surprise. The image she had created was so vivid that I didn't feel at all self-conscious questioning her as though she were that reality.

"Your spirit was leaving your body, even as they were praying over you?"

"The shell was worn out. No longer good for anything. And I was leaving it just like they told me the crabs did down on the beach. They crawled out of their old shell and left it, and that's what I felt like I was doing."

"And your recall?"

"It stopped when I saw myself going toward the light. I went toward the bright light, and it absorbed me. I was part of it; it was a wonderful feeling. I was just light."

In her short and tragic life it was the only happiness she had known. Cayce, if John Bainbridge, had good reason to help the people he had in the present lifetime. For, if nothing else, he was driven by a past that would not die as long as he remembered it. He had reached a spiritual low since entering the earth plane in Atlantis. And he knew, in his soul consciousness, that he would have to dwell again in the light of the Lord who made him, to go back spiritually to his beginnings in Atlantis, and rise up once more, stronger and purer than ever.

Part II

EDGAR CAYCE'S COMPANIONS THROUGH TIME

CHAPTER 9

The Sister of the Master

I didn't know what to expect. So Edgar Cayce in a life reading had said Irene Seiberling Harrison was Ruth, the sister of Jesus, both children of Mary and Joseph in the days of turmoil and of glory in the Holy Land two thousand years ago. She was of a humble family then, in moderate circumstances. In this lifetime she had been born to privilege, the daughter of Frank Seiberling, founder of Goodyear Tire and Rubber Company, who made Akron, Ohio, the tire center of the would. But as I found, she was still humble, still pious, notwithstanding being raised to wealth and distinction on a storybook estate to which presidents and kings had beaten a path. She was forty-seven years old, listing herself as a house-wife and a Protestant when she asked Edgar Cayce for a life reading more than fifty years ago. Now she was ninety-eight, still pretty and petite, with a sprightly manner and a smile for all of humankind.

Her looks and voice belied her age. She was not old in any sense. She looked ageless. There was a freshness about her pale face and a merry twinkle in her eye. Her hair was combed back like that of the Judean women of the biblical time. Her voice was strong and modulated, her stride sure, and she sat erect in her chair.

When she recently fell and broke her hip, her doctors were amazed that she healed more rapidly than some young athletes they were treating for a similar break. But not Irene. All her life she had been inspired by the boundless powers of the mind, which, of course, had made it possible for her to accept the unique powers of Edgar Cayce. She liked what he had to say about natural, healthful foods and exercise. For she was an advocate of both, as witness the trampoline she jumped around on every day and the natural fruit and vegetable juices she favored. Her husband, Milton Harrison, a banker and lawyer, whom she loved dearly, was long gone.

"Of course," she said with a shrug, "he traveled a lot and ate a lot of hotel food."

She spoke often of Jesus, not as she did her father and husband, both of whom she venerated, but as somebody to worship, but not as a god.

She was religious and spiritual and believed in reincarnation, for she had many life readings with Cayce. I also knew she had a delightful sense of humor, for when I phoned to tell her I wanted to discuss her past life, she had said with a laugh, "Why don't you use your imagination?"

And I had responded in the same vein, "I'd much rather use yours."

All imagination was not necessarily an illusion. I recall having regressed the author Taylor Caldwell, trying to find the source of her nostalgic novels, jogging a memory from which flowed a remarkable chronicle of ancient Greece, the best-selling book *The Power and the Glory*.

Irene had married and, I believe, had three children. She was known with her husband for her charities and good works. She was not one to sit back and let the world roll by. She was a Christian, very conscious of the burdens of those less fortunate.

With a psychologist familiar with Cayce's work, I had flown to Akron to meet with this remarkable woman. She had greeted us warmly and, though living in the small gatehouse, had somebody show us through the Seiberling manor house, with its many rooms, and the sprawling 3,000-acre estate. It was impressive, yet its spacious gardens and great halls were overshadowed by the simplicity of the woman whom Edgar Cayce had spoken of in the same breath as Christ.

Cayce had said she could remember the past through introspection, looking into her deeper self—her subconscious was that close to the surface. There was no need to regress her, no need to even ask, for Cayce, speaking of her life as Ruth, had said she would have no difficulty remembering what had lain dormant for so long in her deeper consciousness.

"And those [Ruth's] experiences may be recaptured, as it were, by the entity by introspection. For he has

given, that they that call upon him or upon the Lord in
his name may know what has been the experience from
the foundations of the world. Even as thou has seen him
before those people that doubted, so may ye see him in
this experience standing before the door of those that
would proclaim some other way."

As I looked at this woman of substance I could see
the faintest hint of a smile. And I knew that she had
remembered and that the meaning of death had become
clear to her.

She nodded solemnly, and her eyes closed a moment,
as though she were drifting back into a wonderful time
that knew only the limitations of the spirit.

Her eyes were clear, with the sparkle of youth. Again
as I marveled how ageless she seemed, I wondered
whether a joy of life, with thoughts of timeless futures,
once again with the people she had loved, did not somehow have a lot to do with the calm and steady gaze that
mirrored an ancient soul with no confusion about life.

"I do feel at times as though I had been there," she
said at last, in a quiet voice, "and that all I have to do
is close my eyes and it will all return."

It had been years since she had seen any Cayce readings on herself. But some of it appeared to have clung
to her, just as Cayce said it would.

She frowned a moment, and for the first time, I saw
a wrinkle of concentration, which disappeared as quickly
as it came.

"At first," she began, "Jesus seemed remote, not as
real as when I read about him in the Bible. He was of
the family but not in the family. Of course, we all know
now that he said something like this when told his mother
and brother waited without. And he replied in effect that
he had no family, the world of man was all the family
he needed.

As she hesitated, the thought passed through my mind
that she wasn't claiming very much (considering a belief
in reincarnation and in Cayce, as we were told) for his
having saved a dearly beloved friend still alive on this
plane fifty years after the doctors were ready to draw a
sheet over his face.

Yet as I looked at her and saw the serenity in her eye,
I realized she was thinking it all through, putting it all

together in some orderly fashion consistent with what she was and had been.

She had thought a lot about this very special life she had known before.

"I did and do have a feeling Jesus was not on my horizon until he started his two years of preaching before the Crucifixion. Then he became an entity that began to draw my attention. I have a feeling of my being active when he became active, of suddenly being aware that this brother, who had not been part of my childhood, was attracting attention and crowds wherever he went. But, you see, he wasn't in the home. He was out on the horizon. Naturally, I was deeply concerned with everything that happened. And I can—with imagination—see myself attending some of these public appearances. But I was like a face in the crowd, not like a relative. I would kneel and look up with awe at this man, that was my feeling. He was with the Essenes, and they were a very special group."

Accounting perhaps for this remoteness was the age difference, she being the much younger. And there were the lost years, preceding his ministry, when he was said to be in Egypt and India studying and making himself ready. It was no secret that Jesus may have been an Essene. There were scholarly claims that both Jesus and John the Baptist were of that religious order originating in the Holy Land in the second century B.C. because it was a monastic order calling for abstinence from conjugal relations, purification through baptism, and a belief in immortality. Essenes denounced slavery and banned trading because it encouraged greed and cheating. This was all what Jesus and John believed in. And so the label seemed to fit.

She was still speaking of that other childhood, a time she seems to treasure, a time with fond parents, Joseph and the mother of Jesus.

"As a child, I had little idea of the ferment of the times, of the nation's cry for a Messiah to deliver them from Rome, of Isaiah's prophecy of the coming of a son of David, a man of peace, riding into Jerusalem on a donkey, to become, as the prophet Isaiah said, a light unto the world, Gentile and Judean alike. Not until I was eighteen had I any sense of any intimate knowledge of him. He was thirty then, beginning his public career. But even then, he was still somebody off there, not somebody in the home. I went to many of his discussions, and I was a very sympathetic person in the audience, very proud that people would listen so closely. He would be in our little village on a certain day. He would be gathering people here and there, and I would listen with open ears. I was impressed with everything.

"And it was not because he was my brother. I was very young and very critical then. Even now as I analyze the character, the historical character of Jesus, I have very different feelings from most people. The things he said that make an impression on me now, that are recorded in the Bible are, 'It is not of myself but the Father in me that doeth the work.' This I use in my own life to guide me. This is what helps me."

The connection had heightened this sense she had of caring for people. She concerned herself with the underprivileged and was involved enough to write to the privileged about helping the less blessed.

"I'm always writing letters to the president of the United States and senators and representatives, and I will be surprised sometimes at my own letters. They're right to the point, they ring bells, and I have a very definite feeling they are meaningful to the people I write them to. Yet, I always say to myself, as Jesus did, 'It is not I, it is the Father in me that doeth this.' "

She had the same reservations about Jesus today that she had as Ruth. "By himself he could do nothing. And I think this turning to God helps me to be meaningful with my life. As far as I know, Jesus never said, 'Now I want you to worship me.' I never got that impression, as far as I can envision, from my contact or awareness of him, if I were Ruth. How can I say for sure that I was, even though I have these impressions that come at me strongly at times. If I were Ruth—and it seems a presumption at times—it was high respect, regard, belief in what he was doing—accepting that he was healing people. But he himself didn't claim that he did it. It was the great Divine Intelligence, whom we call God, with which he was in perfect attunement. And what is this life, this death we speak of? 'If you would do the things I do, ye shall do that and greater, for I go unto my Father.' What did he mean by that as I look at it in my present consciousness? He meant, 'I am in tune, right here and now with my earth-vehicle to work through with my Father in an absolute oneness.' "

She was still very much the sister, not wanting a god as a brother she had sat down at the table with.

"He was at one with the great spiritual intelligence of the world," she said. "And this was where his power came from. But Jesus of Nazareth was a human being as we were human beings. And he was letting this absolute consciousness of God flow through him. But he didn't take credit unto himself. He gave the Father the credit. People put him on this pedestal, but I don't think for one minute he wanted that. His idea was to make people know that he could do what he did with the help of the Father.

"He said, 'The things I do, ye shall do.' For a long time I puzzled over that. And I said, 'Oh, no, that's foolish. We'll never do it. And then I began to realize that in a little simple way it worked, by my saying when I was tackling something, 'Look, it's not I but the Father in me that will get this accomplished.' That's what he was trying to teach us."

I had to smile to myself. For she spoke and acted like the sister of the Son of man, despite her denials.

"And that is exactly what you believe?"

She gave me an inquiring look, and I went on. "You put it all in the hands of God, this infinite, universal intelligence you speak of?"

She nodded, and the ghost of a smile was on her lips. She had enjoyed the discussion, just as she must have relished being the missionary Ruth with her husband, a Roman, two thousand years ago. For insensibly, I paired the two in my thoughts—Ruth and Irene—as the dialogue developed, and it became obvious where she was coming from, despite a modest disclaimer every now and then of an exalted past.

One thing still puzzled me. Had she ever resolved in her own mind a difficulty with the virgin birth, as described to her in her past life?

"In the Cayce readings," I said, "you questioned the virgin birth. You couldn't understand that, however you tried." I managed a smile. "Perhaps you were too close to it."

She nodded, and her face brightened like the face of spring.

"I have done some thinking about this, now that I am alone so much with my thoughts. And I can say that as far as the Immaculate Conception is concerned, I accept it one thousand percent."

It was not always thus. In her reading as Ruth I had been struck by her sharp questioning of the Holy Mother as to whether "Jesus was the natural son of Joseph."

As Irene Harrison, she had asked the same, and Cayce had replied, "As ye questioned in Athens. A conception through the Holy Spirit, to those that open themselves to the will of the Father-God. In such, even in the earth there comes the natural to be unnatural. For nature proclaims God, as the unnatural in nature magnifies God."

At length, Cayce gave Irene an insight into her mother's feelings, an insight that had been denied her because of the holy mother's wish not to talk about that which was the Lord's.

"Hence, as the body grew, as the body was held by the mother in its sole purpose of 'thy handmaiden, O God, use me as thy will—let my cup be filled with thy purpose, thy desire, because of thy love for man, that I may be a channel, through which the world may know [of the Son's birth], though I be doubted and spurned by those that are worldly wise.' "

As Ruth, she was a believable, questioning sister. Why, she asked, should her brother be out saving the world, going here and there, when in his own family it would have been as easy to save an ailing Joseph as a Lazarus, already dead when raised from the grave.

Cayce replied, "In thine own physical reaction there was the reasoning, 'If he healed, why did he let Father [Joseph] die? If he is such as so many proclaim, why hath he been so long away?'"

Jesus, said Cayce, had his reasons, stated throughout his ministry. Had he not said the world was his family, appearing to renounce the mother and brothers who awaited him, only to point up the universality of his love?

Not unnaturally, Ruth had not understood the nature of this brother, so distant at times yet so impressive to

others. She had stood with her mother in a synagogue in
Capernaum (upstairs, the Judean custom for women) as
he discoursed on the prophets Moses and Isaiah and Elijah. She saw the wonder in the eyes of the people, for
some knew they were listening to one anointed of the
Lord, the Messiah for whom all Israel waited. Ruth
looked at her mother and saw the mist in her eyes, sensing with her mother's exaltation a secret sorrow as she
marked the passion of the crowd. For Mary knew, as she
had known at his birth, that this son was not hers but
the world's and not long for this world.

As he spoke of the patriarch Abraham, saying, "Before Abraham was I am," Ruth saw the mingled looks
of ecstasy and dismay. For how could this beardless
youth have preceded Abraham, when he was not yet
thirty years of age?

And she still doubted, not his mission—for that was
clear in the eyes of the people—but a deification that her
own bloodline denied. For how could a brother be that
which the sister was not, in the eyes of God?

As Ruth, she had a certain detachment yet awe of this
brother who was in Egypt when she was born twelve
years after him. She did not get into what he was doing,
nor believing in it, until the last two years of his three-
year ministry when all of Israel was talking about him.

After the Crucifixion, with a reinforced belief born of
the Resurrection, she carried his message of eternal sal-
vation into the world of Rome, which was to become a
conduit carrying the enduring faith to the far corners of
the empire.

"The entity became closely associated with the Roman
influences after the death upon the cross. And after some
beautiful experiences with the disciples and apostles,
came that in the entity's activity as it journeyed with
those that brought to the Roman power the awareness
of the Christ influence in the man Jesus."

As Irene, she asked Cayce about the man who had
walked with Jesus after the Crucifixion and vouched for
the Resurrection.

"Did I know the Roman who walked with Christ to
Emmaus?"

Cayce replied, "Married the one and returned to
Rome with him, there helping others to understand the

message that Jesus brought." And she had married him in this lifetime as well. Coming together in the same fashion as old companions so often do to carry on from the past.

As a Roman, beloved of Christ, he carried the word to Antioch, Athens, and Rome, meeting with scorn and approbation in a wide-ranging empire that almost seemed to have been established to facilitate the spread of Christianity.

Irene had not known what to make of that first reading. She was without pretensions. It humbled yet troubled her to think she could have been related to the messenger of God.

A few months later she asked Cayce for another reading on the biblical period. Jesus emerged as large as life. Cayce drew a vivid picture of him as a youth, moving about, schooling himself before the return to Judea and to Jerusalem for the Passover instruction. "We find that James—the brother of the entity [Ruth] was born into that experience."

Then came a glimpse into the "secret years" of Jesus as he was preparing himself for his ministry and the birth to Mary of Ruth, one year after her brother James.

"When there had been by the wise men of the East, the beginnings of the teachings of Jesus and his sojourn in Persia and India and when those activities brought about the change in the financial status of the family, Ruth then was born in that city of Capernaum."

From the vividness of this description, it almost seemed as though the words were flowing from the lips of an eyewitness—Lucius of Cyrene.

The reading Cayce had given the woman he called Ruth seemed to take on an added reality. For Lucius (Cayce) had stood at Paul's elbow in Antioch and in Rome and Judea as well. And it was in Antioch and in Rome, said Cayce, that Ruth and her Roman husband had served under such missionaries as Paul, Lucius, Mark, and Timothy.

Irene had been thrilled that day as Cayce called out "Hold fast. Even as thou hast seen him in this experience standing before the door of those that would proclaim some other way. Turn not away because of those who would bring thee to material understanding, as thou didst

bring the heart of the people to him, as thou didst bring
thy younger brother Jude—though he faltered much. As
thou didst bring strength to thy elder brother James, who
was made first head of the church in honoring the
brother."

It all seemed so far away and yet so real. For we were
very conscious of the power Christ exerted over people's
minds and that he lived in them as they lived in him. We
were not dealing in abstracts or ancient myths but with
a spiritual force that pervaded so much of humankind.
Still, as I sat across from Irene Harrison and her daughter, Sally, sitting protectively close, I couldn't help but
wonder what had led this conventionally bred woman to
ask for a life reading, presupposing reincarnation, of a
mystic like Cayce, twice jailed for his clairvoyant readings, once in New York for fortune-telling, again in Detroit for practicing medicine without a license. Yet Irene
didn't find it at all odd that people in trouble should turn
to him.

"He was a leader, a man ahead of his time." She
paused. "And he saved a beloved friend's life. There was
no question of that. Four doctors had given up on him.
He had been in Europe, taking graduate studies and
working on his doctorate after getting through college.
He became deadly ill while traveling in Italy. His lungs
were congested, and he was wasting away with fever.
The Italian doctor telephoned his parents in this country
and said, 'If you want to see your boy alive, come and
get him because he can't do it alone.' "

I was listening closely, as was the psychologist, for we
could see that it had been an emotional experience Irene
would relive over and over until it came time, as the poet
said, for the crossing of the bar.

The friend was brought back to the States, where a
team of specialists, consulting together, thought it could
be tuberculosis. For one lung was congealed, and he was
running a high fever. Every morning his temperature
was down, and every night it went up. It was like this
for months, and finally having nothing better to offer
in the way of a cure, the doctors decided on solitary
confinement.

" 'Complete quiet,' they said. 'Nobody goes into his
room.' Nurses and doctors were excepted. Nurses around

the clock watched him like a hawk. But they could do nothing but hope."

Irene was living in Bronxville then with her husband and her family. In constant telephone communication with her friend's parents, she could sense their despair. It was just a matter of time, the doctors said. There was no chance of recovery. Each day her friend was a little worse off. To ease her own feelings she had mentioned the illness to a friend in New York, and the friend said, "You should get a psychic reading from this man Edgar Cayce. He's a wonder at things like this, when the doctors are stumped."

Irene had her misgivings, for it seemed like voodoo to her. But then the friend mentioned that one of New York's leading Presbyterian ministers had been impressed by Cayce's gift.

So she got a reading for this friend, mortally ill at thirty. And she could hardly believe her ears. For Cayce turned directly to the nature of the illness. "Yes," he said, "we have the entity. Yes, he is very ill, but he can overcome it." He cautioned against telling anyone of the reading as their predictably negative thoughts could only block its success.

This was in March 1932. Cayce offered no immediate turnaround. "He's going to get worse and worse. But in three months, on June 28, when no one will think it humanly possible for him to live, the fever will break, and he will be on the road to recovery."

The Harrisons had three months to wait and to invoke the power of God and Christ. "If," quoting Cayce, "two people stand together at the last moment, when hope is gone and know there is a power greater than the minds of men that has the entity [the friend] in its keeping, then this will pull him through. And there's nothing you can do between now and then. The fever will have to get higher and higher. When it appears as if it will kill him, it will burn out the infection in his lung. And when the infection is burned out, the fever will immediately subside and his life will be saved."

They told nobody, as he had said. And they put the date in a drawer—the twenty-eighth of June. Meanwhile, as weeks passed, the date slipped their minds. And then at 2:00 in the morning on June 28, the friend's mother called and said, "Robert is dying. The doctors say he has a temperature so high it won't register. There's no hope whatsoever."

I had been listening quietly, and my companion was equally silent. It was as though we were watching a Greek drama unfold in which a tragic finale was inevitable. And yet we knew the victim had survived. Still, how and why had the Harrisons in Bronxville, New York, been so confident of the friend's survival when his doctors and family on the spot had said it was the end?

Irene's eyes glowed with the remembrance.

"You see, here we were, not thinking of the reading, dickering for a summer home in August on the ocean at Fire Island in New York. And suddenly we remembered that Cayce had said that on August 12, six weeks from June 28, we would be going to the seashore, because my friend would need to breathe the iodine from the sea air.

"If not for that reading, which I saw developing, I would have been sobbing the way Robert's mother was."

But instead, she reassured the youth's mother in no uncertain terms. "You believe in God. You know God is in charge of that boy and that he brought him into the world and he can save his life. The Bible says that where two or three are gathered together in my name there am I in the midst of you. Milton, my husband, is one; I am two. You can go to bed and know the Infinite Intelligence is in charge and will be in charge until the work has been accomplished."

And so on the strength of what Edgar Cayce had said—not knowing of Edgar Cayce's existence—that dear, sorrowing mother went to bed and slept that night, buoyed by the confidence in Irene's voice.

I wanted to make sure of one thing.

"Nobody knew of the reading, not even the family?"

"We had told no one, as Cayce said."

Later that morning, after a sound sleep, the mother called Irene. She reported a miracle.

"The doctors are all marveling. The high temperature that they said no one could survive suddenly broke, and our boy broke out in a sweat, and his body, which was so bloated and congested, began to turn back to normal. And then they tested the lungs. The fluid had all drained off."

At this my companion seemed to come to life.

"And this was on what date?"

"On June 28."

The two of us exchanged glances, which seemed to say, "If he could do this, what couldn't he do?"

But this was not the end. For though the friend's life was spared, his days were still numbered, the doctors said.

"He only has a few months to live," they said. "This terrible fever has so affected his blood that he's in a state of pernicious anemia. He can never build his body back. We can keep the nurses and feed him fluids, and he'll be around for a few months."

The lung infection was gone, the doctors acknowledged. But nobody could see the patient. He was too weak. By now Cayce was no longer a secret in the family. And Cayce had said that when the patient pulled through, Irene's husband was to tell their friend what had happened and ask him if he wished to continue the Cayce readings.

Milton Harrison was a businessperson. He specialized in getting things done. He had to get that youth to the seashore. All his life he had put people first, like the Roman of old who had walked with Christ. He had been told that the young patient could see no one. But somewhere deep inside of him was a spirit of the past that would not be denied. The man from Emmaus, with Jesus' sister at his side, had gone from Rome to Antioch and Judea healing the sick and counseling the troubled in Christ's name. It was nothing now for him to take the overnight train from New York to Detroit. The doctors said, No visitors. But Harrison strode resolutely to the sick man's door. He wouldn't be dissuaded. "I will not leave without seeing him."

"All right, two minutes," they said.

He needed less.

Robert was so weak he could only nod and murmur a feeble yes.

Nothing seemed to help. There was no sign of a normal convalescence. They put him in the sun, and it only seemed to tire him the more. Cayce, in a reading, recommended a drop or two a day of Atomidine, an iodine compound, to stimulate the nervous system and charcoal tablets to encourage a response to the sun's healing rays. These were given by the family. The doctors knew none of this but were encouraged by an unexpected improvement. Milton and Irene, heartened as well, counted on what Cayce had said about their friend being healed by the sea air.

No team could have worked more in concert than the Harrisons, working together in the name of the Almighty and of the Promised One, Jesus Christ. And doing it the way Jesus said it should be done and as Lucius of Cyrene had counseled in the days of the Coming.

What had Cayce said that appeared so consequential now, speaking of another dear one—and husband—at another time and place?

"Returning from that meeting where for the first time she had heard the utterances of Jesus as to the prophecies of Isaiah and Jeremiah of the Coming, and the consequent uproar among the skeptics, the entity Ruth encountered that one now the husband.

"Being not only beautiful of body but active in those conditions of helping people, which became the interests of the unusual Roman, there were the natural consequences that brought about a bond of sympathy between the two. Then began the travels to ascertain the truth of what had been told by the mother of Jesus' birth, as to the experiences in Bethlehem, and in Bethany where the raising of Lazarus from the dead was witnessed by Ruth and her companion, that brought a change that made for a new life, a new understanding of the Creative Force.

"Just before the Crucifixion there was the consummation of the wedding. And Jesus attended that wedding and blessed them."

And now Irene Seiberling Harrison was being enjoined by Cayce—or was it Lucius of Cyrene?

"Study that, as he has given in those last words of his to the apostles and disciples, to become not only by word but by act, the living example of that as he taught. 'As ye do it to the least of thy brethren, ye do it unto thy Maker.' "

It was all being done for a dear friend; Irene and Milton were doing now what they had been doing all their lives together, as Cayce had said.

"If ye would know good, do good. If ye would have

life, give life. If ye would know Jesus, the Christ, then be like him, who died for a cause without shame, without fault, yet through that bringing the Resurrection."

And to get Irene's friend back they needed what inspiration they could get from that simple injunction. For to the doctors in Detroit the projected move to a spot off Long Island, where the Harrisons were to summer, was a mission impossible.

"He can't even sit up in bed," said the attending physician. "He's dead on his back. He regurgitates half the food we feed him with a spoon. He can't swallow it. He couldn't sit up in a plane, and to put him on a train that rattles and shakes would be the end of him. His body couldn't take it. He would die, and you two . . ."

The implication was clear. His death would be on their heads.

They didn't know what to do. There seemed no way out. But they remembered what Cayce had said about the Higher Power.

Without realizing it then, both were joined with an old companion—Lucius of Cyrene—in the healing of a dearly beloved companion of the present.

And again, as many times before, Milton rose to the occasion.

"There is an intelligence above man that knows," said Milton, for he had worked with this intelligence long before.

"But how will you get to that intelligence?" asked a practical Irene.

"I don't know, but there is that power."

With that declaration of faith he went to sleep.

But the channel to the Higher Power never slept, for Milton woke in the morning, crying, "I've got it!"

Milton suddenly recalled that the president of the Baltimore and Ohio Railroad, to repay a favor, had offered him his private railroad car anytime he wanted it. And now, as good as his word, the man arranged for the car to be trans-hooked to a succession of trains, so the ailing man wouldn't have to leave the car till they got to Long Island.

Cayce had said the youth would be able to make the trip and the sea air would cure him. The doctors said he would die en route. But as they saw how determined the

Harrisons were, and how the patient had perked up at the suggestion, they grudgingly gave permission.

"He's only got a month anyway," they said. "So he may as well die happy."

So on the twelfth of August, as Cayce said, the Harrisons brought Robert to the summer home on Fire Island. The doctors predicted he would never come back alive. But they reckoned without Cayce. For in one of his readings, without having consciously heard of her, he recommended a remarkable masseuse named Dolly Pan. "Get her address from a cousin of yours who has used her as a masseuse. She is the only one to touch the body of this entity. She works with zone therapy"—meaning she touched certain pressure points on the soles of the feet and the back to stimulate various deadened areas of the body. There was similar advice on how to get a trained nurse and how she should handle her patient.

"So," said Irene, as we marveled at her memory, "these were Cayce's instructions. He said that the first day our friend arrives at Fire Island no one is to speak to him, except the trained nurse who will be on the shore waiting when he gets off the ambulance. 'She will cross on the boat, then go up with him to his room. And this nurse you will find by putting an ad on the Unity Church bulletin board in New York City, saying you want a retired nurse for two months for a cottage on Fire Island.' Sure enough, a retired nurse answered the ad, and we told her, 'Now, whatever you've learned to do, it's not medical stuff you follow, but you will follow what the Cayce readings say, if you want this job.' "

For five days the masseuse and nurse were the only ones to enter the sick man's room. Cayce's instructions were specific. "The first night she was there, Dolly Pan was told that for five minutes she was to touch pressure points on each foot and five minutes on the back." By the fifth day, the treatments had gone to ten minutes, and the Harrisons could visit for a few minutes. By this time the youth could talk normally. And soon he was well enough to sit up and eat whatever he wanted.

All this was remarkable, but more of the same was to come. In less than a month, Robert was walking, and the little family group was looking forward to another month on Fire Island. Then, in September, just before

Labor Day, there was a stunning message from Cayce. Despite the good the ocean air was doing Robert and the beautiful sunny weather, an unsolicited Cayce reading said the family must leave the island within twenty-four hours and return to their suburban home in Bronxville, outside New York City.

"This is a very important message," Cayce stressed. "We are telling you that you will take this entity tomorrow to Bronxville. And take him by ambulance. No other way. You are not to tell him until the night before because otherwise he may refuse to leave. Move all the help out, move Irene and the children, all the family, all the day before. Let the nurse remain with your friend overnight, to leave with him on the 5:30 boat in the morning for the mainland. Have the chauffeur there so he can help lift the body on a stretcher into the ambulance."

I looked up at this, marveling what was to come next. Cayce was so remarkably explicit.

"I thought he could walk and was almost well."

Irene nodded, but she had a twinkle in her eye, like a child about to spring a surprise.

"Yes, but Cayce didn't want him to expend any extra energy, what with the strain of moving when he didn't want to leave. We thought it was crazy. We had the place for the entire month, the weather was beautiful, and everybody was happy. And here we were bound for Bronxville. It didn't make sense. But Cayce was so right in everything we didn't dare question him."

So a rather depressed and confused family slept that night in the Bronxville home. The next morning as they awakened, they found the weather had changed. It was cold, foggy, and gray. There was a chill in the house. Harrison lit the fireplace and turned on the radio.

Irene looked at us bright-eyed.

"And what do you think we heard? A hurricane had unexpectedly struck. A tidal wave had hit Fire Island. The water had swamped the cellars of all the homes and the lower floors. There was no communication between Fire Island and the mainland for ten days. No boats could get across due to the fog. There was no power. Fire Island was marooned. There was no heat in our cottage.

Our friend's lung, still delicate, could never have withstood it."

My companion, the psychologist, was frowning.

"Are you saying this was in a Cayce reading?"

Irene nodded. "The reading saw it. There had been no suggestion from the weather people. They had no briefing of this tidal wave. And to think, when we left Fire Island, we felt like crying. We wouldn't have been human if we hadn't thought that maybe Cayce was pushing the alarm bell."

Robert stayed on with the Harrisons for four months, until January 1. He was completely healed. He had improved so much he was able to visit Cayce in nearby Scarsdale and have a reading with him. And this time Cayce had a vision he disclosed to Irene when he came out of trance. He shook his head in wonder and said, "I never remember what I tell my people, but I will never forget the wonder and beauty of meeting Jesus on this occasion. He must have been with your friend during this healing time. Because there he was, and I talked to him."

All through our lengthy discussion, a tireless Irene Harrison had been incredibly communicative. Her hearing was excellent, as was her eyesight and all her senses, including a keen sixth sense that Cayce had perceived to be almost clairvoyant.

It had been a day that neither I nor the psychologist would soon forget. We had traversed many lands and crossed many horizons, and the wonder of it was that it had all been as real and as moving as anything we had ever known.

It was with some regret we made our good-byes. It would be a long time before we met up with anybody like Irene Seiberling Harrison again. Irene took us to the door of her little gatehouse and gave us a firm handclasp and a blessing for the road. She had been with us for hours and yet there was not a trace of fatigue in her unlined face. She had made this journey into the past before, and that past only served to freshen her.

There was a feeling as we departed that we had made an adventure into time and found it timeless.

Later, on the plane, my companion turned to me with a quizzical smile.

"Who was saying all that, Ruth or Irene?"

"A little of both, perhaps," I said. "I'm sure Edgar Cayce could tell us."

His eyes had closed; he seemed half-asleep. It had been a fatiguing experience, for we had the feeling of having lived through two lives, not that much apart, as one measures different states of consciousness.

His head nodded, as he murmured drowsily, "How could Cayce be so right about Irene's friend and not be right about Irene?"

CHAPTER 10

Of Love Possessed

"Of course, I felt close to Mister Cayce," Gladys Davis said. "Why shouldn't I? I was his wife in one life, his daughter in another, and his mother in still another."

She laughed.

"And don't forget Atlantis. We were soulmates then, thought-forms in the beginning that split off into separate souls with the capability of loving one another."

Though she spoke lightly, her voice admitted of no doubt.

"And all this you are sure of?" I said, rather lamely.

"Of course," she said. "It's all in the readings and in our lives. Everything we feel and are is there. All we have to do is look into ourselves, and we know how we came to where we are today."

I didn't quite know what to say. For this was many years ago, and I hadn't yet come to believe in reincarnation. But when Gladys spoke about anything dear to her, I listened carefully, for I had never known anybody with a greater regard for the truth.

We had been friends for a good many years. She was always unfailingly kind and helpful. And more than anyone had helped me put together the books I had done on Edgar Cayce, including *The Sleeping Prophet*. She had been a unique part of the Cayce household for twenty-two years, working with Cayce and his wife, Gertrude, until their passing, three months apart, in 1945.

I had never heard her speak of Gertrude Cayce, except in a tone of warmth and sometimes with a misty eye. As we talked together then over lunch she sat back and reflected for a moment, lost in thought, as she often was when her thoughts were with the Cayces.

"Gertrude and I had a great love for each other," she said finally. "She was like a mother to me, and I like

170

her daughter, as we had been in time past. There were many things to work out, and we managed, believing as we did that we had all been brought together for a purpose."

She referred to this previous relationship so casually, that it almost slipped by me before I could lift an eyebrow.

"Oh, yes," she said, "in Egypt, I was a child then, and she left me. That was one of the things we had to work out, and I think we did very well."

She was speaking of a past life, of course. And I didn't know what to make of this at the time. But I had never known her to make misstatement or exaggerate a point or condemn or criticize. She was indeed a model of restraint, almost too good to be true. But this goodness had not come easily. It was a virtue dearly earned during some very trying days in a household that, at times, was a little island unto itself and, at others, a goldfish bowl.

I had heard all kinds of gossip about these two, Edgar and Gladys, long after Cayce's death, but I gave it little attention. Though a skeptical reporter, all I had to do was look at Gladys's guileless face, and I knew that no breath of scandal could ever touch her. There was invariably gossip about young, beautiful women and older men. And I supposed a lot of it in this case came from a tendency to link the lives so real in the past with the nebulous present.

Looking across the table, as we were fiddling with our lunch, I could see the vestiges of a fresh-faced beauty that had launched these countless rumors, and I knew they would never have been made of a woman less attractive than Gladys. The sparkle of youth, still in her eye, reminded me of pictures I had seen of her when she was eighteen or nineteen, first hired as Cayce's secretary. I was sure she could have won any beauty contest she had chosen to enter. She was tall, slim, stately, and fair, with a smile that could have captured the heart of any man with blood running through his viens.

Yes, she had been a beauty, and the tawdry newspapers of the day made capital of this when Cayce was arrested in New York with Gertrude and Gladys on a trumped-up charge of fortune-telling. There was that suggestive front-page picture of Cayce and Gladys together, with Gertrude's likeness carefully snipped off to support the spicy headline: "Mystic Arrested In Hotel With Blonde Secretary."

She could laugh about it as we dallied over our food, but it was no laughing matter then. Cayce so keenly felt the humiliation of being booked as a common criminal that he considered giving up the work that had brought him so little of the world's rewards. But what troubled him most was the distress it caused the two people he cared about.

"It was all part of what Mister Cayce had to put up with all his life," Gladys said, a shadow crossing her face. "He didn't like seeing anybody hurt because of what he was doing. He was a proud man, and though the charges were thrown out, the whole episode left a nasty taste."

She had a mercurial smile. "Of course, it set a lot of tongues wagging. You can't keep tongues from wagging, whatever you do—or don't do. But he was always Mister Cayce to me."

I looked up and smiled.

"I wouldn't have thought," I said, "that he could ever be anything else."

After Gladys's passing in 1986, I remembered our conversation as I began delving into the Cayce life readings. The rumors were still alive, though the three principals had passed on. And as I was about to begin my research, one of the people presently on the scene admonished me, "I hope you're not going to perpetuate the picture of Cayce as some goody-goody who never looked another woman in the eye."

I shrugged and said, "That is not what he's all about."

But I realized, of course, even as I said this, that people were interested in anything that affected Cayce's heart and mind—and soul. And each had his notion of what that was.

I had my own picture of him in my mind. He was a homespun personality with a keen sense of humor, a psychic gift that, while it sometimes confused him, still gave him a lively appreciation of his worth, and a boyish charm that attracted women, even as as it drew him to them in his inoffensive way.

As I got into the readings, my curiosity took me not only to Cayce's file on himself but to Gertrude's and

Gladys's as well, which had been made available by an A.R.E. justly proud of all three of these people.

I was somewhat surprised, but not at all startled, by the depth of feeling between Cayce and Gladys, transcending in its intensity anything that could have grown out of one lifetime. It was matched only by the understanding and love that was Gertrude's for a husband so different from her in temperament and by her compassion for a younger woman anyone else might have considered a rival. I saw nothing uncommon about the relationships, since they proceeded quite naturally out of the past Gladys had so cheerfully talked about. The principals in this little drama accepted that past because of their understanding of karma.

"If there was ever a test of reincarnation," said one observer, "this was it. For each had something out of the past to struggle with, and something to give the other."

Nobody knew better than Cayce that the joining of people for a useful purpose was never accidental. "It is the future that shapes the present," said the French philosopher Tardieu. And only a few like Cayce understood that a predictable future could only occur in some foreseeable way if the design was already established by a designer modeling a congruent chain of events out of the past and present.

"They were drawn together out of the past," said Jeanette Thomas, the keeper of the readings, "and the meeting was anything but chance, though it may have appeared that way. Mister Cayce had put an ad in a Selma newspaper for a secretary, and twelve applicants for the job showed up and were sharpening their pencils when Gladys arrived with an older friend, Miss Willie Graham. The reading was for Miss Graham's little nephew. And though she wasn't applying for the job, Gladys took down the reading with the rest, at her friend's request."

Cayce found something wrong with the boy's nervous system and recommended a treatment, which Gladys set down with all its unfamiliar anatomical terms as though she had been born for the job. She had a feeling of easy familiarity as well with the man who was speaking in his sleep.

"Gladys," noted biographer Mary Ellen Carter, "was

increasingly at ease as the procedure focused on the words of the sleeping man. She was aware of a new sense of well-being that increased with each passing moment. She felt warmed and drawn to this man as she would be to a member of her own family. There was a feeling of belonging, and a knowledge that she had been led to this moment. . . . Suddenly, she was alert and earnest, her facility for taking notes and catching each syllable never sharper, her sense of purpose never keener."*

Although she wasn't a candidate, Gladys was the only one considered for the job after she produced her copy of the reading.

"We need a full-time secretary," Cayce said.

"I'd like to be considered," said Gladys.

"Fine, Miss Gladys," he said, "consider yourself hired."

"Again," observed Mary Ellen Carter, "she felt that lovely sense of renewing an old friendship. His presence seemed to remind her of some warm emotion dimly spiraling down the passages of time. So strong was the notion that she tried to place him in her memory, at the same time wondering why she did that."†

I felt almost an eavesdropper as I noted the entry of Gladys into the Cayce household—with a magnetic current as disturbing as it was pleasant. While it heightened the awareness of the three concerned, it was somewhat of a mixed blessing because of the sometimes uneasy remembrance that went with it. After some months of this disquietude, the mystified mystic decided to give himself a reading, with the concurrence of the women, to throw some light on the familiarity of the various parties after Gladys's entry into the family fold.

Gertrude conducted the reading, taken down by Gladys. Cayce in trance was asked by Gertrude, "What should the relation between these individuals [Cayce and Gladys] be at the present time on this earth plane?"

It didn't take much imagination to visualize the eagerness with which the sleeping Cayce's answer was awaited by the two others in the room—the long-enduring, forty-

*From Mary Ellen Carter, *Miss Gladys and the Edgar Cayce Legacy* (Virginia Beach, VA: A.R.E. Pub., 1985), 6.
†Ibid., 8.

seven-year-old Gertrude and the dewy-eyed nineteen-year-old Gladys, sitting demurely with a pencil in hand, ready to take down whatever Cayce said.

Cayce finessed the question for the moment. "We find these in the present earth's plane have had many experiences together. Their soul and spirit are well knit and must of necessity present each that they may be one. In the beginning these two were as one in mind, soul, spirit, body, in the first earth's plane (Atlantis) when the earth's indwelling of man was both male and female in one.

"In Atlantis, there came the separation of the body. For the desire being to give of self in bodily form to the other, it brought the separating of the spirit and soul from the carnal forces. But there was no physical joining, only that of the spirit."

He presently came to the current embodiment of Gladys, indicating the stringent lines of behavior they were to follow despite the intimacy of the past.

"The lives of each have ever been bound in the other's life, the conditions as exist are only the outgrowth of endeavor in the earth plane. They—the relations in the present—should be the ever innate affection as is necessary in the lives of each, for the satisfying not of the earthly forces but of the soul and spirit which find manifestation in material affection. Let that affection be such as gives of self to each, in no uncertain terms or physical manner, but ever in the answering of each desire toward the other in the way that gives self's affection. That is, the outward manifestations of the inward desires of the heart and soul, which find in each the answering chord in the other's affection that will never, never, never be found in any other."

The answer, with the wife a rapt listener, obviously confirmed the honesty of Cayce's readings. For what husband, in his conscious mind, would make such a statement in this circumstance? I put down the reading with the uneasy feeling I was opening a whole Pandora's box of revelations recalling the Knights of the Round Table as the Lady of Shalott looked down to Camelot and saw "the web that floated wide, and the mirror cracked from side to side."

I reverted to the reading, for curiosity, frankly, got the better of me. And so I came to Cayce's enjoinder:

"Be faithful one to the other, irrespective of earthly conditions, yet in that way that there is that consideration of other relations that are necessary and existing, for other conditions as have been met.

"Be kind, affectionate, one toward the other, in the heart and soul preferring the other, giving of self in physical manifestations of the affections of the heart, of the soul, of the mind, of the body. For these are souls in the making and were united in the beginning. And though their bodies may burn with their physical desires, the soul of each is and will be knit with the other when presented before the throne of him who said, 'Be fruitful, multiply, give of the best that the best may be presented to him [Christ].''

I thought of the tremor that must have shaken that little room. Of Gertrude, the loyal wife, and Gladys, too, still a teenager, thrust into this uneasy spotlight. But Cayce would go on with his reading undisturbed. For he alone was unaware of what he said, as he ended the reading on an upbeat note.

"Be thou faithful unto the end and receive that crown that is ever for the faithful in heart, soul, and body. Be kind, affectionate, loving, ever-giving, ever-preferring the other."

I had come to the end and all I could do was sigh, thinking of the frustration and strain that must have invaded that little room.

What must have gone through Gertrude's mind as she sat and listened? Did she visualize her marriage of so many years crumbling? What were her feelings toward this much younger and prettier girl, this virtual stranger, who was herself in a state of confusion as she crossed the last *t*, and dotted the last *i*? And what of the great man himself, as he awoke from his sweet dream and was told what he had said? Comb my memory as I would, I could find no clue in anything Gladys had ever said to me of such a distraction in the long closeness of her relationship.

I understood better now her passionate attachment to the Cayce work, the years of going without a salary, the restlessness that affected her at times as she saw her youth dwindling away, and perhaps above all, the special insight she now had of the lives expressed in the past and their bearing on her present and future. But I was still puzzled, still concerned by the provocative vistas plainly opened up by the reading, and the questions left unanswered.

I could not turn to Edgar or Gertrude or Gladys, in the physical plane. But their spirit lived on, the essence of their soul, in their common questing, their testing of the truth, in their mutual effort to accommodate the past and resolve the present.

There was a manifest desire by the Cayce people to tell the story of Cayce's lives plainly and openly. "Just as he was open, let us be open," said an inheritor of the Cayce legacy. "For that, above all, was what Edgar Cayce stood for—the truth."

No one in Gladys's final days had been closer than Jeanette Thomas, the understudy who succeeded her. Though I had found Jeanette cooperative in the main, I wondered if she would not be somewhat defensive in her zeal to keep Gladys's pure, white light forever shining. Any misgivings I had were soon dismissed. For the trials and tribulations of the three people she loved were an inspiration to Jeanette in their heartrending revelation of love and self-denial.

"You will see what very special people they were—and are—the more you get into it," she said. "They had a great capacity for living life to the hilt. There was nothing namby-pamby about them. They were essentially kind, gentle people, feeling the bittersweet of life just like the rest of us—facing a challenge that became more of a challenge because they knew what it was."

"After that one reading," said Jeanette, "Gladys naturally asked for a life reading on herself. Cayce had mentioned a French existence, when she gave up her child—Cayce—when he was only three, and was consigned to a convent where she pined away for the child who had died for lack of care. She thought she would like to know more about it—and the rest."

Jeanette had marked that one section of her Cayce file: "The affection which was lost in that plane should be manifest in this present. For only in this will this entity [Gladys] find its rest in this earth's plane with that entity [Cayce].

"Then give of self that the bonds may be united again,

that each may give of their better selves in their developing to that land where no partings are known and affection is the rule."

I had no doubt what he meant by their better selves, and neither did they. Cayce then described the meeting of Cayce and Gladys, as Uhjltd and Ilya, in Persia, when they were husband and wife and loved each other as they pleased.

"With the meeting, there is the realizing of the oneness of their souls (from Atlantis). There we find both of good stature, beautiful in figure and in form. In their close association they become enamored of each and give of themselves in the pleasures of the bodily forces, and a satisfaction not understandable to others was experienced and known."

Again the injunction to remain constant, as though Cayce's subconscious was all too aware of what this teenage girl must be feeling, together with its effect on the woman she was beginning to love as a mother long lost in Egypt land.

Even the thought of that other life together in Persia had the effect of awakening long-dormant affections and leaving tangible marks that lent credibility to Cayce's recollections.

"In these associations both suffered physically, and each bear in the body at present a mark designating these conditions. On the female body, just below the left breast, to the side and on the edge of the breast itself, the mark, and an answering one on the body of the male [Cayce], in the opposite proximity of the breast."

Jeanette nodded solemnly. "Yes, I know about Gladys's mark. Toward the end, I would often massage her, and I saw the birthmark, a strawberry marking in the described position."

"And Mister Cayce?"

She shook her head. "I know nothing of that."

The Persian reading, as detailed by Jeanette, suddenly took on the lusty flavor of the Songs of Solomon: "The charms in breast, neck, thighs, navel, all gave of the beauty as would reach the soul of the mate, and the crying of the soul's desire, both in the carnal and the answering of oneness in each."

Only a man who had experienced such a love could

have remembered it as he did: "They watch the sun's slow sinking over the desert sands. And in this fading hour they first find the answer of body to body as they melt into one, giving them an offering (a son, Zan) who gave the first philosophy of life and love [Zoroastrianism] to the world.

"Meanwhile, in this future they need only remain faithful, one to the other, ever-giving, ever-retaining those joys of the relations that give of self in service to others. These bring joy, peace and, again, uniting of body, soul, and spirit in the next. Remain faithful, therefore, unto the end, through daily acts of selflessness for and with others, remembering that they and all souls in these manifestations become knotted one with the other."

I now had a better understanding of the dedication of these three. For the remembrance of the past, instead of separating, only served to deepen the feeling of one for another and stir a compassion for humanity. Gladys was the only one of the three I personally knew. The two others I knew by their activity. I understood by this time Gladys's unfailing tolerance of any human foible, which gave her an almost Pollyannaish visage, and her immersion in the Cayce work, to the extent that she never thought of marriage until after the deaths of the two people she loved most—Gertrude and Edgar Cayce.

Whatever Gladys suffered, it was in silence. Not once in our long relationship had she mentioned any past life experience, nor had I any separate inkling of her romance with Uhjltd (Cayce) in the exciting days in Persia-Arabia. Still, in my mind's eye I can visualize this strong-minded, warmhearted friend, poring over the readings that described her love for her warrior mate in the brief interlude they shared. In that day they had lived on the fine edge of life, and so they died, one after the other, in a treacherous assault by a rival chieftain on the Persian city of the hills and the plains, during which Ilya was stabbed to death. And the grieving Uhjltd, courting death, was slain in a subsequent skirmish with his adversaries.

"Only with the treachery of others afterward," said Cayce, "was the life of the female taken. Hence the dread of knives in one and the mistrust of friendships in the other."

Long after this reading, Gladys looked back and described a few of the things Cayce said of her that were obviously true: "Loyalty to friendships, fear of knives and cutting instruments, distrust of the opposite sex, and that all must be used in God's service."

She became more and more involved in the work, not only compiling and collating the readings, but interpreting them as well and keeping in touch with people who had readings, checking their accuracy from time to time.

She had quite understandable fits of depression. She was beginning to develop little aches and pains from the frustration of a love that could not be fulfilled on this plane. At twenty-seven, she sought advice on how to meet the disappointment in her life from the man who knew what that disappointment was. Gertrude conducted the reading.

"As has been given from the beginning," said Cayce, "there is set before thee good and evil. In the choosing of thine will, the influences of the past become magnified or lessened by that. So when you are beset by those forces that would unbalance or uproot what thou hast believed, rise up and say, 'Get thee behind me, Satan, for thou savorest of the things that are of the earth.' Narrow and straight is the way that leads to life everlasting, and broad and crooked the road to self-destruction."

Jeanette's heart went out to Gladys, troubled by the rumblings of the past and the desire for a normal life in the present.

Seven years later, at thirty-four, as she saw her youth slipping away, she asked Cayce if she should marry, as she had a strong desire for a son, doubly felt because of the lost son in France.

Cayce replied, "If so desired."

"Why do I have such a restless incomplete feeling," she asked. "And how may this be overcome?"

Cayce, in trance, replied, "There is the constant warring between the flesh and the spirit. Thou knowest the way. Then open thine self to the spirit. 'Thine will, not mine will, O Lord.' And thus may come harmony and even those material manifestations which may bring contentment. Hold fast to that which is a creative force in the spiritual, not as indulgence. And we may bring harmony and peace."

Her relationship with Gertrude was also very much in her thoughts. In the fifteen years she had lived with the family, she had come to regard Gertrude as a saint, always forbearing, never complaining, forever putting others first.

"What is my relationship with Gertrude?" she asked.

As always the ghosts of the past haunted the present.

"That of a protection, as a protectorate over those activities or influences that would bring either mental or physical hurt. These are the expressions, as from the experiences in the Egyptian sojourn, as well as in the Persian. Hence these may be cultivated in a way that may be a strength, or a helpmeet, one for the other."

At this seemingly gratuitous advice, I looked somewhat askance at the keeper of the records.

"What he was saying," said Jeanette, "was that in her past ties with Gertrude, in Egypt, where she was Gertrude's daughter, and in Persia, where Gertrude, as the alien Inxa, became a close friend, she had a strong supportive figure in the present situation."

Jeanette smiled, but there was a sadness in her smile.

I'm afraid we were both thinking the same thing: poor Gladys.

But then we had not experienced the great love of other times when the sun gave way to shadows and two bodies joined together as one—dreams to sustain the spirit if not the flesh.

Two lifetimes, more than any others, gave some insight into the patterns of the present. Jeanette had discussed these lives—the Egyptian and the Persian—with Gladys. For in these experiences the lives of the three—Edgar, Gertrude, and Gladys—seemed so inextricably interwoven they could not help but influence the present.

"Just think of the loyalties involved—and the love," said Jeanette, "and so much becomes clear. In Egypt, we have Gertrude and Edgar together in good and bad times, forced to give up the child through no desire of theirs but nevertheless remorseful where that child, Gladys, was concerned.

"Gertrude as Isis was so beautiful of body, so graceful as a dancer, that casts of her divine form still survive in Egypt today. But she cared nothing of this. She was obsessed by the child, held in bond in Egypt."

That feeling was still so strong in Gertrude that she asked Cayce about the child, Iso, who languished and died before they could get back.

"In the Egyptian period, why was the child kept by the king?"

"The mother being the favorite, the father being rejected, the king in power being thwarted by the acts of the priest, the king took vengeance on both through the offspring, keeping it by the counsel of those advising same as a lesson to those guilty and to the populace as a whole."

"Why did it die so early?" she asked with a mother's concern.

"Being withdrawn from in thought, in counsel, by those responsible for its entrance (Ra and Isis)—being not hated but an outcast."

"What effect did this have on this entity (Gertrude) in this present experience; what urge comes from the same?"

"That of the protective urge, yet ever-fearful of the variation of experience that may exist between those of the associations [Cayce and Gladys] and self."

The picture that had been forming in my mind of the household I thought of as "these three" had taken a definite context. Whatever the world believed, these three accepted without question the intimate disclosures in the Cayce readings as they did everything Cayce said in trance. So I could divine Gertrude's guilt at the desertion of the helpless Iso, the love child born of her relationship with the high priest. And it was no help that Cayce in his readings cast the blame for his fall from grace on the shapely shoulders of his Egyptian love mate.

"In the Egyptian forces the entity (Gertrude) was of the household of the assistant priest to the leader (Cayce) in the religious cult. And being of beautiful face and form, brought through her seductive forces such troubles to self and that entity (Ra). This bringing banishment to the group brought distress and physical suffering to each in the enmity of the many."

There was still a holdover of old grievances, for which Cayce chided Gertrude as he had prodded Gladys about holding to ideals, which she appeared to do without this prompting.

"And in the present," speaking of Gertrude, "we find the grudges easily held that the entity must overcome to reach the development that will bring the best of mental, physical, and spiritual forces.

"Let the entity gain the understanding that self must be made as nought, if we would manifest the spiritual elements in the physical plane, and that it is hard to kick against the activities that would bring only condemnation of self, for each thought and deed must be met and paid for."

Gladys had no pleasant memories of Egypt. In the happier Persian period, when she was wed to Uhjltd, Cayce incarnate, Gladys saw the clearest karmic connection to the present. "For in that life," she confided in Jeanette in a rare moment, "everything was quite the reverse of what it was in this life. At that time Gertrude, as Inxa, came to live with Uhjltd and myself and was protected by us, just as I was taken in and protected by Mister Cayce and Gertrude. So I understood very well how Gertrude felt. For after Inxa wandered the desert, ill and alone, my husband came to her aid, as he had helped me when I was once pushed into the desert and left for dead. We then took her in and restored her health. She was the fairest of the fair, a very powerful figure with a magnetic look."

In believing as the principals did, it all seemed perfectly plausible—for one life experience affected the other in some consequential way.

"It was quite natural for Inxa to be drawn to the man she had been married to in the Egyptian past," Jeanette pointed out, "in much the same way Gladys was affected in this life. For those knowing the people involved, believing in Cayce and reincarnation as we do, there was no surprise, only admiration for the restraint observed in trying circumstances."

For a while it seemed as if everybody was stepping on everybody else's toes. But, as Jeanette observed, the same characters had to keep coming back in some connected way to work out a future largely shaped by the past and present.

"All the energy was there for powerful interactions, with resulting complications. It would have been surprising had it been any different—not if karma was to be worked out, in which Edgar Cayce's spiritual growth was the principal stake."

Cayce summed up the issues in a reading for Gladys on her Persian experience with him.

"That period as indicated may be well paralleled with the entity's experience and activities in the present. For when analyzed it comes to this: Know that good lives on. It is creative and eventually finds its period of activity in which the opportunity is given for the completing again in the material associations and activities."

There was always free will to be considered. For it was the choices we made, the responses to events not the events themselves, that ultimately determined our eternal well-being.

"Problems, disappointments, or setbacks may be periods in which there may be the arousing of the latent urges to accept the opportunity presented or periods in which the failing to keep the ideal might lead to a turning aside from that ideal."

Gertrude would have been less than a woman if she had not asked about that past life when Edgar Cayce and Gladys, as Uhjltd and Ilya, husband and wife, were so much in love that the birds sang of their love.

Only she attended the reading.

"You will give a detailed life history of this entity's [her own] appearance in the Persian desert and her associations with those of that period with whom she is closely associated in the present."

Cayce remembered it well.

"The name then was Inxa. With her nomadic people, Inxa had been pushed from place to place by Uhjltd's warrior bands till she came to the city of the hills and plains. And there, sick and friendless, she met Uhjltd.

"As a virgin damsel, the entity was healed from emaciation and want by the leader of this place. With the return of health, strength, and vitality, that beauty which brought so many under the influence of the entity was apparent. For the body was then considered the most beautiful of any in that locality."

Gertrude, in her devotion to Edgar Cayce, was undoubtedly selfless, and the burden of her questioning focused on how she could be most helpful, not only to her husband, but to the young woman she thought of as her sundered daughter out of the past.

"You have to realize," said Jeanette, "that with Gertrude's confidence in Mister Cayce's powers, there was no doubt in her mind that Gladys had been her child. This explained her feeling of acceptance and compassion for these two troubled by the remembrance of things past."

Gertrude's questions were designed to give her a better understanding of how she should conduct herself. Cayce, perhaps out of his own projection, saw some underlying resentment in his wife, not of the present so much as the past. He counseled her, as he did Gladys, to find peace of mind by being more giving in thought and action.

"Often does the entity find rising as antagonisms within self, respecting the activities of others and their associations, as may be easily surmised from those experiences. So in the associations, with personalities with whom it deals most, there should be more of the cooperative influences brought to bear. He (or she) that makes himself a channel in giving, receives the satisfying contentment of body, mind, and soul."

It was easier said than done. At times, Gertrude found it hard to deal with that past, as did Gladys. In Persia, Gertrude as Inxa had become a leader, rivaling Ilya in influence, with the force of her magnetic personality. "The latter then developed in the later portions of the experience the abilities to control more and more by the eye and by the prayer, that oft brought many to submission, who were not able to be conquered in any other manner."

The rivalry with Ilya, bitter in the beginning, later blossomed into a close and loving friendship. "In the latter portion both became closely associated in ideas and ideals and in material things. The entity [Inxa] then was one who aided in the care of Ilya in her last days."

Gertrude and Gladys confided more and more in each other, as the bonds of the past overcame any superficial uneasiness. Toward the end, Gertrude had lost the sight in one eye. She confided to Gladys that she felt this was a karmic outgrowth of her experiences as Inxa. "I realize all of a sudden," she said, "that this blindness in my right eye is no doubt a direct result of my misusing my eyes in my Persian-Arabian incarnation to subjugate others to my way of reasoning."

It was my first intimation of the seriousness with which Gertrude viewed the karmic changes that manifest themselves physically in this life. I had seen the subtle acceptance of emotional confrontations brought over from the past, but this requital of an eye for an eye, so to speak, puzzled me. And yet, I had no trouble accepting the birthmarks on Edgar and Gladys as a throwback to some previous experience.

"I think," said Jeanette Thomas, "that it's the idea of punishment that bothers you. People don't like to think of the Creator as one who may not like us for some very human failings that a stranger might overlook."

Gertrude was troubled and frustrated as she saw the years slipping away without her having formed any clearcut view of her own purpose, apart from her help in her husband's work. And in this role she now had a partner.

It was no surpise that she should go to the fount of knowledge she had gone to so often.

She was fifty-two when she asked the sleeping Cayce, "Why do I feel at war with myself so much and so often?"

Cayce replied, "Because there is too much self-condemnation in thy feelings respecting others and their attitudes."

"What," she asked, "causes physical suffering at times from mental worry?"

"Fear within self. Fear is the fruit of indecision respecting that which is lived and that which is held as the ideal. Doubt is the father of fear, fear the beginning of faltering. Faltering is that which makes for disease throughout the soul and mental body."

As so often in the distant past, Gertrude was assailed by self-doubts about her purpose and position.

"Please clarify the karmic conditions which I should understand and meet, in order to be a better wife, mother, and friend and fill more adequately my place in this work."

Cayce picked up on the "associations with individuals who comprise the household in the present. . . . Then there may be seen the varying forces that bring karmic influences. Where fear comes from faltering, force self to know there is the expression of God in every soul. Then may the body in the present have that peace that passeth understanding."

Both Gertrude and Gladys appeared to reconcile themselves to their situations. There was in time great harmony in a household that revolved around Edgar Cayce and his work. Under no circumstances was that work to be disturbed, which meant that Cayce was not to be disturbed in either the conscious or the unconscious state.

Gertrude and Gladys were not alone in their soul-searching. Edgar, disturbed to the core of his subconscious, was so affected by these delicate readings that he sought some direction for himself in his confusion. He gave himself a number of readings and, in time, came to a resolution that stilled any doubts of his own course.

"The experience of each has brought those things that in their associations in the present make for doubts and fears and desires and disturbances that burn and burn, yet all must be tried as by fire. And the fires of the flesh in material associations must be purified in the love, as the Father gave, that all may know that each walk together with the Son. Be thou then those that will make his paths straight. For narrow is the way, yet straight is the gate that leads to that knowledge that may be had in him."

Speaking of being together with Gertrude in the Egyptian experience, he said the exile brought destructive elements to the body and that the karma of that past was to be overcome in this lifetime. There was no mistaking what their present position should be. "That same entity [Isis] that was taken then is at present in this earth's plane the companion, as should be, in the present sphere."

In the end for Cayce, it was a clear triumph over the past and those "secret sexual urges" that had plagued him for many lifetimes. He remained true to his marital vows.

After experiencing all this, feeling something of the voyeur, I found myself with little to say. I returned the various readings to Jeanette and gave her a questioning look. She nodded, with a little sigh.

"In a way," she said, "it was a triumph of all three.

For their sacrifice made it possible for the work to be brought out pure and untainted. Any other woman but Gertrude might not have harbored Gladys as she did, not only in her home but in her heart. Anybody but Gladys might not have given her youth to the cause, making the work her total obsession in the end.

"But as you think about it, the greatest triumph was Edgar's. For, plagued in many lives by sexual urges normal in any man, he finally conquered what he considered his carnal self to become a clear channel of the soul."

Cayce didn't have to be intuitive to know that malicious tongues would wag about his closeness with Gladys. He knew that small minds, in and out of his own A.R.E., would never comprehend the valiant efforts of all three—Gladys, Gertrude, and himself—to expand spiritually out of a crucible of fire that brought out the truest flame in each.

In a special work reading, deploring the tongue-waggers, he stressed that appearances were as vital as substance in keeping the work free from criticism. Yet, at the same time, he knew in his heart that the scandal-mongers, fed by malice and envy, would persist in projecting their mean-spirited outlook onto natures nobler than their own.

"Better," he said, "that there be someone else with these two than alone, because of the attitude that some snobs take toward such relations. For it has often been given that relations with the opposite sex in psychic forces bring the carnal forces to that not understandable condition in other minds that are shut out to the higher, finer, and ennobling things of life and who only see that which is of the earthly. This then should be done in the manner that there may be no questioning in any manner or form, or—as given—present the body, the life, the work wholly unspotted from the world, avoiding even the appearance of evil. Let the two in their attitude, which is above reproach in their own lives and bodies, be circumspect in their actions, for they will be enjoined by such."

I thought now of my friend Gladys, always self-effacing, always putting others before herself, but still wanting the world to know that the work, as its workers, remained untainted to the end.

All the wagging tongues, all snide comments, might never be stilled, for as Gladys said so aptly, "Wagging tongues will always find within themselves the reason to wag."

But as recently as 1980, in a terse notation on a Cayce reading counseling a spiritual course, Gladys Davis had the last word: "Continence was certainly maintained. For sexual intercourse was never experienced with Mister Cayce by me. In all other ways, I feel there was the perfect union as described, not only with him but with all those dear to him."

CHAPTER 11

Auld Lang Syne

All Harold J. Reilly would do is lay his hands on a patient and a surge of healing energy would flow through his body. It was a mystery nobody quite understood, not even Reilly. For at the age of fourteen he had left school to help support his mother and a brood of younger brothers and sisters, and he was a man more interested in results than reasons.

I met Reilly when he ran the best health club in America. He was taking care of people like Nelson Rockefeller, Eddie Rickenbacker, Sonja Henie, Bob Hope, Bing Crosby, and a lot of other luminaries of the day. I had been assigned by my newspaper to do a story about him and the people he kept in shape. Though only in my twenties, I had to hobble into his place because I had a sciatica condition so painful I could hardly move one leg after another. I was in total despair, for I had to stop every few moments to lean against a wall, then push on a few steps at a time. Two doctors had told me I would have to undergo back surgery or be crippled for life. I didn't know what to do, for I dreaded the surgeon's knife as much as I did the alternatives.

With it all, I managed to interview Reilly and the people he helped. I marveled at his eclectic background. Before moving into New York's Rockefeller Center he operated a health center on Broadway, where he conditioned the likes of Jack Dempsey, perhaps the greatest of heavyweights, and his conqueror, Gene Tunney. He appeared in the ring himself on occasion and was known more for his brute force than his boxing skills. He never backed up. He was that rarity, a man born without fear.

He was a functioning physiotherapist and chiropractor. But he was like no other therapist his clients had ever known. "He just touched you, and you felt better," said a newspaper colleague who had been nursing a traumatic hangover.

I saw him work his wonders on the sick, the lame, and the halt. No ailment was too much for him. They were challenges to be met and conquered. There was the elderly stockbroker who was told by a prestigious clinic that he would never walk again. He was helped bodily into Reilly's health center, looking, as Reilly said, like death warmed over. In two weeks he was able to walk out with a spring in his step, to resume his busy brokerage business.

I would never have believed it had I not seen it for myself. "How did you do it?" I asked, for the man, in his late sixties, was in a truly moribund state.

Reilly smiled. "I gave him hope," he said, "and hope is a sick man's best medicine."

"And that was all?"

"Oh, there was some treatment, straightening out his back, but others had treated him before me."

Reilly liked the story I did. Since it appeared in the largest paper in the country, it was widely read and brought him many clients.

"You wrote about my magic touch," he said with a twinkle in his eyes. "Now let me try that magic on you."

As I hesitated, he laughed, "Don't you believe what you write?"

I hobbled into his office the next day, so depressed by this time at my condition that I felt I was only making a courtesy call.

I can still recall how gently he stretched me out on the table and ran his powerful hands over my body. Even through my clothing I could feel a significant relaxing of the areas of pain.

He measured my legs with a tape measure, first together, then separately. "Your sacroiliac, or hip joint, is out two inches," he said. "No wonder you're in pain. Every step must be murder."

As I felt my body relaxing under his touch, he made a swift movement with his hands, and I felt a pop.

"What was that?" I asked in alarm.

"That," he said, "was your sacroiliac going back into place."

What about my sciatica?"

"That's only a symptom of a displaced sacroiliac. Fix one and the other disappears."

He gave me a scrutinizing look.

"Now stand up and walk around."

I rose gingerly and cautiously put both feet on the floor.

I could hardly believe it. There was no pain.

"Walk around," he commanded.

I took one step, then another, and another. Still no pain. "It's a miracle," I cried.

"A miracle," he rejoined, "is only that which we don't understand." He gave my reporter's body an appraising look. "Keep coming in, and we'll do another miracle."

His deep-set blue eyes beamed, and for the first time I realized what a handsome figure he was, looking more like a centurion of old with his bold face than a New York Irishman who had put on the gloves with the boxing immortals of his time to test his prowess in the ring.

"Did anybody ever tell you," I said, "that you look like a gladiator in ancient Rome?"

He dismissed this with a smile and a wave of a hand.

"I never listen to what people say," he said, "unless I've known them for five years. Unless, of course, they're patients. And they often tell me what I need to know without even knowing they're doing so."

As I got to know him better, I realized what a complex man he was, appearing hale and hearty to his multitude of clients but owning, in fact, a nature that harbored many secret matters.

"What's your honest feeling about psychic phenomena?" he asked one day, as we worked out in his gym after my brief encounter with Cayce's friend Dave Kahn.

I looked at him in surprise, for I had already mentioned I was doing a series of articles on extrasensory perception for my paper.

"I think there's something to it," I said. "Some time ago I ran into a woman who predicted everything that happened to me for the last five years. Her name was Maya Perez. She called herself a mystic."

He put down a barbell fifty pounds heavier than the one I was struggling with and studied me for a moment.

"You know, you gave me credit for a lot of cures that

really weren't all my doing. I'd like to give credit where credit is due."

"You certainly fixed me up," I said.

"Yes, but I had a lot of help."

He laughed as he thought about it.

"It's hard to believe even now. But this man sent me patients by the carload, and he hadn't even heard of me except when he was sleeping."

He had my complete attention. I put down my barbell and stared at him incredulously, for I knew next to nothing of Cayce then, not having had the opportunity to investigate Kahn's claims.

"Keep lifting," he said, adding a weight to his own load. "We can talk as we work; it makes the burden a little easier when you forget about it. The mind is the builder, you know."

"What do you mean sleeping?" I said, hoping it might be some sort of joke.

"Just like I said. They came from all over the country with slips that had my name and address on them and the treatment this man wanted them to have, even to what vertebra or cervical should be adjusted. And to top it all off the man was in trance. Can you beat that?"

I had some idea by now of who he was talking about, without knowing any more about it. But Reilly painted such a graphic picture that I shared his reaction of wonderment and surprise.

He had a small gym and steam bath on Broadway in those days, and to say the place was obscure would have been an overstatement.

"Nobody would have known I existed," he said, "if not for Jack Dempsey coming in every once in a while for a rubdown and a workout. So you can imagine my surprise when some of the most unlikely looking people started streaming into my place. The treatments varied; for some, manipulation of the spine; for others, some form of hydrotherapy. Or it could be exercise or massage, sometimes a colonic. It so happened I had just bought a colonic machine and wondered how anybody would have known that."

All the slips stressed the same basic thing: proper *assimilation* of food to be consumed in a relaxed mood; good *circulation* of the lymphatic and cardiovascular systems; and regular *elimination*. What Reilly got to call the ACEs of well-being. Every slip bore the name of the man prescribing the treatment, a name Reilly had never heard of before—Edgar Cayce.

"Who is this Doctor Cayce?" he asked a patient, pronouncing the name as Case.

"His name isn't Case, it's Casey [Cayce]," said the patient. "And he isn't a doctor."

"What's he look like?"

The patient shrugged. "I wouldn't know. I never saw him."

Reilly thought he was being kidded.

"Where did he get my name?"

"I wouldn't know that either," the man said. "All I did was make a phone call to Cayce's home in Virginia Beach, asking about my aching back and how to relieve it. He went into trance and said that a nerve was pressing against a displaced vertebra in my spine. And he mailed me your name and address with the instructions."

"And he spelled out my name?"

"Just as it is on the door of your health club."

Reilly shook his head as he thought about it. "I thought the whole world was going mad. But in every case when I applied the treatment he recommended, the patient got better. Actually, I had been doing some of the things he advised, just different little ways of massaging and manipulating people that came to me as I was working on them. I could see there was nothing harmful or drastic in what he was prescribing, not when I had been doing some of it myself."

In only one instance did he have no luck with a Cayce patient. At the time I didn't understand why it bothered him as much as it had, for the patient had rejected his treatment and gone elsewhere.

"I could have saved him," said a frowning Reilly. "I could have let him think he was having his own way and then slipped in Cayce's way of doing it. But he got a little nasty, and I let him go. He was a high-liver, used to doing as he pleased. The Cayce slip he handed me said he should have light massage for a circulatory problem. He insisted on deep, heavy message, which Cayce had warned would be disastrous and lead to his total disintegration."

I thought Reilly was taking a lot on himself.

"Well, you did what you could," I said.

Reilly's chin shot out, and for a fleeting second he looked like one of those old bare-knuckled fighters whose pictures I had seen lying around in barbershops. "I should have tied him to the table and given him the treatment, like it or not."

"But it might not have worked, and he could hold you accountable."

"The man who sent him to me was never wrong."

"How is this patient doing?"

"He isn't. He went elsewhere and died three weeks later, totally disintegrated after receiving treatments he had been warned against."

By the time scores of Cayce people had beaten a path to his door, Reilly's curiosity had run over. "I wanted to meet this Cayce and find out how he knew about me. I was hardly a household word at the time. I had a lot of things to ask him—how he had diagnosed these people without seeing them, prescribing remedies that cured them. The more I thought about it, the more I had to know there really was such a man."

He had been a little uncertain when he picked up the phone and asked for Edgar Cayce, not knowing precisely what to say about the most remarkable thing that had ever happened to him. "I didn't want to appear to be questioning. So I just thanked him up and down. Then as we got to talking, I found myself feeling as if I were talking to an old friend I hadn't seen for some time. I felt his warmth and friendliness, and I responded in kind. I heard myself saying, 'I know we're going to be friends.' I had never said anything like that before, because I was never one to make friends lightly. He didn't seem at all surprised to hear from me. I told him I would like to meet with him the next time he came to New York and get to know him."

Reilly looked forward eagerly to the meeting. And he was not disappointed. Neither was Cayce. There was instant recognition that this was no ordinary meeting. "I looked at him and felt somehow I was at one with this man I had never seen before. I could tell from his look that he felt the same. He was very open, completely frank, and I liked that in him. I half-expected it, any less and I would have been disappointed. We were old friends, having a reunion. That's what it felt like."

But the mystery deepened. For Cayce offered no explanation of why he had sent so many of the lame and halt to this sturdy, capable-looking man with a touch of the healer in him.

"You know," Cayce said, "I never heard your name, nor did I have the slightest idea of your existence in my conscious mind. But as I look at you, I know that we are not strangers."

Startled as he was, Reilly was not one to kick a gift horse in the face.

"I ask only one thing of you," he said. "Will you let me give you a treatment? It will be one I learned from you, of course."

Edgar Cayce gave his newfound friend a penetrating look from his deepset, grayish blue eyes. "I have an idea it was something you learned long ago."

I was intrigued by this extraordinary experience and by the sudden openness of a man I had thought of as only physically oriented.

"Why are you telling me this?" I asked.

"Because the man doing a series on ESP is ready for what I have to say," he chuckled. "Can you imagine telling the scores of physicians that come in here, along with people like Bob Hope and Nelson Rockefeller, that they're being treated, indirectly, by a sleeping psychic? They'd skin me alive."

At that time I had never heard a stranger story.

"When you say you felt you knew him, what did you mean by that?"

"I wasn't sure. I just felt as he put his hand in mine that here was a man I could trust with my life. Such a man was hardly a stranger. Yet I knew at the same time I had never seen him before. This bothered me a while until I got to thinking there was more to life than there was in books or lectures. But I had a feeling even then that he knew something about me that I didn't know. It was not so much what he said but the way he looked at me, as if he were sizing up a friend he hadn't seen in a long time and noting the changes in him."

The friendship flourished. Cayce was a frequent visitor to Reilly's health farm for the fresh air set in northern

New Jersey, just an hour's drive from New York. They had many discussions and Cayce would say, "You know, Reilly, you're a natural-born healer."

Reilly didn't have any idea what Cayce meant, for he wasn't aware at the time of the extent of the Cayce readings.

And then one time, looking at Reilly speculatively, Cayce said, "I think we ought to trade off one of your treatments for a life reading."

Reilly frowned. "A life reading? Now what would that be all about?"

"Oh, your past, present, and future. Give you some idea of what's going on in your life and why."

"My past?" said Reilly with a puzzled frown. "That's an open book."

Cayce smiled. "Further back, into your past lives."

Reilly laughed. "Well, we've always been Irish on my father's side. Right from the Old Sod."

At this time, Reilly had been trying to move his health club from Broadway to the more prestigious RCA Building in Rockefeller Center. But he hadn't been able to get the space he needed at a price he could pay. He had no idea what his next step should be. So he took the life reading, which he wasn't terribly interested in, thinking he would slip in a few questions about the Rockefeller Center move. "There was no doubt in my mind that a psychic who sent people he had never seen to a man he had never heard of could answer any question I wanted to ask."

The Reilly reading was given in November 1933, ten years after Cayce's first reincarnation reading for Arthur Lammers in Dayton, Ohio. Present were the mystic's son, Hugh Lynn, later president of the Cayce Foundation, who put Cayce under while Gladys Davis took notes in shorthand and members of Reilly's family looked on in varying degrees of wonder.

Reilly didn't know what to make of the past-life phase of the readings. As a practical man, the only life that mattered to him was the one in the present. He was more interested in what Cayce had to say about Rockefeller Center than about an adventurous life as the Norse warrior Eric the Red, who discovered North America, and before that as an Egyptian and Roman. What would an Irishman be doing in those countries?

"Can you imagine me as a redheaded Scandinavian?" he said with a laugh.

"No," I said, reviewing the blunt-featured face with its smiling blue eyes, "but I can see you as a gladiator in ancient Rome."

He seemed amused. "He even gave me a life in Atlantis. I had no idea even where that was."

Oddly, all he recalled of that reading was an unpronounceable name.

"Can you imagine anybody calling me Arptl?" he said with glee.

"No," I persisted, "but I can see you as a Roman."

He did manage to sneak in a few questions about the center and about his 200-acre farm, so close to New York, which he had contemplated selling.

"Is it advisable," he asked, "to continue my efforts to secure an establishment in Radio City?" [The RCA Building housed the Radio City Music Hall.]

"Advisable to continue," the sleeping Cayce replied. "As we find, these negotiations should culminate in the latter portion of the coming year [1934]."

"Should I continue my lines of endeavor as carried on in the city or extend my efforts in my country place?"

"Carry on in the city, but extend the efforts in the country place, for those retreats through which many may find an awakening."

Then Reilly asked, "Any other advice or guidance at this time?"

"Look first always into self and that which prompts self's activities. Do this not for self alone, but rather the love of the Father—as shown in thee—may be reflected in thy acts to thy brethren everywhere."

"Sure enough," said Reilly, "fourteen months after the reading, in December 1934, the Rockefeller lease was sent to me for my signature with everything I had asked for."

And as Cayce suggested, Reilly wound up helping his brethren in what he called a modest tribute to Cayce.

"I told a general meeting of the A.R.E. that anybody sent by Cayce would get the full treatment at my establishment, whether or not he or she could pay for it."

But with all this affirmation of the Cayce readings, even until Reilly's death in 1987 at the age of ninety-two, it remained a mystery to Reilly why Cayce had sent so many people to him for help. I could see why this was so.

In going over Reilly's life reading, I had missed the connection myself, just as Reilly had, until it was pointed out by somebody more familiar with the Cayce readings than myself. For the connection with Cayce was buried in one of Cayce's own life readings for himself years before. He was the high priest in Egypt, and Reilly, anonymous as all were in the readings, was an authority on the purification of the body and the mind and one of Ra's principal aides. And since neither name was mentioned in their individual readings, there would be no way of connecting them unless you already knew who they were by number.

In Reilly's reading there had been only a casual reference to a priest, which Reilly had missed, not being anymore aware of the Ra connection than I. As myself, he was more impressed by the health readings, which proved themselves in the treatment, than by the reincarnation readings, which put a strain on the imagination.

Looking back now, knowing of Cayce's connection with Ra, I don't see how I missed it. Cayce had made it clear enough.

"We find the entity [Reilly] was in that land now known as the Egyptian during those periods now when there were the rebuildings of that which had been torn down through rejecting the activities of the priest and his expulsion from the land." Only on the priest's return from exile, did the Egyptian version of Reilly get involved in the healing work presided over by Ra, and, then, in typical thoroughgoing fashion.

"With the priest's return and the establishment of those things pertaining to the arts of healing, the entity [Reilly] through his activities brought much to a disturbed people. He aided those that would be called physicians of the day in establishing places of retreat and conditions that might aid the individuals and groups in cleansing their bodies, purifying their minds, by the activities of the body and by the classifying of foods."

I had got to know Reilly well and was impressed by

Cayce's accuracy. For Reilly not only worked wonders with the many patients that physicians sent him but also treated some three hundred physicians with his therapeutic baths and manipulations without any of them knowing that they were the beneficiaries of a psychic—Cayce. He was many things, as Cayce suggested, not only a wise counselor but a proponent of a diet of pure fruits and vegetables, which he grew organically at his New Jersey retreat.

And so the mystery had finally been cleared up. It was little wonder Cayce had sent his clients to Reilly and that Reilly had this rural retreat and a health center for them. And no wonder that this natural-born healer knew how to follow Cayce's instructions. It had all happened before in a land we now call Egypt, and the pupil had finally caught up with his teacher. He knew what to do with a patient, in touching him and peering into his eye, just as Cayce knew by his astral journeys into a universal consciousness to which nothing was alien or forgotten.

The connection was very clear to Jeanette Thomas, the keeper of the records, who, like Gladys Davis before her, had a special liking for Reilly.

"Why wouldn't they feel like old friends?" she said. "They had been together when Mister Cayce, as the high priest, established his psychic healing centers and Doctor Reilly was one of his chief supports."

And Cayce had been through it all with his one-time deputy and foreshadowed his development from the old consciousness to the new. "Hence the entity may be said to have developed throughout the sojourn in the Egypt land, and in the present there may be much gained in not only material things but in bringing contentment through the activities of the body, and also as to their thoughts, in those things that create a channel for the mental and spiritual forces to manifest through."

This was a piece of diffused advice that Reilly must have been thinking of subconsciously, dealing with people with emotional problems like the client who had lost his heart to a woman and then regained it in the gym with Reilly.

"And these forces should be stressed, not only in self, but in the advice and counsel that may be given to all whom the entity [Reilly] may contact."

I thought of this one day as I was doing my exercise routine, when on the other side of a partition, secluding the "basket cases," I overheard Reilly saying in a soothing voice, "You can't run away, my boy, for you always have to take yourself with you."

"But I have to get away," a grown man's voice squeezed out in a tone of torment. "Every place I go reminds me of her. I can't live without her—not in the city where we shared so much."

I heard the sound of weeping and closed my ears, thoroughly ashamed of a professional curiosity that couldn't ordinarily afford that luxury.

Later, I saw the man, a South American, as he was dressing glumly outside his locker, knowing who it was because of the acute agony in his face so peculiar to stricken lovers. Reilly took the time to come by and put a comforting arm around the man's shoulders.

"Keep your body occupied," he said, "and that will occupy your mind. Double workouts, every day for the next two weeks. Doing something about yourself, that makes the difference. And put your passport back in the drawer."

To expiate my guilty feeling, I confessed to Reilly that I had eavesdropped. "I didn't realize," I said, "that you counseled the lovelorn."

"I've had a good teacher." he said. "This man will get over it, if he sticks with it. Nobody can stay depressed when the blood is singing through their veins."

A month later, I saw his protégé emerge from the gym, whistling a jolly tune. Though he knew me only by sight he gave me a warm handshake.

"Congratulate me," he cried. "I'm getting married next week."

"How wonderful," I said. "So she came back?"

He gave me a puzzled look. "Oh, no, I met this lady only two weeks ago. She is beautiful." He touched his fingertips to his lips. *"Bellissima."*

There was so much of the old Roman about Reilly that I wondered if there was something I had skipped over in his reading. Still, a gladiatorial role would hardly seem consistent with the deep spiritual quality I had found in his quietly helping the less fortunate, his zeal in making people well, his feeling for people like Cayce who gave

of themselves, even his inclination for people of the
mother faith as an honored trustee of a Jewish medical
school.

He was born a Catholic, and he died a Catholic, but
I noticed that in his Cayce reading he had listed himself
as simply a Christian. It may have been a momentary
whim, but knowing him, I knew he did nothing without
a reason.

I half-recalled a Roman life in the Cayce reading,
which I had skimmed over in focusing on an Egyptian
experience that seemed more relevant at the time. So I
took another look.

"We find," Cayce said, "the entity then was in the
Roman periods of oppression, during those dark days
when certain [Christian] tenets and truths were being
taught in the land."

His name was Pompeanel then, and he was the kind
of warrior only Rome could produce: fearless and strong,
neither fearing death nor courting it. "The entity," said
Cayce, "was among the soldiery of Nero, the oppressor
of the Christian peoples, and had the abilities to be mas-
terful in the games of the arena."

He was to herd the despised sect into the field of combat, to goad them into making a fight of it for the pleasure of the mob. "To make by force the activities of the
sects that were being persecuted by the resentment in the
emperor."

I could see it all: Emperor Nero blaming the Christians
for the fire he set, turning the gladiators and the lions
on these hapless people, and fiddling while Rome burned
and martyrs were made. And the gladiator, this same
Pompeanel, marveling at the Christians not cringing or
bowing down, holding their heads high, singing hymns to
their God as they embraced death, knowing they had
found everlasting life in the life of their Savior. And then
the miracle occurred. Pompeanel, the pride of pagan
Rome, crossed from one side of the arena to the other,
to stand with the Christians whose courage in the jaws
of death had drawn him to the Master who inspired that
courage.

"Thus came the period to meet those in physical combat, and he later went to the death, or to the end, with
those peoples whom the entity had come to love."

And so in the end he had become a Christian, that which he had declared himself in the present.

He gained in Egypt, and I would have thought in Rome, but Cayce saw it differently.

"The period may be said to have been one when the soul forces lost and gained. During the period came much that gives the abilities in the present to be of aid to others ill in body and need those influences within themselves [like the deranged lover] to meet the needs in physical derangements."

Even in Reilly's health center, Cayce saw the old Roman influence. Reilly's clients, fitted with white robes and sandals, went from one room to another in the course of various treatments, led from one therapeutic table or bath to another.

"Hence," said Cayce, "the games of the Romans [boxing], the baths of the Romans, dress of the Romans are to the entity in the present—from that period—of particular interest."

There was something else Cayce had said, of a material nature, that had slid by me and that as a prophecy was validated spectacularly in time. Cayce had told Reilly to hold on to his two hundred acres or so, within forty miles of New York City. As he sat on the land, using it as a retreat for himself and his patients, it made a rich man out of him, constantly escalating in value.

"Better than an oil well," he told me once, "for it will never go dry."

I was not much for feeling presences, or seeing ghosts, but I never felt that I had to look very far to find Harry Reilly. I recall his telling me, "Never mind the past or the future, live every day as if it's the first and the last day of your life. For as Cayce said, this is the life that counts. Here we triumph over the past and materialize the future."

I never knew until the end how much this great disciple of a great man believed in reincarnation. For he was a hardheaded Irishman in this lifetime who had to experience something to believe it. And yet I recall something he had told me not long before his death, after he came out of a prolonged coma.

"I crossed over just long enough," he said, "to know there was more out there waiting than I had ever realized. It will not be a difficult transition for me. When you feel a pat on your shoulder and a voice saying, 'Stand up straight, back arched, chest forward,' you will know who it is."

I have heard that voice in the wee lonely hours of the night, just as plainly as I heard it years ago in a Rockefeller Center gym, saying, "Yes, I was with Edgar Cayce before, and I will be with him again one day. He knows where to find me. He always has."

CHAPTER 12

The Ties That Bind

There was a bond between Edgar Cayce and David Kahn that nobody seemed to understand. Cayce appeared to be everything that Kahn was not. Cayce was a devout Christian, almost ministerial, quiet and reserved, jealous of his privacy, with no ambitions outside the advancement of his metaphysical work. Kahn was Jewish, with no allegiance to the Master to whom Cayce had dedicated his life. He was also an extrovert, inclined to be aggressive, and no shrinking violet when it came to his accomplishments. Nobody had more Cayce readings than Kahn. He appeared almost importunate at times, to a point where Cayce's associates wondered why Cayce put up with it.

Cayce would wave his hand and say with a smile, "Sometimes I'm not sure myself. But I just know that it is impossible for me to turn Dave down."

Kahn seldom made a decision of any kind without asking Cayce for a reading on it. He had more than two hundred trance readings, not to mention help given by Cayce in the waking state, when he could also be quite clairvoyant.

"Dave couldn't sneeze," a friend said, "without asking Cayce what it meant."

He was a man given to exaggeration, and when Cayce's friends scoffed, Cayce would again smile and say this was only Dave's way of getting attention for something of benefit to people. Kahn recommended the readings to so many that there wasn't enough time in the day or night for Cayce to handle them all. And then, and only then, would he ask Kahn to desist. "You have me all balled up," he would say, but still with that twinkle in his eye that acknowledged their friendship.

They had known each other for what seemed forever,

since Kahn was a boy in his native Kentucky. But there was more to it than that. For Cayce was a man to whom materialism was meaningless when it applied to him or his family, and Kahn seemed driven by his ambition to make a fortune. It hardly seemed like a match made in heaven.

But while Cayce had no criticism of Kahn, or his goals, in the waking state, he was more plainspoken, though still tolerant and understanding, about it in his sleep. In one reading, in the unconscious state, for instance, he pictured his friend as "one considered at times over talkative, even to self's detriment."

Certainly a harsh judgment but not Cayce's, as he soon made clear. "This," he said, "is not true. Had the entity's words been applied in a more normal or nominal way, rather than extravagant, this would not have proven as beneficial in gaining that attention that is necessary to be felt."

In his picturesque way, he foresaw Kahn's success in the manufacture of furniture, including radio and television sets. He put it this way: "One whose greater powers in earning monies will be in the manufacturing and selling of things made from products of the earth's storehouse, especially in wood or wood and metal."

At times it was almost as though he were trying to tone down Kahn's aggressiveness and preoccupation with success. On still another occasion, he advised, "Ever be in that way of using all force to the glorification of God rather than of self."

The advice didn't seem to faze Kahn. His first questions were

1. What should the body do during the present year regarding the business?
2. What specific request should the entity make of the firm for his financial benefit?
3. What investment should he make this year to give him financial independence, and on what date?

These questions, it seemed to me, were pretty much involved with self. But Cayce was not in the least put out. He told the younger man what he wanted to know.

"Never work for a straight salary, and always be in a position to gain for self the fruits of the labor of self."

It was not like Cayce to respond in an accommodating way when his counsel was glossed over. But he wouldn't have been Cayce if he hadn't repeated his admonition when Kahn's ambitions were being realized.

"Let service be a portion of the commodities as will be given to the entity as the expansions begin, especially in that of service to the individual users of the commodities manufactured."

In his personal life, as well, Kahn leaned heavily on Cayce. Contemplating marriage, he requested a reading of his actress bride-to-be and another for himelf a few days later. Cayce advised that by increasing Kahn's responsibilities and adding to his incentives, marriage would bring him closer to the success that was so important to him. Dave and Lucille were married a few months later. It was a fruitful marriage, interspersed with considerable financial success and achievement.

Meanwhile, Kahn was trumpeting Cayce's talents to a skeptical world. On trains, airplanes, ships, and elevators he would discuss Cayce's exploits, without much caring who he was talking to. He was the first person to mention Cayce's name to me, and he always had a Cayce story for me whenever we met.

"The man was a living wonder," he would say with a shake of his head. "He told me I would head this giant furniture combine. And at the age of thirty-two I was the top man in the business. In World War I, he told me I would come back unharmed. I volunteered for everything, knowing he was never wrong, and came back a blooming hero, making captain and all that."

I got to know Dave Kahn fairly well. He was a pleasant-faced man with a lingering drawl. He was only a youngster when he met Cayce in the Kahn family's hometown of Lexington, Kentucky. Cayce had given a reading for a neighboring homemaker and another reading for one of Kahn's younger brothers, which was quite helpful. A grateful mother had told the oldest son, Dave, "Never forget this man. Help him whenever you can. He has a gift from God."

And this Kahn had done, opening his home in New York to the Cayces, helping the family with food and fuel during the dark days of the Depression, and responding whenever Cayce needed help of any kind. When Cayce, with Gertrude and Gladys, was arrested and put on trial in New York for fortune-telling, it was Kahn who marshaled the evidence to win Cayce an acquittal. He was a staunch friend, which none would deny, but even so there was no accounting for his extraordinary influence with a very private Southern gentleman.

After World War I, to the wonderment of many, the two men came partners in an oil venture in Texas designed to finance a Cayce hospital for the incurably ill. And though the Cayce readings picked out the oil deposits, it remained for others to bring in the gushers and make the money always denied Cayce when the readings were given for any reason but to directly help people. Even though the venture failed, there was still nobody on easier terms with the retiring Virginia Beach mystic than the brash young businessman who had wound up making his mark in New York City.

By 1989, Dave was long departed from this sphere, but his wife, Lucille, was very much alive, and still pleasantly involved with the A.R.E. No wife of a Cayce aficionado had ever become more involved in the Cayce work, even to becoming a president of the A.R.E. She was a frequent visitor to congresses at the Virginia Beach center, and was readily available for somebody like myself who had been on friendly terms with her husband. She had spoken for him often when he was alive, and she spoke for him again as we met for lunch one day.

I was quick to notice a change in her attitude toward me, for where twenty years before she had seemed severe and distant, she was now friendly and warm, bright and amusing, and there was a measure of acceptance in her tone that seemed to say, "You *were* one of us."

Although I knew she believed in reincarnation, it was odd to hear her speak of this belief as casually as another person might mention being an Elk or Mason. There was no nonsense about Lucille Kahn. There never had been. To realize that she believed in reincarnation and its karmic purpose was very illuminating to me. For she had a very logical and probing mind and was not one to waste her time on something that didn't add an extra dimension to her life.

I hadn't seen Lucille for a dozen years, but she didn't seem to have changed. She must have been eighty-five, but she looked no more than sixty, and she had a spring to her step, a light in her eye, and a humor that saw the pleasant side of everything.

"You don't change," I said.

She gave me a demure look and said, "I've always done yoga, you know, and meditated and thought of living the way that Edgar Cayce taught us to live, with a happy collaboration of mind, body, and spirit."

She had some idea of what I wanted to know, for she had been married to David Kahn, Edgar Cayce's close friend, for more than forty years. Now it was twenty years after Dave's death and the shadow of the two men—Dave and the man he called the Judge—still walked with her into the soft and gentle light.

"They were bound together in my mind," she said, "and they loved one another, no matter what the relationship seemed to others. I didn't quite understand all this when Dave was courting me. When he told me, 'You marry me and you marry Cayce,' I thought it was Dave's exaggerated way of often expressing things."

As we had lunch together, I thought of what it must have been like for a young woman out of the Oklahoma Indian Territory to have been confronted with a man like Cayce, who could peer into the past and the future with equal clarity. And he could tell her, as well, about her aura and about her lives in India and Greece, which had shaped her present experience. And if this weren't enough, he could talk about the children she would have one day and how best to guide their present development through their past inclinations and aptitudes.

"It must have been quite a shock to you," I said, "meeting with Cayce and learning about another part of you that you had not known anything about."

She smiled and poked at her salad.

"When Dave proposed to me and told me almost in the same breath that I would have to accept Mister Cayce as a member of his family, I thought it was some kind of joke. But that was before I met the Judge." She laughed. "Dave didn't like calling him Mister Cayce because that seemed so stiff when he liked him so much, and he couldn't call him Edgar because Mister Cayce was so much older. So he compromised on Judge—respectful, yet with a certain familiarity."

But she soon looked on the Judge as one of the family. "He was easy to be with. There were two sides to him: the mystic who went into the sleep state and came up with his wonders and the plain homebody who canned fruits and vegetables, cooked up a great dinner, and talked to plants and flowers, causing them to lift their heads to the sky."

I had heard some of this before. But there was something I wished I had known more about when Dave was alive.

"I've always regretted not asking Dave about that first meeting," I said. "It might have given me a better idea of their connection." I laughed. "You know, Cayce always said that love at first sight came out of some old memory."

"Well, I think I know that story as well as Dave did, I heard it so often. You really should know more about it," she said with an approving smile. "That should tell you something about people coming together because they're meant to get something done. It seems to be full of coincidences, but you and I know there is no such thing. Everything happens for a reason. Anyway, the Kahns and the Delaneys lived next door. The name was W.I. Delaney, and he was a lumberman. He was much older than Dave, but treated him like an equal. So one day he takes Dave in his confidence, saying, 'Dave, you know that my wife has been in a wheelchair, and nobody can do anything for her. So I heard about this farm boy in Hopkinsville who they say can go into a trance and tell what's wrong with sick people. So I telephoned him, and he agreed to come and see my wife and bring a doctor with him. But he tells me somebody will have to take down what he says, as he doesn't know what he's saying in his sleep.' "

So then he gave the fifteen-year-old Dave a hard look and said, "Will you take it down in longhand? I can't trust myself."

Lucille laughed a little as she conjured the picture of the tall, lanky Cayce arriving at the Delaney home and being told by Delaney, "Well, here's the young man who is going to conduct the reading for you.

"Mister Cayce just gave Dave a look, without blinking an eye, and said, 'Here's a little booklet, and in this booklet it will tell you what to say when I go into trance. When my eyes begin to flicker, then you give this suggestion: " 'You are now going into trance. You are going to give a reading for Mrs. Delaney. You will speak slowly and distinctly because I'm taking it down in longhand. Add that. But if you don't give the suggestion as I blink my eyes, I will go into a deep sleep, not say a word, and may not wake for hours.'

"And so Dave kept watching Cayce's eyes like a hawk and, just as Mister Cayce said, told him to give the cause of Mrs. Delaney's paralysis and tell how she could be helped. So the reading was given, and it said the problem was caused by an accident she had when she was was holding her infant child. She was in a horse and buggy— this was 1908—and the horse reared, and she flew out of the buggy and hit the base of her spine on the step. Sometime later, she was in another accident and this revived the original injury.

"The Delaneys didn't know what to make of this man who went to sleep and said all this hocus-pocus, but they did remember these accidents, and so they took heart and were ready to listen to what Cayce had said.

"Delaney had insisted the doctor be at the reading. So this doctor wrote out the prescription for the drugs Cayce said she should have. Dave rushed down to the drugstore with the prescription. The druggist shook his head over it, not having seen anything like it before, and said, finally, 'Well, there's nothing in it that could harm anybody, so I'll fill it.' Dave took it back and gave Mrs. Delaney the prescribed dosage. And two days later she broke out in a rash, and her husband, who was a devout Catholic and somewhat skeptical of black magic, calls Dave and says, 'You see, Dave, I told you we're not supposed to deal with this nonsense,' just as though Dave had anything to do with it. 'Look at my wife; she's got a terrible rash, and she still can't move.'

"And Dave, who's strangely drawn to the farm boy who takes pictures for a living, says, 'Let's call Cayce and find out what happened. He seemed to know what he was talking about.'

"And Delaney laughs and says, 'In his sleep?'

"So they called Cayce, and Dave says, 'Can you give another reading and find out what caused the condition now appearing, and what shall we do?'

"So the reading was given, this time back in Hopkinsville without a doctor, and Cayce calls back and says that had the prescription been properly filled there would have been no complications. Black sulphur, one of the main ingredients, was missing."

Somehow it seemed quite natural for the fifteen-year-old boy to take over. For all of Delaney's suppressed doubts had returned. So it was Dave who went back to the druggist and asked, 'Did you use black sulphur in that prescription?' And the druggist said no, he couldn't get it and had used black molasses instead, since it was a sulphur compound. So Dave calls Cayce again and asks where they can get the black sulphur. Cayce gives a reading and says that a drug house in Detroit, Parke-Davis, has it. So Dave calls Parke-Davis, and they have it, as Cayce said, and Dave asks them to send it immediately. Then Dave goes back to the druggist in Lexington with the black sulphur and asks him to refill the prescription. And he takes the compound back and gives it to the Delaneys."

Lucille had been telling her story with obvious relish. I could see the gleam in her eye as she mentioned Dave's name. As she paused for a moment to catch her breath, I said, "Doesn't it strike you as a bit odd that a fifteen-year-old boy should have instant command of a situation that would have baffled an older and wiser head?"

She gave me an enigmatic smile.

"Look into the readings," she said. "That may give you a clue."

I figured I could get into that later. But right now all I wanted to know was how all this wound up.

"So with the black sulphur, Mrs. Delaney begins to improve. Soon she was able to comb her hair and feed herself. But she still wasn't walking. Cayce also said she should have osteopathic treatment. But there were no osteopaths available, and so Dave called Cayce again and said there were no osteopaths in Lexington, and Cayce said, 'Don't worry about it, there will be.' And a week later an osteopath moved to Lexington and set up an office, and the Delaneys called him for treatments."

"You mean," I interrupted, "that Cayce saw this osteopath establishing an office there, without even knowing who he was?"

She nodded. "In the same manner he sent people to Harold Reilly without knowing who he was. It just came to him, or he wouldn't have mentioned osteopathic treatments. There was nobody like Cayce. He was in tune with the subconscious minds of everybody."

In six months, Mrs. Delaney was able to leave her wheelchair and take a few steps at a time.

In the Kahn household next door, this was considered a miracle. Dave's mother, one of Cayce's biggest boosters, told her eldest son, "Promise me that you will see that the work of this man is made known to the world."

Dave had given it his best effort, and he drew Lucille into the act. In time she fell into it with his enthusiasm. As a fine actress with a great degree of sensitivity, she knew enough about the inner nature of people to know that the great ones of this world were usually quite different from the norm. And so she was open.

She had played on Broadway and was an up-and-coming young actress touring with the renowned Otis Skinner in a play, when, at the insistence of Dave, she got her first Cayce reading in Dayton, Ohio. Cayce had been living there, working with Arthur Lammers, for whom he had given his first life reading, and he was pleased to read for the bride-to-be of his young friend.

The reading so impressed Lucille that she wrote Cayce expressing her wonder at his analysis of her character and personality and his delineation of her theatrical gifts from a past she had never even dreamed of. Already she was beginning to understand something of her husband's affection for the remarkable seer who, with his tall, spare figure and gentle eyes looked more like the man next door.

I had known Lucille to be a very private person, an elitist who had run a successful lecture program for twenty years, recruiting such eminent speakers as the British scholar Gerald Heard and Professor C.J. Ducasse of Brown University from the ranks of the intelligentsia. I never quite understood how she had entertained a newspaper reporter like myself as a speaker in this exalted company. And I was somewhat abashed when, after I had casually made a reference to the Cayce "movement," she had gently but firmly reminded me that there was no such movement. "For we are definitely not cultists."

I could subscribe to that and to a certain remoteness as well, which conveyed a sense of her being very much her own person.

"I would have thought, I said, "that you would be the last person in the world to take in strangers off the street."

She went back pretty much to what she had said before.

"In marrying Dave, I married Cayce."

I persisted.

"But there had to be a reason behind it. If this had been some average man from Chicago or Milwaukee or New York, would you have felt comfortable with him and his wife and his secretary and his son lounging around your house for a month at a time, making telephone calls and having a business going on the side?"

She nodded thoughtfully.

"In the beginning I did it for Dave, but as I got to know Cayce I did feel a certain connection with him, more of a mystical than an emotional thing, a feeling of being completely comfortable, like family."

"They were the only family you treated as your family outside your own family?"

She smiled. "Yes, that's right."

"Didn't you find that significant?"

"Actually, it was a very natural thing. I didn't give it that much thought. He was very special. They all were. I found myself concerned about him, his health, and his work, that he not overwork. He didn't give his readings for the money—anybody could see that—but as a contribution to humanity. I recognized that early on. Throughout his life, whenever there was a family illness—my own, Dave's, or the two boys—there were physical readings given voluntarily. We followed them to the letter. And as far as our meals went, they were all very natural, as outlined by Cayce—not very much red meat, plenty of fresh fruit and vegetables, not eating when upset emotionally, things very commonplace now in diet but very new then."

She had become enough of a believer to request a Cayce reading for her infant son. "We had a life reading on him when he was five months old, and it told of his many incarnations and guided me on the pitfalls that might occur in his upbringing. One of the things it warned me about was that he was a very quick study and could skim over something and not be very thorough because he was very bright. So I watched that as he was growing up. He used to say to me, 'Well, what does that word mean?' Instead of giving it to him the easy way, I decided I'd stress a study pattern as Cayce suggested. And I'd say, 'Well, let's go look it up.' So we'd go to the encyclopedia, and he got into the habit then as he got older to use the encyclopedia and other reference books for the information he wanted. It created good work habits, and I'll always be grateful for the readings because I never would have recognized this tendency on his part in those young years. But he's very thorough now, so thorough that when I make remarks off the cuff, he'll say, 'What's your authority?' So I smile to myself and think, 'Well, it's all coming back.' "

The readings said this son had been a doctor in the past and could be so again if he chose to make another contribution in this direction. Sure enough, as he grew older he was drawn to medicine and the role of the mind in human health and behavior. It was as though there were nothing else he had ever wanted to be or do.

"And so he went to medical school at Harvard and then to the Columbia Psychoanalytical Institute and became a psychoanalyst, and this is what he's practicing today. He has this background of reincarnation and karma. While I'm sure he doesn't bring it up in his sessions, I don't doubt that he often thinks about it."

She was fully aware that the two preeminent figures in psychoanalysis, Jung and Freud, were both involved in parapsychology and reincarnation. "Oh, yes," she said, "Freud said that if he had his life to live over again he would devote himself to the psychic world."

I had to laugh at this.

"He may very well get the chance," I said.

She joined in the laugh. "Yes, we're all in it together."

By this time it was obvious the Kahns were as tied to Cayce as he was to them.

The second son was a lawyer, and Cayce had seen this aptitude from the past as well. "The reading had mentioned he could go into the law, but he should never be confined to an office or a closed space. As he matured and had his own family, he became interested in environmental problems, getting out of his office constantly to deal with people and their environment."

She felt that the readings for the "Cayce babies" were particularly evidential of reincarnation. "Dave, of course, felt that everybody should have a reading with Cayce. He didn't see how he could have survived without it. As he said, 'If you didn't know where you came from, how did you know where you were going?' "

The husband of a friend of the Kahns had died, and the mother was having problems with the young boy. She turned to Dave and said, "He misses his father and needs a man in his life. Would you help me with him?"

Normally the most genial of men, Dave made a condition, reflecting the longtime dependence on Cayce.

"I will help you," he said, "if the boy gets a reading from Edgar Cayce to guide me."

The mother agreed.

"He got the reading, and it said he should prepare himself for the kind of work that would make him a city planner. This was the furthest thing from his mind, and I thought that was the end of it. And then one day, some years later, I picked up the *New York Times*, and there was a picture of this boy grown up with his name under it, and it said, 'New City Planner.' "

She smiled. "You see, Cayce saw it all in a future influenced by the past. And so again it was a case of somebody wanting to go in many different directions and eventually coming back and doing what the readings said he should do and could do."

The Kahn home, on swank Park Avenue, provided a protective umbrella for the Cayce readings. New York City, at that time, had stringent regulations against both fortune-telling and practicing medicine without a license. As fate would have it, Cayce and Gertrude, with Gladys, had chosen to stop at a New York hotel on this one occasion because so many of their appointments were for people living in or near the hotel.

To the horror of Cayce's friends, that week Cayce and

the two women were trapped into a reading by a plain-clothes policewoman. They were arrested for fortune-telling and held for trial. It was a Roman holiday for the newspapers. The newspaper that cropped off Gertrude's face from a picture taken of all three, as a token of instant karma, is now defunct. But it was to be one of Cayce's darkest moments. For he had to wonder why he had been so chastised if he was meant to be doing his psychic work? And why, with this gift of his, hadn't he been able to discern that the woman requesting a reading was a police officer trying to trap him? But, again, it gave Dave Kahn the opportunity to manifest his loyalty to the man he called Judge.

"Dave," Lucille recalled, "made a great witness. The trial judge became so engrossed in Dave's sketch of Cayce's work that he called him to the stand and began to question him. It was easy to see how fascinated he was. In the end, throwing the case out, he quoted from Shakespeare to a crowded courtroom: 'There are more things in heaven and earth, Horatio, than are dreamt of in your philosophy.' "

No such intimacy as that shared by two diverse people, Cayce and Kahn, could have come out of thin air. There had to be a reason. For every effect there was a cause. And the loyalty of these two men, so different in so many respects, was so evident that it colored virtually every aspect of their lives, as reflected in their going off together for two years to explore for oil.

It had been a learning experience for both men. Cayce never again set out for himself on a financial venture, though a rich oil field was eventually found in the area where he said there was oil.

There had been a break in the conversation and Lucille was looking across the table at me a little speculatively, not wanting to lead the questioning, waiting for me to push the right button.

"Was there anything relevant about your reading that you recall?"

She smiled. "How could I forget it? It would be like a girl forgetting her first date."

It had been a notable experience. Cayce had given her past lives in Germany, India, and Greece. And these lives, he said, had an ennobling influence on this life and her artistry in music and the stage.

There was an interesting bit about her Greek experience. She had come under the influence of the Roman historian Tacitus, and being beautiful of face and form and having this sponsorship, she became a widely acclaimed thespian. And with this celebrity, she had developed a case of ego.

"The love of stage and of applause is innate from this appearance on the earth's plane," said Cayce. "Well that some of this be kept under the control of the will."

Nobody knew better than Lucille how right Cayce was. But there was still nothing to link her with Cayce in a past-life expression, or with Dave, for that matter.

It had been a long session, and I could see that she was tiring.

"We will get together again," she said, "but first go to the encyclopedia."

I knew what she meant.

I was beginning to understand something of the ties binding these two diverse men. Jeanette Thomas, having waded through Dave Kahn's readings, was looking rather triumphant, as though she had made a great discovery.

"It goes back," she said, "to Egypt when Edgar was the high priest and there was that movement to throw him out of the country. Some stood by him and some didn't."

"And Kahn did?"

"I deserve some kind of medal," she said. "There were so many files to go through."

She had the one paragraph yellowed out.

"The entity [Kahn] was in that experience in that defense of the priest Ra-Ta, who was driven into exile by the aggrandizement of self-interests and of the fleshly desires. The entity, a priestly aide, though, remained faithful to that priest. Hence the inner attempt at times for the exaggerations by the entity, especially when they are felt at the moment beneficial to that priest."

No wonder that from the moment they met, Kahn, even as a fifteen-year-old boy, seemed to fully understand what Cayce was all about. He was an intimate of long standing.

Jeanette plucked a letter out of the files.

"Look how happy Cayce is about paying that old debt. After being inundated by requests for readings, Cayce still finds time to write Dave about how glad he is to be of help."

I scanned the letter. It was not that of a man who felt put upon.

"I certainly am in hopes that everything works out to the very best for all. And I'll certainly be glad to know that I have had some little part in being of assistance in some way."

Cayce's old aide seemed to be growing spiritually, with a nudge from Cayce every now and then. For in 1938, some twelve years after the Egyptian reading, Kahn asked for advice in "the developing of service to his family, associates, and mankind, for the balance of the days of his life, to improve mentally, physically, and spiritually."

Subconsciously, this may have been the request the Sleeping Prophet was waiting for. For it gave him a chance to expand on the reincarnation process.

"Each soul as it enters into material manifestation," he said, "enters to fulfill a purpose. God hath not willed that any soul should perish but hath with every temptation, every fault, prepared an opportunity for the entity to become as one with him. For that is the purpose of the soul's being in a beginning without end."

Dave was content. For he knew what his friend of old expected of him in this life. And in return he delivered a last valedictory: "I believe that thousands can be thankful that I was able to talk about you. And, more important, that you did as much as I said you could."

To this Cayce could say amen. For he had chosen his emissary well—out of the time-tested past. They knew better than anybody, these two, seemingly so different and yet so alike in their beliefs, that they would return again and again until the meaning of death was made clear.

I had a number of questions rolling around in my head and looked forward to seeing Lucille again. She had the effect of making me aware of the closeness of the various people who had flocked around Cayce.

"You know," she said, as we again sat across the table, "that Paul once said that if one man lives again, then all men do. Cayce said pretty much the same, but in a different way. He showed their lives coming together and the reason for it."

I smiled. "And what do you think of Dave's role as town crier?"

She shrugged. "Things haven't changed much. In Egypt, Dave stood by Cayce when he was banished and served as an intermediary in bringing him back. And when Cayce, as a channel in a small town in Virginia, was looked on with suspicion and ostracized, Dave again made it his business to see that Cayce was accepted."

She gave me a penetrating look.

"You should know about that. Dave was the first to mention Cayce to you. And you turned around and wrote *The Sleeping Prophet* and other books that spread the work around the world. And there's been a cascade of books on Cayce ever since."

"And how about you and Dave?" I said, restraining a smile. "There doesn't seem to be any connection between the two of you in any of the past we know about."

"Oh, yes, there is," she said, giving me an innocent look. "Cayce said I collaborated with Ra-Ta in an exchange of ideas in my India days. And Dave was at Ra-Ta's side and assisted in the collaboration that took place in India."

She paused dramatically, as befitted a former star of the stage—in two lifetimes.

"And that's what Dave and I did again in this life, collaborating with Cayce and each other."

She looked over my head into the distant horizon, as though peering through the veil of time. "And that's what we will do again one day," she said with a little sigh, "collaborate with the greatest of joy from the lessons we learned this time around."

CHAPTER 13

Dreams I Have Known

Elsie Sechrist was known as the dream woman because of the many books she had written about dreams and Edgar Cayce's interpretation of them. One of her books, *Dreams: Your Magic Mirror,* had become so popular that the Russians, who had banned God from their vocabulary, had invited her to Moscow and Leningrad not only to talk about the subconscious mind and Edgar Cayce but to touch on the spiritual with perhaps something of Jesus and the Almighty thrown in.

She spoke in Russia on three occasions. Two of the meetings were open, attended by scientists, but, on the third occasion, she went underground, with many of the audience ducking up dark alleys to attend her lecture and the private session later when they freely discussed reincarnation and dared to speak of God.

She was not surprised by her warm reception all over the world, for her mentor in many lives—Edgar Cayce— had foreseen all this activity on her part and had prepared her for it. He had taught her to meditate, to visualize, to dig deep into her subconscious, waking her up with his own mind at two every morning to meditate with her and help develop her dream state and her waking state as the readings said he had done before in ancient Persia.

He had a unique way of building up a student's confidence in the subconscious path he had put them on, in their dreams, in their visions, in the lives they had lived before. He would tell them little things in this life, sending out messages, which had great impact because of the direct effect they had on the lives of his pupils.

With her husband, she had met Cayce at a lecture he gave in the backyard of his home in Virginia Beach. She was almost immediately confounded by his wonders.

"There were about thirty-five or forty people there for a conference," she recalled. "Bill and I felt right at home. We had been drawn to Cayce as though by a magnet. There was no explaining it in rational terms, though we had been interested in reincarnation. We had heard about him and felt we just had to meet him. We would sit for a long time on his porch, and he would talk to me and Bill about everything under the sun.

"During his lecture, he asked, 'Is there anybody here who would like help in their meditation?' And without knowing why, it was like a compulsion, I raised my hand.

" 'Yes, I would,' I said, 'I would like it.' I didn't even know what meditation was.

"So, he said, 'All right, I'll awaken you at two in the morning.' And I said, 'Oh, I'm sorry, but I don't have a telephone.'

"And I thought, is this man who I just met, who seems to have a spell over me, is he going to come into my bedroom?

"And he said, 'I don't need a telephone.'

"He just sort of grinned. He could read your mind, and he said, 'I'll awaken you. Don't worry. Two o'clock in the morning.' So for over a year he awakened me, wherever I was, at two in the morning. Every morning he would help me with my meditation, and after that I started visualizing and remembering things long past.

"I got very good at it. I would stay up fifteen or twenty minutes and had no trouble going back to sleep. I would meditate on creating a pure vessel of my self and made an affirmation for each day . . . helped through by my belief in God, my neighbors and myself.

"I remember one morning it was 2:20 when I woke up—twenty minutes late. By this time I had begun to visualize so well that I saw Cayce in my mind's eye, and he was laughing. So I called him later that day from New York, where I was living at the time, and said, 'Why were you laughing at me, Mister Cayce?' And he said, 'I wasn't laughing at you. I was laughing because you thought you had overslept, when the truth of the matter was I had overslept by twenty minutes and didn't wake you up until twenty minutes after two.'

"We both laughed over it, but I realized again how

connected we were in our subconscious and universal mind."

I wondered how she had progressed so rapidly that she could tune in to him while he was tuning in to her.

"I saw him in a vision. I had been seeing him in a vision for some time now. It stimulated the whole process of visualizing. For once you start having visions of things, and you validate them as I did, they just keep coming, stronger and stronger. For you have joined your subconscious mind to the universal mind, which remembers just about everything."

Elsie was a formidable lady, physically and mentally. And as a good nurse should, she had aged well. She was hobbling about with a cane because she had slipped and broken a bone. But it didn't keep her from getting around and dining with old friends of the past and present. She was known for her candor, which could be bruising at times, but at heart she was a gentle soul who thought nothing of taking on a tiger if there was a matter of truth involved.

Many thought the Sechrists independently wealthy. But this wasn't always so. And there was a metaphysical assist in their riches—a vision, which she was not quite ready to tell me about. "Later," she said. "I have to keep some mystery about me."

Almost nothing happened to Elsie that didn't have a touch of the esoteric or supernatural to it, though she thought it all perfectly natural.

As I looked around her spacious home on one of those Virginia Beach inlets that seem to dart in and out of narrow slips of land, I was not only struck by the costly decor and furnishings but by the bric-a-brac and pictures that adorned the walls.

My eye was caught by a picture of some ruins that seemed to jump right out of the frame.

Elsie saw my look, as she saw everything.

"That's a picture of the ruins of Persepolis, some three hundred miles or so southeast of Shūshtar, in Iran. This was home to me long ago; Bill loved it. It was one of the most peaceful places I had ever been in my life. This is the remnant of the big temple built there thousands of years ago."

I had some confusion jumping around in time with her.

But she only shrugged. "I knew it then, and I know it now. The architecture may not be what it was, but our reactions were the same as when Persia was the flower of the East. We were overwhelmed by the sounds and voices of the past."

Voices were nothing new to Elsie. They were responsible for her best-selling book on dreams. She had written a book about general philosophy that Cayce had talked about, and she was meditating one day, asking what publisher she should send it to, when a voice said, "Drop that book and write one on dreams."

She felt it was the Cayce influence. Messages were nothing new between them. Some time after that, she was again meditating, wondering how the sum of $5,000 her husband and she had managed to save could have any influence on their life-style.

She chuckled. "That was really the mystery—how $5,000 could turn our lives around. But I meditated on it as Cayce had taught me, and I was filled with a feeling of confidence. I knew we were going to be poor no longer.

"Bill was going to put the money in the bank for interest, and a voice said to me, 'Take that $5,000 and buy property in Virginia Beach.' Which we did. It was wonderful. We paid $5,000 for it and sold it for $279,000.

"The land we bought was originally a worthless swamp. They filled it in. And now it's all built up. There's a street there today named Sechrist Court. We had owned that property, across from the Virginia General Hospital. And that started our fortune."

With the money made in real estate, they went into other ventures with another follower of Cayce's and were soon among the nouveau riche.

Cayce had seen it all, while alive, advising his people to buy to the north in Virginia Beach, then a sprawling small town, now the largest city in Virginia with 400,000 population.

As he had in life, Cayce, after his death, had sent Elsie all kinds of messages, contacting her in the wee hours of the morning. Nothing had changed.

"It was almost," a friend said, "as if he wanted the Sechrists to have enough leisure so she could do missionary work for the Cayce readings and reincarnation."

The Sechrists became world travelers, moving into the Holy Land, Egypt, and Persia, all places they had shared with Edgar Cayce, trying to retrace the steps they had made in these earlier lives given them by Cayce.

Because of my earlier books on Cayce, I knew the Sechrists as I did so many of the people who had a vital part in Cayce's life. Her husband of many years had recently passed away, but Elsie, stifling her grief, maintained her place in the continuing Cayce argosy, settling in the Virginia Beach environment she had found so stimulating. There the Cayce old guard hung on, calmly awaiting the crossing that held no fears for any of them. Elsie said it for all: "Death is just a comma in the book of life.

"Those of us who were with him before will never be very far from Mister Cayce. We still have much to learn, and we're still hearing from him."

Feeling a significant loss of energy just before his death in January 1987, Bill Sechrist had turned to his wife and said, "Would you mind contacting Cayce and see if there's anything I can do to get some strength." But instead of hearing a voice, or having a vision of a living Cayce, as sometimes happened, all she saw was a black velvet cross fall to the ground. She didn't know what it meant, but she had a feeling of foreboding. "I couldn't get anything," she told him. "I'll try again tomorrow." And the next day when Bill passed over, the meaning of the vision became clear.

It was a great loss, assuaged somewhat by the conviction she would not be long apart from her companion of old. They had been together in many lifetimes, knowing Cayce as well, and the great love they bore for each other was the product of that past. In all my obervations, I had never known a pair who seemed to enjoy each other's company so much.

I encountered them frequently, and they always seemed like young lovebirds to me, teasing each other good-naturedly, and unselfconsciously walking arm in arm as young lovers would. Though by now a successful businessman, Bill Sechrist, as in the distant past, took a great pride in his wife's brush with fame, and was always the first to encourage her literary efforts. There was never any suggestion of *his* or *hers*. When she was invited to lecture, he lectured along with her. Theirs was a joint caring, what Edgar Cayce called an eternal love. They were soulmates, and soulmates built no condition around their love. And in this love and the mutuality of their thinking, they shared a love for the man who had added an extra dimension to their current adventure, and to the past as well.

Just as she felt Bill's presence after his passing, so did she gain strength from the knowledge that the departed Cayce was not very far from her. He was a great buttress in this time of sorrow, her continuing connection with him bolstering her faith in humankind's immortality.

"Cayce knew Bill was going," she said. "He gave me a sign that I would know after the event what he knew before it. For black had always been symbolic to me of death."

Based on the Cayce readings, it was no surprise that she had dreams and visions that were prophetic. Cayce had said in one of her readings, "The entity was in the city of the hills and the plains when the activities of the teacher [Uhjltd] there brought many helpful influences by the practical application of healing in that experience. The entity became what would be called today a seeress or a prophetess among the natives. The abilities of the visions, of the experiences, of the dreams, arise from the application of self to certain tenets—the meditation and mind development—in that sojourn."

She had been the leading nurse at that time, working at Uhjltd's elbow, dressing the wounds and helping with the ligatures, just as she did in this life as a registered nurse who taught other nurses their trade. But she was also a psychic reader then, telling fortunes in the sand.

She had lives with Bill in four experiences, including the present.

"I remember very well," she said, "how we were connected in the city of the hills and the plains.

"I was working with him. I was a nurse at the time as I was and am in this lifetime. I had visions and dreams in which I went in and examined the cavelike homes. This was a very primitive period; the homes were sort of carved out of the hills, some of them big rock slabs, and the insides had been carved out for rooms so the people could have their homes there.

"They were rather short. I still remember them very clearly. They looked about five feet tall, the men, a little more maybe, very black hair, flat heads rather than being sort of rounded like ours were. (For we were from the Egyptian experience.) My job was not only as a nurse, but I also inspected the homes, the caves, to see about the cleanliness and taught them hygiene."

"So Uhjltd was in charge of all that?"

"He was there."

"So you must have a distinct memory of him."

"As I said, I remember working with him, aiding in tying up wounds of the people that had been hurt at different times, and of course, the place was a cave carved out of the rocks or one of the hills. And so he acted as a doctor and I as an assistant, a nurse helping him with these people.

"I don't remember anything except that I was in charge of teaching them cleanliness of the body, of the homes, of their hair, and he would direct me in treating the wounds, and he would help with that, too. As Cayce, he later remembered.

"There was a salve of some kind that worked miracles, but I didn't know its name or what it was made of.

"The scenes that I was shown or that I lived through concerned just Uhjltd and me and the patients. Then when I entered some of these homes it was the family that was involved, and I was instructing them in cleanliness and wholesomeness.

"I knew Bill in the Holy Land, Persia, and Egypt, and we shared our memories together and enjoyed going over the trails we had left behind in these lands. We had the same recollections of Egypt, and these were constantly being filled in by the dreams Cayce said I would be having all my life.

"I had dreamed of a period in Egypt that went way back before our bodies were perfected to the degree they are now, even though we have throwbacks even now. As a nurse I saw a number of those of excessive hair and the vestiges of tails."

"We were hairier then, weren't we?" I said, thinking that it was a natural part of the evolutionary process because of the lack of clothing.

"Many men still are, which is from the primate king-

dom. And then sometimes even today you'll see the body
of a baby that's very much like that of a monkey.

"I know that one of these lives was in the Egyptian
period because I had twins born to me then, and while
their bodies were perfect, they had hooves for feet, and
you see something like that now once in a while. And
so this would be a throwback to one of those particular
periods before the bodies had been perfected."

Cayce had summed it up pretty well: "When the entity
was in the Egyptian land, there were those activities,
just prior to the passing of the priest, when many changes
were wrought by the priest trying to hurry the evolution
of the body and of expression through the activities in
the Temple of Sacrifice. Thus again we find the entity in
pursuit of those activities, to help others help themselves."

There was little question which experience ruled Elsie
in this life. And the depth of her emotional response may
have stretched her memory of the Holy Land and the
Master who walked and talked with God.

"It all flooded back on me like a great tide when I
looked out on the sea that he swam in and meditated in
the garden where he suffered his Father's will.

"My memory went beyond the Crucifixion and the
Resurrection, for I was so young when I saw him. It was
but a moment of time, expanding from one life to the
next. I saw the Apostles and the disciples in the critical
years after he joined the Father. Mister Cayce said I had
a chord of memory of the day when there was the descent
of the Holy Ghost upon the disciples. He said that the
entity—meaning me—had a vivid dream, and in this
dream I saw the disciples standing on the brow of the
hill and saw the bolts of fire that came down over their
heads. I gathered it was the tongues of fire that the Bible
talks about. From time to time I've had other recalls,
especially when Bill and I went to the Holy Land. I remember many things there now, especially the Essene
community, and Cayce had said I was part of that
community."

Having the means to travel as they pleased, they
yielded to a compulsion to go over the areas they had
traversed together before. And it was with eagerness and
high anticipation that they visited these lands. They were
particularly curious about their lives together in the city

of the hills and plains, and Bill, a rather meticulous individual, mapped an area in Iran where the Cayce readings said they had lived before. By Bill's careful computations it turned out to be five and a half or six miles from the main Muslim mosque in the Iranian town of Shūshtar.

"Bill and I went there by helicopter. We knew exactly what the distance was, for Bill was good at that. From the helicopter we dropped a bucket of red paint, as low as it was safe for the pilot to fly with a helicopter. Then we went back and hired a Landrover, and we found what we thought were so many of the markings that Cayce had mentioned, like some remnants of clothing, an altar cloth, pieces of utensils and fragments of pottery, and the huge rock with a man-made door hanging by a cave, but we didn't dare go in because it was filled with all this debris and all kinds of things scurrying about in it.

"Somewhere in the reading, it mentioned a rock that was thirty or forty feet distant from the entrance. And right through the rock there was a hole, through which the setting sun would shine right into the cave. We waited for the sunset and it was exactly as he said. So we were very excited. We saw this as a verification of whatever else he had said about our lives back then. So we met with some explorers from Japan about digging into the cave. They got excited, too. They had heard about Cayce in Japan. And they were willing to pay for all the excavating, everything, if they could have the picture rights to it. We said that's great. We agreed to go back and get all the information we needed, then come back and begin the digging. But the next thing we knew the shah, who was sympathetic to foreigners coming in and excavating, was run out of Iran, and Khomeini came in, and it was all over. He didn't want any Americans or Europeans digging up their national treasures."

They were never able to go back and explore the cave and look for the altar cloths and other relics of gold and bronze that the readings said were still in the cave.

"Bill in that lifetime had been a trader, as the readings said, and traveled with his camel caravan. He always loved camels in this lifetime." She smiled. "He would rather see a camel than a pretty girl anytime. The readings said he took a caravan all the way from Egypt to India to Arabia. He used to sell pots and pans in his travels then by the wayside, which is rather amusing since in this lifetime his biggest success before he got into his own business was pots and pans and pressure cookers for a company in Wisconsin."

They made many trips to the Holy Land, and freshets of memory overwhelmed Elsie, the dream merchant, as she gazed into the Sea of Galilee, the placid body of water by the side of the village that Jesus called home.

Cayce had placed the time and circumstance:

"The entity was in the Holy Land, especially following the persecution of the church. She was rather young when the Master walked in the earth and knew rather by hearsay of those that had seen and known him in his ministry to the earth.

"Yet the teachings of the Essenes were especially close to the activities of the entity. Though she lived not in Jerusalem, she had visited there on feast days, and as a very young person had been impressed by the activities on the days of the Pentecost when there was the first speaking by the disciples in tongues. The entity aided many that faltered, in many various ways and manners, and in part was a teacher, rather than helper, to those in authority in the Holy Land. The name then was Mercia."

Elsie was bombarded by impressions of the past in the Holy Land, some elevating, others depressing, for reasons that were sometimes obscure. She felt at home in the Essene ruins and relived her memories.

"I knew when we went there that I would find two doors in one of the ruins, which had obviously been a house of worship. Women entered through the left, and the door over to the right was for men. The whole area of the Dead Sea and of the Holy Land and of the Essene community, the Qumran ruins, I just loved that. But as I said, it was the Sea of Galilee that drew me. We used to stay in a hotel overlooking the sea, and I could have just stayed there all the time and then gone up the hill where Jesus gave the Beatitudes.

"Cayce said I was a part of the Essene community in Christ's time, and so Ed Jamal, a friend who was with us in Israel, and I went out looking for my bones, so to speak, but we couldn't find them. We weren't looking for anything else in particular, just rummaging around. I was not born in the Holy Land but somewhere just outside it. Cayce said that I was of the Jewish faith but not a Jew, however that could be. He said I often visited there on holy days, and I was there the day of the Pentecost and witnessed the descent of the Holy Spirit on the disciples' heads, and there was a distant chord of memory, as he said. I found the place in the Holy Land where the disciples had stood that day. But for me the holiest place and the dearest place was the Sea of Galilee. I enjoyed the places Jesus enjoyed. In Mary and Martha's home, in Bethany, where Christ visited and found peace, I'd sit in the garden for an hour, and it would bring back many memories of my association with them. It just felt as if I was closer to Jesus there than anywhere else except Galilee. I would sit in absolute quiet and know a greater peace than I've ever known in any church. I also had a strange feeling, as though of a secret fear, of a pit there that people would climb down into as part of their tour. I would take ten steps then become so repelled I had to come back up."

She never knew what she may have encountered there. "Must have been snakes," she said. "I loathe them."

She liked best the bypaths that Jesus had taken and could visualize him walking alone, stopping every now and then to speak to the birds and the flowers.

Jerusalem palled on her, as did other heavily populated places in the Holy Land. "We got so tired of their building a church everywhere we turned, even where one of the disciples supposedly expectorated. We got so we didn't stop at Jerusalem anymore. We would just head for the Sea of Galilee and Martha's vineyard. I loved that place. I'd go in there, and Bill would say, 'All right, but will you please limit yourself to a half-hour?'

"When I sat in the garden and closed my eyes it would transport me back to the time when Mary, Martha, and Jesus were together. I never did get up the courage to go back into the deep hole where Lazarus was supposed to be entombed. Something held me back. But I loved their yard—Mary, Martha, and Lazarus's place . . ."

I had been listening raptly, and it suddenly came to me that she sounded just as casual as a neighbor describing a visit to a friend's home. And so I suppose it was to Elsie. They had all been friends. There was no doubt of that in her mind, or in Cayce's.

She came into Jerusalem then only on special occasions. Cayce said she visited Jerusalem on the feast days as a very young person. There on the day of the Pentecost, as noted, was the first speaking in tongues by the disciples. As described by the Apostle Paul, the disciples spoke in one tongue and people of all the races gathered there each heard them as if they were speaking in the listener's tongue. But it was her overwhelming feeling for Jesus that prevailed over everything else, taking her to Calvary and beyond.

"I had a vision of Jesus standing on a hill with a big orchard in front of him. And he pointed to the orchard, and he said to me, 'The harvest is ripe; the laborers are few.' "

For a visionary like Elsie, the meaning was clear.

"Christ was saying the fruits of his labors were there to be picked, but the pickers were few and far between."

In Egypt, of course, they had visited the pyramids. Sitting in a lofty chamber of a particularly sacred pyramid had seemed like old times to Elsie. She loved every moment of it, visualizing herself as married to Bill then and sitting at the feet of Edgar Cayce, then the high priest, and learning from him to develop her psychic power. As the group was leaving the chamber, she saw one of the women weeping, and she asked, "Is there something wrong?" And this woman sobbed, "I had the most terrible memories. They were so depressing."

And Elsie replied, "I had nothing but the pleasantest remembrances, and that's what you should meditate on— that which elevates you and brings you closer to the helpful reality of the past, not the dregs."

What other people thought about and dismissed as imagination or subtle suggestion, Elsie knew to be true. For she had tested her past in the deeper realities of her mind, balancing it against what she could observe and conceive of in the present.

She had seen the Temple Beautiful in her dreams many times, and she had heard voices echoing from the past, and she had learned to trust these voices, for they had never failed her, in time of triumph or of travail.

I had asked about the Temple Beautiful. The reports I had were fragmentary and not distinctive. She didn't hesitate, for her subconscious mind—and Cayce—had long ago made a reality of the house that Ra built.

"The Temple Beautiful was a real temple. It was for those who were to become teachers. There was one aide to the high priest, who was Florence Edmonds of the Cayce study group in this life, who was able back then to look into your spirit and say whether you were ready to enter the temple to train as a teacher.

"When I met her in this life, I said, 'What is it about your eyes that is so unusual?'

"She asked Cayce about it, and he said it was a throwback to her Egyptian days. It's quite intriguing how the fears or inclinations we have are so often ruled by past-life experiences.

"I had ridden horses a lot, and I loved them, but I had a fear of turning my back to a horse. I was doing a lot of dreaming, as my subconscious opened up, and had dreamed about where I had owned horses in Ireland. So we went to Ireland to a place much like my dream, jogging my memory. And there I recalled how, while raising horses, I had turned my back on a particularly vicious horse, and he bit me on the shoulder. My fear disappeared, lost in the reality of an explained cause.

"I was marked by Ra-Ta. He had marked many from that time so he would recognize them in each lifetime. Somebody who had been through the Egyptian period and had discussed the mark with me mentioned it one day. 'I saw the mark of Ra-Ta on you; it's in your right eye.' People often said to me, 'What do you do with your right eye?' I said, 'I don't do anything.' I asked Mister Cayce about it when we were alone one day, and he said, 'You were marked in the eye because you had misused the eyes in hypnosis, forcing others to look where you wanted them to.'

"I meditated, and I saw this large, blue eye looking at me. I didn't know what to think. But I knew it was from the past."

At this time she was meditating with Cayce at two every morning and visiting in Virginia Beach, attending his classes. She laughed, thinking back.

"So this particular time I tried to meditate on God, to purge myself of this evil eye, as others saw it. I awoke at two as usual, under Cayce's influence, and my hotel room on the ocean was filled with the odor of gardenias. There were no flowers in this area so near the beach, and yet the smell was so strong that it cloyed on my senses. The next morning when I saw him, I said, 'Oh, Mister Cayce, I want to tell you of an experience I had last night.' He said, 'Before you tell me of your experience, let me tell you of the dream I had before I awakened you.'

"He said, 'I dreamed that you and I were walking in the garden, and you asked me for help in meditation. And I said to you, "You need to meditate through the all-seeing eyes of God." And you said to me, "That's not enough. I also need the scent of gardenias.' " By this time nothing he did astounded me. So I said, 'That's exactly what my experience was.' He had projected this into my bedroom."

She looked up and shook her head. "I don't know anybody outside the Bible who can do anything like this."

I wasn't sure anybody in the Bible had sent fragrances flying around. And I wasn't quite sure what it meant, wonderful as it was.

After Cayce's death, even though Elsie found herself still communicating with him, she relied more on her own powers, her own subconscious, stimulated by meditation, and her own little dream world.

She had notebooks full of dreams that she had recorded. "Looking over them I found there was something tremendously prophetical in them. In these dreams, long before television, I saw myself on what looked like a stage, all over the world. In Russia, France, England, Germany, Ireland, South America, Australia, just everywhere. And I thought that was just crazy because in my own mind I said, even if I had the talent or the beauty to be a movie star, it was the last thing in the world I wanted to be."

But it was the lecture platform she was visualizing, and it was Edgar Cayce and the dream world she would be speaking about and about reincarnation and God, to large and curious audiences.

"London, Paris, Dublin, Moscow—you mention any country you like and Bill and I were there. In Russia the first time, there was a group of scientists. They all knew about Cayce. They had books about Cayce there, in Moscow and Leningrad. We spoke on any subject that would fall under the heading of parapsychology. In Russia three times. That was almost unprecedented to be called back there like that. I saw no Bible, but they had my meditation book and some of Cayce's books. They said to me, 'Whatever you do, just don't mention the word God.' "

And she didn't, not at first.

"I was trying to give them the basis of our spritual life without stepping on their toes. But when I got through with my lectures, I couldn't restrain myself any longer. And I said to the crowd of Russian intellectuals gathered around me, 'I must tell you that I personally believe in God.'

"They were nervous about it at first, looking around apprehensively. Then a dozen or so of the scientists started asking me questions, some out of curiosity, others with a desire to make me justify my belief.

" 'God—where is he? What's he like? Is he physical? Have you seen him? How could we prove that it was God?' There were a lot of questions of this kind."

She answered them as best she could, not backing up an inch nor caring much who was listening in, for Elsie was an indomitable woman.

Her first talk had taken place in a large government hall, with Soviet agents presumably in attendance. But when she was invited back to Moscow, there was a smaller hall and an aura of secrecy.

"We walked one mile at night through buildings and alleys to be sure that we weren't followed before we went to this other hall where Bill and I gave our lecture. This time after the talk there were questions in a private room. They were all interested. There were about four hundred people there. It was an intelligent group. I could see that I had gotten to some of them. I would talk about a Supreme Being without giving his name, and they knew what I was saying. They were all interested. I think when the truth hits a soul, it is stirred, and it reacts in some way to many of the things Cayce had said about the fellowship of man.

"I had a private meeting later with some of the Soviet scientists. And this time it was outside somewhere, in a nondescript-looking place. Even there they looked under the table to make sure there were no hidden wires, that we weren't being tapped. They asked very personal questions about the Christian religion, the Catholic church, the difference between Protestant and Catholic, and about life after death. There were many questions about reincarnation. I spoke freely for I felt there was no danger. Since they had so many Cayce books, they were familiar with so much of this. They asked questions about Cayce. What was he really like? What about his education? They found it hard to believe he had never gone beyond the fifth grade. They asked about his family, and I told them what he knew. We didn't get into God this time. I respected their discretion in their godless homeland, and since I had already told them how I stood on God, there was no reason to mention it further. But they did like the idea of many lifetimes. They felt it would give them more of a chance than they had now."

I had listened fascinated, but I couldn't restrain a comment at this point.

"You mean," I said with a smile, "that the government might change?"

"They didn't think this was funny."

She had done what she had to do, not stinting herself because of her age and her health, because she knew that her old teacher—Uhjltd, Ra-Ta, and Edgar Cayce himself would have wanted it that way. She had seen the man she called Papa Cayce for a last time in this incarnation the day before he died, in January 1945, and she well remembered what he had said to her in a voice suddenly grown strong: "Elsie, I expect great things of you."

She sighed, and I could detect the hint of a tear in her eye.

"And whenever I get tired or feel old or feel sorry for myself, I think of this great and good man, and I wonder what I can do to please him—in this world and the next."

CHAPTER 14

The Good Companion

Nobody was closer to Cayce than the man his companions knew as Luke. I had known him since he was a boy. And I saw him emerge as a man, totally respected by those who had been close to Edgar Cayce and were still alive to remember what he was like.

"He reminds me of Cayce," so many old-timers said. "He doesn't look like him, but he has his profundity and love of a joke. He even laughs like him."

I didn't know about that, because I didn't know what it was to hear Edgar Cayce laugh and neither did our Luke. But I had written enough about Cayce, delved deeply enough in his nature, to know there were strong similarities. And the strongest was the pull Luke had on the great body of people who looked on Cayce as their teacher and leader. He was their good companion.

"Oh, yes," he told me, with a disarming smile, "I have heard all that about Luke. And of course, if I was Luke then I must have been related to Cayce back in the Biblical time, for, as the readings tell us, he was Lucius of Cyrene, the disciple of Christ who was a kinsman of Luke's."

He threw up his arms in a deprecation gesture. "But I don't have the slightest idea how accurate all this is. In my conscious state I don't have any specific recall of that period, except for some vague biblical images I see once in a while, which could be related to my reading of the Bible." He had read the Gospel of Luke many times. It had intrigued him. And like Luke, he loved to travel, taking the high road to helping people. No man was too big to be approached, none too small to be reached. Like a true apostle of Christ he loved humanity.

As I thought about regressing him, I had all this in mind and more. For while all of the Bible was exciting,

237

some was more exciting than the rest. One book in the New Testament, the Gospel of Luke, read like no other, so rich in lyrical detail that it put the poetry of Homer in the shade.

Where did it all come from? the Bible scholars have asked for a thousand years and more. Some say that most of Luke was written by others, more in tune to Christ and the Holy Land. The verse is so clear, so strong, so vivid, they say, that only an eyewitness account could explain it. Yet Luke, we are told, never knew Jesus except out of the mouths of others and the beat of his own heart.

For Edgar Cayce it was all clear. There was no mystery. A traveling physician, a healer influenced by his uncle, Lucius of Cyrene, Luke jotted down whatever he heard of the Master and his remarkable healings. That alone drew him to Jesus in the beginning, though inevitably he came totally under his spell.

Lucius was Luke's mentor and guide, until in his own love of Christ, Luke surpassed his teacher. He was at home in his beloved Greece, and in Asia Minor, preaching and healing in the manner of Christ as he kept gathering stories in his diaries about the Son of man.

Nowhere else was there the detail and the personal touch that Cayce provided out of a memory bank that was universally inclusive. The Bible scholars argued endlessly, and about the only thing they agreed on was that Luke hadn't written Luke—not like Mark, Matthew, and John had done theirs in any case.

Dr. Ernest Findlay Scott of the Union Theological Seminary argued there had to be a better source for the Gospel of Luke than Luke himself. "We have seen," he wrote in his *Literature of the New Testament,* "that, according to one recent theory, Luke has built his gospel . . . on this unknown document."*

From the nature of the writing and the narrative itself, two outside sources were surmised, to which Luke had access, since the first two chapters of Luke read like nothing else in his Gospel.

---

*From Ernest Findlay Scott, *Literature of the New Testament,* ed. by Austin P Evans (NY: Columbia Univ. Press, 1932), 83; (Westport, CT: Greenwood Pr., 1985).

"The man who wrote the Gospel," said Scott, "was obviously the man who composed Acts in its finished form. Was this Luke himself or some person whose name is now lost? And who made use of Luke's diary?"

I could not help thinking of Lucius, so close to his relative, and Lucius's mistress Vesta as well. For as Scott pointed out, Luke wrote so sympathetically of women because "he had derived much of his information from women or was anxious to secure a larger place for their ministry in the Church of his time. Here again we need to remember that Luke had access to special sources, from which he borrowed such lovely stories as those of Martha and Mary, and the sinful woman who wept at the feet of Jesus."

The connections were there. Lucius's wife, Mariarh, was associated with Martha and Mary. And Vesta, close to Lucius and the Apostle John, was an obvious channel through which information may have been passed and later collected and published.

I thought it would be interesting to find who authored Luke, if at the same time I could get a clearer picture of his controversial relative from the man the Cayce old guard thought of as Luke.

Cayce identified him as the "physician in the period of the Master, and the writer," undoubtedly the dear and glorious physician of Taylor Caldwell's historical novel—and the Gospel. This modest and unassuming Luke found the designation rather overwhelming. "I don't know how to take it," he said. "But I can't fault Cayce, since he seems to be right about so much I know about."

Of a searching nature himself, this enterprising leader, who I shall call Robert, was willing to be regressed, if not to be identified. "I am sure," he said with an amused smile, "that most people would find it presumptuous if it even looked as if I was Luke."

He was a good subject, sensitive and responsive, eager to understand, if possible, the emotional feeling he had about Christ and the miracles of his healings. He had studied for a while to be a physician, only to drop out, bored with physics and chemistry. Instead, he had gone into the study of the abnormal mind and of healing with prayer. Each day he meditated, applying his mind to the healing of the sick. In a way, he was something of a mystery himself. For where, at an early age, had that calm and spiritual nature that so influenced his elders come from?

I had known our Luke since he was a boy, thirty years ago. Even when he was thirteen, he seemed a grown-up to me. He was contemplative, appearing to take everything seriously, asking questions about the nature of life and God, though he was also quite athletic and good at games. He was well rounded, and he listened. It was a remarkable trait in one so young. He listened, and what he listened to was the conversation of adults as they discussed philosophic matters normally beyond one of his years. Yes, he heard over and over there was a God, and Christ was his only begotten son and messenger. He came to believe in this God and his envoy without the shadow of a doubt, just as some said he had two thousand years before.

I saw him often, for his parents were dear friends. He was uniformly courteous, yet there was a distance between us, something apart, not an aloofness or detachment, but a reserve, as though he were functioning on a separate level. He had a grave smile, and it was hard to tell what he was thinking, for his face rarely showed emotion. I had never seen him angry or upset, though I am sure there were private moments when he would have liked to cry out his anguish to the heavens. For his eyes, even then, told me he suffered when those about him suffered.

He was a Cayce baby, like so many others whose parents, believing implicitly in Cayce, had asked readings for children unable to speak for themselves. These readings delving into the past were designed to help parents know the potential of their children as a help in guiding their rearing of them. What aptitudes did they have, at what would they excel? What quirks of nature and of temperament should they watch out for? These were the questions parents of Cayce babies threw at the Master from Virginia Beach.

Cayce identified the child in an instant. He took an unusual interest in him. In the first year of the child's life, he gave him four readings, touching on such aspects as health, wealth, and profession, but centered mainly on his innate wisdom and his potential as a teacher in the spiritual community. Cayce died when the boy was three, but not before giving two more readings that indicated the boy would be successful at whatever he put his hand to.

Cayce knew the boy's past, not only as the remarkable psychic he was, but with the consciousness of Lucius of Cyrene as well. For had not his readings said that he dipped for his information into the subconscious minds of everybody who had ever lived?

Knowing that he was dealing with the soul of the dear and glorious physician of the Bible, he predictably picked up on this background, saying, "An unusual career may be had as a doctor."

But he saw still another path for the nephew reborn who had followed spiritually in his footsteps, one with a grander design. And he told the parents:

"Educate, put then in the way of the entity those things that may have to do with every form of those activities, spiritual, mental and material, that may be of help in bringing in the material plane a health-giving force to those that suffer. Let all know that He, the Son [Jesus], healeth thy disease, enlighteneth thy mind, encourage those who seek after him—spiritually, mentally, materially."

Just as Cayce knew the boy, so did that boy, at the age of two, seem to know him. In his affinity to the youngster, whom he remembered from Judea and Egypt land, Cayce had been dangling the boy on his knee. As their eyes met the child smiled and reached up and stroked the man's face with his chubby little hand and said one word, and one word alone. But it was a word that sent a thrill though Cayce. For that word was Ra-Ta, pronounced distinctly and clearly, with a smile of childlike recognition.

"May God bless you always," said Cayce hugging that baby boy to his chest, just as he had embraced his nephew Luke in his baby days.

Cayce was to mention this incident often. It reinforced that which he believed in. "We were related in the Holy Land. He helped me then, with his advice and counsel, just as I want to help him now. He will be heard from one day. He has been given much to do, and he will rise to his responsibilities."

He gave a brief outline for the boy's guidance: "Teaching is indicated in the experience. Thus the unusual opportunity of education by travel, as well as by academics. Spiritual precepts should be especially stressed in this entity's early developing, not by force of might but by reasoning."

The parents gave the boy his head, not trying to influence, not even telling him of the reading. Unbidden he seemed to choose a path that Cayce had foreseen. Entering college as a premedical student, he developed a strong interest in the mind and the spirit, turning from conventional medicine, as the apostle Luke had.

After four years of college, he felt a strong, almost atavistic urge to return to the lands that Luke had trod in Christ's time. Before returning for a postgraduate degree as a clinical psychologist, he toured the Middle East for the U.S. State Department, with special emphasis on developing a youth program. He felt especially at home in Greece and the Holy Land, almost nostalgic by the Sea of Galilee, where Jesus had sailed and fished as a boy. He would gaze for hours at the placid sea, as though expecting Jesus to emerge gently out of the waves.

He felt a close sentimental connection with Christ, visualizing him as he moved among the people, reciting his parables and effecting his cures by touching the sick and the blind. Yet he was fully aware, as near as he felt to the Master, that he had not in any lifetime met him. It was a lifelong regret.

He believed like Cayce that the mind rules the body, and like the Luke of the Bible that relaxation and moderation spelled out a long and happy life. He looked forward to the regression, knowing as a psychologist that this subconscious mind, under hypnosis, would tap into a universal intelligence far transcending any other source. "In the unlikely event that I'm Luke," he said, "I would like to ask what I have to do to realize my mission on this plane. I can't let Edgar Cayce down. He means far too much to me."

To help with the regression, I found a man of many talents. He was a college professor, a Bible scholar familiar with the Gospel of Luke, and an expert hypnotherapist. He was eager like myself, though objectively detached, to explore this mystery of the past—and present—through a subconscious mind never very far from that past.

It was the most thorough of past-life regressions. In all, there were six sessions in which, for the most part, I was a silent attendant.

Robert, as we called him, reminded me of Taylor Caldwell in his grasp of the information his subconscious was dredging out of a memory filling in the gaps in history.

He was taken back gradually. Once under, half-asleep, he spoke of his present boyhood with refreshing detail, seeming to remember each and every playmate and teacher. The hypnotist's voice was soothing, reassuring, even protective, for he wanted his subject to feel secure, responding as though to a friend.

"Please focus your attention on a life prior to this life, receptive to memories, thoughts, or feelings that come from an existence before this lifetime. In selecting a life to remember, trust in the wisdom of your unconscious mind to give you a memory that will be interesting and useful. Share with me any feelings, any visions you get as you open yourself to what the Creative Forces may offer."

He paused, waiting for a response. There was none. Our subject's brow was knotted in a frown. His eyes remained closed, his breathing steady. His body was motionless except for the rippling effect of his respiration. My first feeling of anticipation was giving way to disappointment. The hypnotist seemed unperturbed. He spoke again in a soft voice, crystalizing his question in four words: "What do you see?"

Robert responded in a hesitant voice. "I see a brown robe."

The hypnotist nodded. "A brown robe? Are you wearing this robe?"

Robert's voice was stronger, as though the pictures assembled in his unconscious mind were being blended into the conscious.

"Yes," he replied. "I have a beard, hair on my face, but not much brown curly hair."

Robert was obviously in a different time frame in which he designated the type of dress I had imagined an apostle would wear: simple to the point of plainness, drab in color and design.

"What about your physique?"

"Stocky, shortish, thick forearms, dark brown skin."

He saw himself at that moment as a passenger on a sailing vessel. He was standing on the deck and could see land dotted with houses and larger buildings made of stucco. He was traveling on a body of water known simply as the sea. That would be the Mediterranean, known to the ancients as *le mere*.

"Why are you traveling?"

Robert responded quickly now, in a resonant voice. "I'm going from one place to another, doing my work."

"And that work?"

"I'm a doctor, a physician."

There it was at last, a beginning.

"And you go from place to place to minister to the sick?"

He nodded. "Yes, for wealthy families and others. I give my patients medicines, but it takes more than that very often to heal."

"Do you have some impression of where you live?"

"I live in Greece. On a farm. A little white house. Olive trees. I have some sheep. I live alone."

We still didn't know who he was.

"Do you have a name that you remember?"

"Yes, Luke."

I felt a little thrill. Here without prodding, the man on the couch had given us a name to conjure with, a connection perhaps to Lucius of Cyrene and to Christ.

He had traveled in Greece and Rome, and he had healed the sick and lame wherever he went. He was not yet a Christian, nor had he met any of the apostles, only his uncle, Lucius, the disciple people praised and castigated in the same breath. For while Lucius had done some public good, there were dark whispers about his private life. The hypnotist seized on Lucius as a connecting rod, a recognizable link to the past that could open the floodgates of memory.

"At that point in your life, can you describe Lucius? What did he look like? What kind of a person was he?"

Our Luke had no trouble with this.

"He already had white hair and a sharp nose. He was tall and slender with a little stoop. He had a gentle smile and deep blue eyes." He paused a moment, then said as though in recognition. "He looked like Edgar Cayce."

I didn't know why a soul returning should have a similar face and body. But if he thought the same, as he grew older, there was no reason why his thoughts shouldn't influence his appearance, as often happens with married couples who have lived tranquilly together for a long time.

Robert made a plausible Luke. His responses were typical of that time frame, direct and cogent, to the point. He did not know everything. He found it easy to say, "I don't know," generally the mark of an honest reaction.

I leaned forward as the hypnotist asked, "What was your connection with Lucius?"

There was no hesitation.

"An older uncle. He was with my family in Greece where I live now but moved to Palestine."

"You see him often?"

"Not now. His house in Greece was like mine. White walls, orange and olive trees. We saw each other every day."

I had to laugh at a bit of unconscious humor that slipped into the dialogue.

"He was older than you at that time?"

The sleeping figure replied, "He's still older."

He didn't mind talking about himself, but he was entirely protective of Lucius, veering off when it came to personal issues. "Lucius went on to become an official of the church. I had little to do with the church. I couldn't stand the politics."

What did he know of the man known as the Master?

He had not known him personally, and yet there was a book about him, in Luke's name.

How then had he written about him?

"Knew many who knew him. He interested me because of his healings, so I put down what I heard about him. Kept records of my talks with others. Very important in my learning about healing."

"And you wrote about the Master from your notes during your lifetime?"

"A record in journals, just my own writing. Like a

diary to help me in my work, so I could refer to them from time to time."

He traveled through Greece into Antioch and in the Holy Land, where he would retrace the steps of the Master. As he traveled, he shared his stories about Jesus. He told of a friend named Amos, a Jew, whose whole life was changed by a look from Jesus.

I forgot for a moment it was Robert speaking. I sensed with a thrill that this must have been how Jesus made it all happen: with a look and a touch, capturing the minds and hearts of people. He didn't have to say a word. Amos had helped Jesus step out of a boat. He felt a shock as Jesus touched him, and the look in Jesus' eyes changed his life. He felt he was looking into eternity. He became a new person, leaving his home to study healing and become a missionary. Like Jesus—and Luke—he made the world his family.

Luke himself took a similar course. He never married, though he had female friends and enjoyed their company.

"I was uneasy about marriage, uneasy about its commitment, uneasy with ties. It would have affected my freedom to move about since I traveled a great deal. I had friends and patients in many cities. They paid for my services. I enjoyed the exchange of ideas with so many different people in so many different places and areas of thought."

"You were a traveling physician, making house calls, as it were?"

"It would have been hard with a family."

"How did you travel?"

"Boat mainly, over the sea."

He had begun as a trained physician, tutored in Greece at a school of healing. But he learned much more of medicine in his practice, even before the knowledge of Christ's miracles turned him to psychic healing.

"I treated all forms of illness. Herbs and poultices were the treatments of the day. That was the way I was trained. Later, I got interested in a self-healing energy in the body, healing through the spirit. None of this was taught in the schools."

He used different techniques in his psychic healings.

"There were songs and prayers to stimulate the healing forces of the patient. By the physician alone, not by groups or chanting, nothing like that, but by stimulating energies inside the patient. So he could mobilize the natural immunity in his system."

Luke depended less and less on herbs and other medicines and more on the mustering of a healing vibration from the atmosphere by these stimulating forces he spoke of.

"I was more involved in using prayer and touch as part of my healing. Exciting for me and for those I work with—physicians I have taught these arts of the Master."

With others he had established schools of healing in various cities in the coastal areas of Greece.

"And you teach in these schools?"

"Yes, and speak about the Master. Although that has to be done carefully. The teachings of the Master are not accepted in these schools for the physicians." He would obliquely inject his stories of Jesus' miracles. "I read from my journals the stories of Jesus' healings that had been told to me, and we would talk about those healings and how they could have occurred. And then we'd try them, putting the spirit of the Master in the healing."

I was acceptive of all this, since I had seen how healings worked through the action of the mind and had done some myself in a spontaneous way, knowing from a buzz in my solar plexus, a center of energy, when the effort was effective. I was always surprised when it worked. For there was no visible exchange of energy, only a warmth that came out of the healer's hand that the object of the healing felt as well. It reminded one of what Jesus had said about others, with faith in the Father, being able to accomplish what he did. I had the feeling there was a healing vibration in the atmosphere. The healer was obviously only a channel through which this vibration passed into the subconscious of the individual to be healed.

The hypnotist was obviously intrigued by Robert's command of the subject.

"You said the healing powers were developed over a period of time and improved with understanding. Did you get better at it?"

Our Luke was very sure of himself and quite expansive. I felt as though I were attending one of his lectures on spiritual healing.

"The beginning premise is that it's possible to awaken the healing forces of each cell or each part of the body. And from there we go to how best to awaken those healing forces. We saw how the Indian gurus would shake their rattles and chant, how the prayer group meditated together, and the passing of hands over the body. We experimented with all of these, incorporating ideas from the Orient and from Africa and other cultures as well.

"Students of healing would write the stories as I told them. They shared the stories with their friends and families, and others wrote them down. They would take notes as I read from the journal, and this pleased me, for it introduced an energy exchange important in healing, by evoking the memory or the energy of the event as it happened."

Our Luke's great love was children, as it was in this life. He had pored over many stories of Jesus' healing before he turned to the Master's way in the case of a twelve-year-old girl who was paralyzed from the hips down after falling from a tree. The conventional therapies he applied had failed, and only then did he apply the spiritual treatment still untried in his own experience.

We could almost see it happening, it was such a vivid picture he drew. "The child's legs had begun to lose their tone. We exercised her legs, manipulating them back and forth, and gave deep massage. There was not that much improvement. Unknown to us at the time, her spinal column had been injured in the fall. We realized after months of massage that it would be physically impossible for her to walk unless she could get help from another source. I finally decided to test what I had been hearing about Jesus' healings. A group of our physicians joined hands, forming a circle with the girl in the center. We prayed and meditated, putting a white light around her. You could feel the energy rising in the room, all directed at her, like a physical force."

The girl's face took on a new tone. Her eyes began to glow. She pushed down on her hands to thrust herself out of her chair. She made a strenuous effort, gritting her teeth. And then, to their delight and amazement, she stood up by herself and took a few tentative steps.

"She fell a few times as she walked, for her legs were weak from disuse, but she continued to walk the next

day and the day after. That was the important thing. She
never gave up. Her spinal column had been normalized
by the energy given off by the healing treatment, stimulating her own energy. She was cured. The rest was up
to her."

It was an emotional experience he never forgot.
"Whenever we physicians met after that, we would em-
brace each other and weep. For it marked our birth as
a spiritual community."

And that, as I looked at it, was where he stood today.
The leader of a spiritual community with Cayce looking
over his shoulder and guiding him as he had before. Like
others in his group, he was not alone. He had never been
alone, no more than Cayce or the rest.

I found myself in a strange dichotomy of time and
place. Robert was so much as I imagined Luke to be that
he seemed out of place lying on a couch in a small room
in Virginia Beach. I fancied him striding along the roads
of the Middle East, sailing the inland seas, helping people as help was needed, not giving a thought to his own
comfort or convenience. And so he was in this life, an
indefatigable counselor, with always a kind word for old
companions, much older than himself, who beat a path
to his door. Nobody was turned away, and each and
every one—man, woman, and child—felt better for
knowing him. Many of the elders, confident they had
known him long ago, nodded wisely and said, "He was
born with the wisdom of the ages."

The impulse to be a physician had been strong in his
youth, as it had been for Luke, but he resisted this, waiting for a post where he felt he could do the most good.

Not knowing that Cayce had spoken of him as the
sainted physician of antiquity even as a child, he had still
maintained a lively interest in the Luke of the Bible.
During a break in the sessions, he plied us with questions, saying he had felt some sort of transformation taking place inside him. "It's probably the usual reaction to
an altered state of consciousness," he said lightly.

I laughed. "Hardly usual."

Like Luke, he was always probing, always looking for
reasons. He would have liked knowing that Luke had
rummaged around for whatever remedy had cured his
twelve-year-old patient.

The answer came in meditation. "As I thought about what had transpired," said our Luke, "I had an idea that it was possible to raise the vibrations or the energies of the body to a level at which a healing of any illness could take place."

The concept of Jesus the Healer had burst on him like a bombshell. When he first heard the Master's name and what he did for people, he had been emotionally overcome, and wept, without knowing why he should be so affected. Perhaps he had felt the lingering presence of the Master himself, for he had first heard of Christ's healings in a home by the sea where the Master had once visited.

"My friend, who knew the Master, told me one story after another about his wonders, and with each story my eyes would fill up, and the whole course of my destiny changed. I was his, and in a way, he was mine."

Luke, with each new record of Christ's miracles, began to assume a different and more exalted view of the Master he loved, without having ever known him except by the tremor of his own mind and body.

As our time frame advanced, the Luke of our regressions advanced with it. Eventually, listening to Lucius and other eyewitness accounts of Christ's uniqueness, he came to believe as Lucius did.

In a sense, it was Lucius's views that dominated so much of the Gospel of Luke. "Lucius worshiped the Master," said our Luke, "and considered him the only begotten Son of God."

The hypnotist, a staunch Christian, had seemed shaken by our Luke's earlier impiety. Ironically, we were seeing a transformation. The hypnotizer, insensibly, was becoming the hypnotized by the reality of Luke's image under hypnosis.

"How," he asked, "did Lucius reach this conclusion when you didn't?"

Our Luke didn't seem at all nettled as he explained the love of Christ presumably astir in Cayce even then. "It was an inner conviction from Lucius's own observations, seeing the look on his face as he was led off to the cross, the glow in his eyes at his liberation, to become again a companion of the Lord. Then learning of the Resurrection, Lucius, imbued with Greek mythology, saw Christ as a god who could give his life or receive it as he wished."

So far there was nothing about Theophilus to whom Luke had addressed his Gospel and Acts.

"He was a follower of the Master, a Greek, a close friend. He stayed with me often in my home outside Athens, and he looked through the journals with me. I wanted to acknowledge his support and interest. I thought it would please him."

But it was Lucius he listened to by the hour, with whom he shared the joys and sorrows of the Master and eventually his beliefs.

"We influenced each other in a good way. He was interested in my ideas of healing, and I in sharing his stories of the Master."

So there it was, perhaps, that hidden source, that eyewitness account that came alive in so many passages in the Book of Luke and Acts. Was it Lucius then who was responsible for some great moments of Luke's Gospel, as when Jesus rebuked his disciples for suggesting he destroy those who did not receive him?

"For the Son of man is not come to destroy men's lives, but to save them."

The reality of Luke was so strong that we could not resist the opportunity to inquire about Lucius's controversial personal life. Our Luke, in the role of a loyal nephew, was reluctant to discuss Lucius's affairs with women except to acknowledge that it did create a problem in a young church struggling to survive. "Some people were upset." But Lucius was an important cog in the Judean-Greek church, serving in his travels as a bridge between the groups, just as Edgar Cayce with his broad philosophy was a bridge in this lifetime between the East and the West.

Since the soul was a continuing entity, did he recognize the presence of Lucius's soul in this lifetime?

He nodded, his lips barely moving. "That soul was Edgar Cayce."

How, I thought, would he as Luke have known that, living some two thousand years before Edgar Cayce was born? But then of course, Robert was a continuing soul, Luke reborn, if he was anything at all of what he said.

"He came forward in the present to serve the church

again, in a different way. As Lucius, a bishop, he was caught in the structure, without much latitude. But in this life he triumphed over the past and was liberated, becoming his own man, healing people in his own way.

Luke, as he lay there, presumably author of one of the four Gospels, seemed an ideal channel to pose the question that all humanity was eager to know—the mystery of death.

The man on the couch did not hesitate.

"A part of us survives the death of the physical body. That is the soul, which exists forever."

"And what happens to this soul?"

"Continues in its relation to the one force, the Divine Intelligence."

"Can you share with us your thoughts as you approached death and passed over?"

"A sense of peace. In my home in Greece. It was a bright day, birds singing, the smell of ripe olives and olive oil and warm dry air. A sense of peace and comfort, no fear at all of dying, excited at the prospect of what lay ahead. A sense of certainty that with the death of the physical body that connection with the Creative Force might be felt more clearly. And with that a sense of anticipation. I had led a full life, lonely at times, but I brought that on myself. I was happy to be moving on."

How wonderful, I thought, for this great and good man, believing in an afterlife, to lie peacefully in the home he loved, looking out on his gardens. How wonderful that he could contemplate his renewal in spirit before he returned one day, fresh and vigorous, to again do battle with life and get on with what he had learned.

And now that he, the spirit of Luke, had tasted deeply of life, how did it affect his present lifetime? Wasn't that what reincarnation was all about, doing something about your karma, not talking airily about it and not moving about in the clouds, rubbing elbows with kings and queens and the like?

"In light of those lessons as Luke, can you conclude any direction in this life to continue your spiritual growth?"

Our Luke was ready. Not for nought was he called the good companion.

"To build on that commitment to help awaken that

potential for the action of the One Force in our lives, to work toward that in myself and others. To awaken the specific skills developed in that life, to be applied especially to children, and to spread the word of healing in the Christ way."

All this, we agreed, this Luke was already doing. He believed in the word of the Master. He was into holistic medicine and all healing with the power of the mind, the human and the universal mind. He was the Luke I would have chosen for the role, full of love for humanity, dearly loving to work with children. He may never have known Christ in person, as he said, but he lived every day in his image, a Christian in thought and deed. Lucius would have been proud of him.

He sat up and rubbed his eyes, the last of the sessions concluded. He gave me a questioning glance and said with a twinkle in his eye, "How did I do?"

"You sounded more like Luke than Luke," I said with a laugh.

And the Bible scholar added with a smile:

"And that is the Gospel truth."

CHAPTER 15

Hail, Hail . . .

"Yes," said ninety-eight-year-old Helen Ellington, "the whole gang of us were with Mister Cayce in Egypt land, and the Lord only knows where we're all going to be the next time around."

Her daughter, Margaret Ellington Wilkins, who was a youngish seventy-five, laughed. "Never mind mother," she said. "She likes to startle people. But the fact of the matter is that we all were in Egypt with Edgar Cayce: my father; my husband, Mac; my aunt; and my niece; and all thirteen members in the first Cayce study group; and then some.

"Most of our group were also in colonial Virginia, in Jamestown and Williamsburg, as Cayce was. This is the way, I suppose, that incarnations have to come in, with the people you have to do with. In one incarnation, like Williamsburg, you deal with certain people, and in Egypt with the same people or others, depending on what you're aiming for in this life."

There was one fixed point—Cayce. "Everybody close to him came back to him. He was Ra; he was Uhjltd. He was a disciple in Christ's time. We all came together to be with him and each other. We were innovators then, as we are now, in the metaphysical. We started something in Virginia Beach, and it's still growing. People thought my mother was crazy in the beginning because she became such a leader in something most people sneered at. But she persevered."

She looked fondly at her mother, who was sitting sedately on the sofa in their comfortable living room, looking from one to the other with a questioning face.

"My mother doesn't hear that well anymore," Margaret said, "but she can pick up things just looking at you."

I could see why Edgar Cayce had singled out Helen

254

Ellington to be a leader in his cause. Just sitting still,
looking out calmly, she conveyed an impression of ageless wisdom. I had been told of her fabulous memory
and her positive outlook on reincarnation specifically and
life generally. She was one of the special few, Edgar
Cayce had said, who could invoke the distant past almost
at will.

Unlike so many others with life readings in ancient
Egypt, she had never felt the need to wander through its
pyramids and mosques or meander through the Holy
Land and mark the Fourteen Stations of the Cross. She
had been in Egypt many times in her past, when it was
a far different land from what it is today, when the man
they called Ra was the leader she followed into exile.
She had gone over it all many, many times in her mind—
a mind still sharp, which, in the twilight of life, was more
soul than body, more spirit than flesh. She carried herself
proudly. For she, with Irene Seiberling Harrison, was the
oldest living member of the A.R.E. and the dear friend
of Edgar and Gertrude Cayce. And she remained the
reigning head of her family, clear and bright, mobile,
sensitive about her diminished hearing but pointing out
that, in walling her off from casual conversation, it had
made her more introspective and sharpened her memory
of things past.

"Not seeing as well as I used to, or hearing, I stay by
myself a lot. But I never get lonely. You need to be
alone sometimes to get acquainted with yourself. Mister
Cayce taught me that. And I guess that's what I try to
do, get acquainted with myself."

She had come to the realization that nothing was accidental. It was no accident, she knew, that a friend had
prevailed on her to attend a lecture at the A.R.E. some
sixty years ago. Nor that she picked out a man sitting in
the front row.

Helen Ellington's still-handsome face broke into a
smile. "It turned out that was Mister Cayce. And that
one look was all that was necessary. I wanted to be a
part of whatever it was he was doing. There was a feeling
of familiarity, a bond I couldn't explain at the time. It
was as if it were the most natural thing in the world."

She had made the calm assumption, as her daughter
had, that I believed in reincarnation. But now she was

not so sure. She was able to divine my thoughts perfectly, by reading my mind or my face. It was not so much that I was questioning reincarnation as their easy acceptance of it. This, too, she saw with a trace of amusement, though I had said nothing of my feelings.

"You remind me of this young man who had just graduated from college and had his master's degree, a good job, and a new car and all that. And he said to me, 'You believe in reincarnation, don't you?' " She smiled sweetly in return. "I was just a nobody sitting there next to him, but something inside of me said, 'Be careful how you answer that.'

"So I said, 'No, Bob, I don't believe in reincarnation. I believe reincarnation is a fact. If you believe in something, that makes it some kind of ism. The way I feel about it, it's a fact.'

"So after a while this young fellow said, 'I never heard it explained like that before.' And I had to laugh to myself, for I really hadn't explained it.

"Edgar Cayce told me one time, 'If you know the question, you know the answer.' So this was a question from within myself. And the answer, born of the same energy, followed it."

"Do you think that made a believer of Bob?"

She shook her head. "Not till he's ready. But it did give him something to think about."

What, I wondered, had made her ready?

"Had you a feeling you had known Cayce before?"

"Oh, yes, but it was more than that. I had many readings after that. I took a great delight in seeing people get help from the readings. Yet as often as I went there and saw all he did, it still looked like the impossible. I said to him one day, 'I guess you get tired of me sitting here watching the readings. But something about them just holds me.'

"He said, 'I'm glad to know that. I can give a much better reading when you're sitting at my feet.' " She sighed a little, "I felt as if I'd always been at his feet. He didn't seem strange, and Mrs. Cayce didn't seem strange. None of her family and none of his family was strange to me. They'd come over whenever they liked, and we'd wander over to see them. I'd fall right in with the people that came to see him as well. I had the feeling I belonged

there. Reincarnation was new to me then. I hadn't
thought it out yet. But the friendships I understood, for
they were heartwarming and tangible, even before I realized from exchanging readings with friends that we had
all known each other before.

"I'd never heard the word *psychic* before I knew Mister Cayce. My sister, Jane Williams, had called me one
day and said there's a new hospital being built in Virginia
Beach and a doctor's going to run it. She said, 'They tell
me this doctor goes to sleep and tells you what's wrong
with you.' I said, 'Hooray for that. I don't even listen to
the ones that tell me what's wrong when they're awake.'
But, as I said, when I met Mister Cayce that all
changed."

She had said that to believe, a person had to be ready.
I was sure something of a practical nature had occurred
to make this strong-minded woman ready. There had
been the tug of an old life perhaps, a comfortable feeling
of déjà vu, something one could put a finger on. And,
of course, there was. One of the impossible things Cayce
had done was to get a friend's handicapped child to sit
up in a high chair and hold a spoon when it could do
neither before.

"This got me thinking about Mister Cayce helping my
daughter, Thelma, whose nervous system had been affected by a respiratory infection. You never knew what
she was going to do or say. She had all kinds of little
nervous habits, like twisting her arms and legs around
while she was walking. And then as she got older, she'd
use bad language; I didn't know what to make of it. One
day I thought I'd take her and walk into the Atlantic
Ocean, and neither of us could swim. But I knew that
wasn't the answer. I had gone to the best doctor in Nor-
folk, and he said, 'Maybe if she'd get married it might
help.' But I knew it wasn't a sex problem. It was deeper
than that. So then I went to my minister, and he shook
his head and said, 'I don't know what to advise you.'

"So I decided on a reading for Thelma, since nobody
else could help. Mister Cayce had a hospital going then,
and he had a Doctor Lydic running it. His reading said
Thelma should get treatments for eight or nine weeks.
This was during the Depression, and I didn't have money
for the hospital. So I told Mister Cayce to please go back

to sleep and give me another reading telling me how to carry it out.

"He laughed and said, 'Why do you feel like that?'

" 'Because the reading said she had to go to the hospital, and I don't have any hospital money.'

"So he told me to talk it over with the doctor and make what arrangements I could. There was no difficulty. Mister Cayce made us feel like a little family, which we were. But it took sixteen weeks because neither the doctor nor I understood the importance of sticking to every little detail of the reading. The reading said she had to be directed closely in everything she did: her school, play, dressing herself, everything, to bring some order in her life. So I saw now I had a part in it as well. The readings continued every two weeks, and in time, with her walking so many hours on the beach, her embroidery, resting, getting her electrical treatments, every minute of her day was occupied, and soon her nervous habits disappeared, and she was normal. And I didn't have to walk into the ocean after all.

"So I decided I'd get a reading from Mister Cayce and look into this reincarnation business. I figured if he could help Thelma, so that she married and had a family, he could do anything."

Again and again I noted that it was through his miracles of healing that Cayce brought his people, as he thought of them, to an acceptance of the lives they shared in the past and their influence on the present. His message was more important than a healing, however helpful, for it was a message of everlasting life.

"When you got to thinking about it," Helen Ellington said, "it all became clear—his being with us and our being with our little group. It was the most natural thing in the world, if you were coming back, to come back with people you knew before. How else could you work things out?"

She smiled as she thought about it. "That put me into Egypt and Persia and all those places and gave me something to think about, for I had been with Mister Cayce many times before."

In Egypt she had been a teacher and a counselor, just as she had been in this life, and she had ruffled the feathers of the young Pharaoh who was trying to resist the

Ra's extensive building program. She joined with Ra after his exile to build up the schools of religious thought, namely the Temple of Sacrifice and the Temple Beautiful.

"That was a long time ago. And before that I was with him in Atlantis, where we all started, and after that in Persia, where I came under Mister Cayce's influence when he was a tribal chief trying to make something of people by healing them. So it became obvious to me why I had this connection with him and why I was so interested in what he was doing. In the same way I thought it might be a good idea for everybody in the family to get a reading, so we'd have a better idea of why we all came together."

It was natural for Helen's daughter to become interested, not so much because of the parental relationship, but through a tendency to be drawn in from a past they had all shared. And this feeling increased, as Margaret grew older, in her marriage to Mac Wilkins, the only sweetheart she had ever known—now and before.

As a teenager, Margaret had no way of knowing why she was so interested in Cayce, attributing it to her mother's activity. But she was so carried away talking about Cayce that the other children would poke fun at her. The explanation came in her first Cayce reading, which revealed to her that she had been with her mother in Egypt, joining Ra in his exile.

"What made it so realistic," said Margaret, "was that we had all this closeness before we got the explanation. So it wasn't like Mister Cayce was influencing whatever had occurred. He only explained it."

I had been sitting with the family in their comfortable Virginia Beach home, looking out on a lake, thinking how much they reminded me of the average upper-middle-class American family. Margaret's husband, Mac Wilkins, was a practical man, a successful plumbing contractor. And as he remained silent through most of the discussion, I had the idea that he was not a believer. Though he had a physical reading with Cayce, he had not shown any interest in the Cayce study groups or any affiliation with Cayce.

Margaret found this lack of enthusiasm quite understandable. "We were in the same Egyptian experience with Cayce," she said, "but Mac was among those who counseled that the priest Ra be sent into exile." She laughed. "Mister Cayce hit that one right on the nose." She gave her husband a tolerant look. "I guess," she said, "nothing has changed."

It was a family divided, where Cayce was concerned, said Margaret, just as it had been in Egypt. Her father, Alex Ellington, had never joined any Cayce study group. But he did have a Cayce reading that presented the family with a satisfactory explanation. "He had been a judge in that experience," Margaret said, "representing the throne in mediating with the rebellious Atlantean émigrés headed by Ra. He had never approved of Ra—or Cayce—and, like Mac back then, was happy to see him banished."

She smiled.

"He couldn't do enough for Mac, taking him into his plumbing business and all that. They were like two peas in a pod in their convictions. Never disagreeing. Just like old times."

Helen Ellington's keen intellect and her enduring quality, her deft handling of the vicissitudes of life, lent a semblance of reality to her convictions. She had not come by it easily, not without reaching deeply into her own soul mind. She had asked all the questions I had and marked each and every turn in the road in understanding humanity's purpose in life. It was the soul she had finally become concerned with, that continuous denominator in human existence, surviving when the transient body had become dust. She became everyman—everywoman— looking to find herself, to become a child of the universe to which she had previously been alien.

"What happened to me," she said, "could have happened to anybody who wasn't deaf and dumb and blind. I didn't know enough about reincarnation to even ask questions about it. Then after I got into Mister Cayce's work, I got more and more interested. And I began to think of reincarnation and evolution together."

Like others in the room, I had been listening intently, for whatever she said was meaningful, based on her many sojourns on this planet.

"By evolution, do you mean we came from the sea?"

"No, does a rosebud grow in the sea? It grows in the earth . . ."

"So what do you mean by evolution?"

"I mean growth. Development of the body and mind, as there was in the beginning in Egypt under Ra." She gave me a gentle smile. "And reincarnation, of course, involves the development of the soul, the learning process, and the awakening of remembrance."

What growth could there be for millions of babies who die every year around the world? What had they learned of life before they were so tragically lost to disease or hunger?

"A little baby dies at three or four months or is stillborn. A young girl is killed at twelve. How do you account for a soul coming into earth and dying before it has a chance to learn anything?"

She had no trouble with that, for she had studied at the feet of the great Ra.

"The reasons are varied. Sometimes it's to teach the parents a lesson. Other times a soul needs to stop over—perhaps to help somebody on its way to another plane. The soul is in the subconscious, and every child has an active subconscious. They remember even before they're born."

With a start, I suddenly remembered my novelist friend Taylor Caldwell (in an earlier book) recalling in a hypnotic regression her mother falling down stairs to dispose of the fetus she was carrying.

And that unborn child had remembered.

For Taylor, it explained, as nothing else could, a lifelong hostility for her mother. In Helen Ellington I had found a voice close to the source of universal knowledge here and in ancient Egypt for nobody had been closer in thought to Edgar Cayce than she. It was almost as though I were questioning Cayce.

"When we die and the soul goes to another level of consciousness, will we get together with the same husband and wife as before to overcome the mistakes of the past?"

"Not necessarily. Jesus answered that pretty well when he said, 'In heaven there are no marriages.' And in the end, we become companions of the Lord."

"And how often do we come back?"

"As often as a soul needs. And whatever it needs depends on what it has done. You can't blame anybody else for what's happening to you. That's one of the hardest lessons I had to learn. You blame no one but yourself. And don't waste too much time on that. Just do something about it. Try self-control. That's important in life. Mister Cayce often stressed that. And the only life that counts is the present. For the now is always with you; it is the future before you know it."

Oddly, with all her hearing problems, she had no trouble understanding me.

"I see it in your mind, just as you do," she said, with a twinkle in her eye. "Mister Cayce did that all the time. He knew what you were going to say before you said it. It could be distracting, but you got used to it."

I returned many times to the Ellington home in Virginia Beach, going through a learning process, not so much on reincarnation itself, but as to how people responded to it and made it work for them. They were so amiable I found myself wondering whether I had known anyone in this family before, thinking that if I had known one I must have known all, for they were as congenial as so many seals on the beach. There was nothing esoteric—or exotic—about them.

What impressed me as we talked was their down-to-earth humor. They could not only laugh at a joke but at themselves.

Since Mac's name was D. J. Wilkins, for Dempsey James, I had wondered where the Mac came from.

Margaret Wilkins laughed.

"Remember the old comic strip, Tillie and Mac? Well, Mac as a youngster had a date with a girl in the office where he worked . . ."

"And her name was Tillie."

"Yeah, somebody said there goes Tillie and Mac. And Mac it was. Even when there was no longer a Tillie."

Mac was a bit of an enigma to me. For while acknowledging that a Cayce reading had saved him from an appendectomy, he was loathe to discuss the mystical, though quietly accepting his Egyptian experience. Yet he did not hesitate to consult Cayce on practical matters.

After the marriage, now in its fifty-seventh year, Mac had asked Cayce, "Which name should I use, my given name, Dempsey James, or my nickname, Mac? And why does my wife prefer the nickname?"

Cayce replied, "Use the nickname. James Dempsey or Dempsey James does not coordinate with the activities of the entity or the entities associated with him or its activities in the past. Mac becomes rather a part of the whole of the association of the entity with the mate."

And to be sure, Margaret and Mac had a ring to it.

And so Mac it stayed. And it may very well have had something to do with Mac's success. For he was a born salesperson, as his wife said, and the easy informality of the name seemed to suit him.

"Looking back," said Margaret, "I can see where Mac's reading fit him pretty well. Mac had a lot to do with sanitary conditions in this lifetime, people having the water they need. And he had that to do in settling in Jamestown, so there may be some influence there.

"The readings said he should have gone into music. And he should have. He had a beautiful singing voice and would sing in church and shows we had. But he never did anything with it. He became a plumber and did very well with that, as Cayce said he would."

When I saw Helen tiring, I would address my questions to Margaret, for mother and daughter thought pretty much along the same lines.

"Have you any idea," I asked, "why you all came together?"

Margaret had no trouble with this, for she and her mother had lived it many times. I saw Helen Ellington nodding with a smile as her daughter replied, "So we could work things out. Mac and I were always together." She smiled. "In Palestine he was my father. I always think of it as incest somehow. I guess the condition had to be worked out. We were together in Williamsburg, and that wasn't too many incarnations ago. Edgar Cayce said I looked out a window in that life and saw Mac, and that was it."

It had been almost like that again. "Mac recognized me the first time we met. I was fifteen, and he was seventeen, not old enough to know what we were doing. But there never was anybody else. That may account for the comfortable feeling I've always had with Mac. There was never any rivalry."

Mac was still uninvolved. He didn't seem very interested, for somebody who had knocked around in Egypt and Williamsburg and God knows where else. Margaret agreed. "He's into what he sees that's working or is of benefit practically. He had a condition where the intestines were pressing against the appendix, and it looked serious for a while. Cayce gave him a reading, which kept him from an appendectomy. He had no trouble believing that."

She laughed, as though Mac weren't sitting there. He didn't seem to mind.

"Another time he was having a physical reading. And he was out working on the Getty horse farm and moving around. Cayce, given the address, opened the reading by saying, 'Now keep still for a moment.' " She gave her husband a fond smile.

"Mac can't get away from being in Egypt with us. And he knows it. Ra got us all together in the temples. It reminds me of that old song, 'Hail, Hail, the Gang's All Here.' Dave Kahn was among the first from Egypt. And there was Harold Reilly and Eula Allen [an author of the Search for God series]. A whole slew of them. It accounts for Mister Cayce's feelings and our feelings. Egypt was a time of crisis when it all could have been swallowed up if people like us hadn't rallied around Ra in exile. Just like now. Dave Kahn was one of the early boosters. He was pushing Edgar Cayce even before World War I. Mister Cayce used to say, 'When Dave got on a train or a bus, he'd stand right up in front of everybody and tell them about Edgar Cayce and the things he did, as though it was the most natural thing in the world.' It sort of got that way in our house, too."

Although the A.R.E. was Christian-oriented, with a sleeping Cayce proclaiming Christ's word, there was a strong Judean influence. A few of the Jewish members in Cayce's inner circle had been with Cayce in many lives— Egypt, Palestine, Persia, Arabia—and had hearkened to a call out of their pasts. And Cayce himself, as the Judaic-Christian disciple Lucius of Cyrene, had a good understanding of the Jewish faith.

Margaret, particularly, with a life in ancient Judea, felt very much at home with Jewish people, though of an old Southern family herself.

"The Jewish people in the A.R.E., like Dave Kahn, were back many times, before Palestine, learning to develop the soul. We are all meeting again. We're searching for the same thing, our own soul development, so we will one day be fit companions for the Lord. Abraham was the first to accept one God. Before that everybody worshiped many gods. But Abraham gave the Jewish people the one supreme God, and God said, 'I choose you because you have chosen me.' " She laughed. "Some say you had to be a Jew once to be a Christian."

In Palestine, Margaret had been a young mother whose son had been wrested from her by the cruel edict of King Herod, who ruled the Holy Land by the sufferance of Rome.

"The entity," said Cayce, "was then among those mothers whose young were taken from them at the edict, for the destruction of the children that the son of Mary might be destroyed also."

Margaret was twenty-one, married but still childless, when she had this reading, which had its reverberations even in this lifetime.

"Why do I have fear especially in darkness?" she had asked the sleeping Cayce.

"This," he answered, "is from those periods when there was the destruction by the soldiery; for the young were hidden in darkness, and they took the body unaware."

"Are the eyes I see when meditating an optical illusion or something with meaning?"

"Rather of meaning; for that soul thou lost in Nazareth may again come to thee in this experience, if ye would make thyself as a channel for such an event in this sojourn."

And there was a child to replace that which had been taken—but, ironically, a girl.

"Why do I have such a great love for children?" she asked.

"For as he gave, 'It is as Rachel weeping for her children and is not comforted until she knows that which was lost there is in her arms again.' "

There was a note, attached to this reading, that caught my eye. "Her daughter had been such a blessing, more

so now that she is a mother and a home builder. She feels
one of her daughter's children is that son in Palestine."

And so through the daughter had come the lost son,
warming the grandmother's heart and quickening the
bonds of affection.

In time, the whole family became involved. All her
life, Ann Lynne Wagner Tynes, Helen's granddaughter,
had been aware of a heritage inextricably tied to the past.
Once a Cayce baby, with a reading when she was eighteen days old, and now an attractive woman of fifty, she
was as fascinated by her past as the others of the Ellington clan. Judea, Egypt, and colonial Virginia were all in
her background. During a field trip when a schoolgirl of
ten, she had a strong feeling of recall as, sitting in the
school bus, she looked out on a restored government
building in Williamsburg. The 300-year-old replica was
totally familiar, though she had not seen it before.

She was eager to be regressed, for she felt it might
turn up something from the past with some bearing on
the present. She was regressed on three occasions, and
each time she had a tendency to analyze the images that
came to her under the shallow hypnosis characterizing
many time regressions. Nevertheless, she drew a connected narrative of the ritual in Egypt's Temple of Sacrifice, rounding out a still incomplete picture of the mating
process.

She was, first, an altar girl and later an aide to the
priests supervising the healing program. And then, passing muster, she became a participant in the project to
produce the perfect offspring, this being one of Ra's most
cherished dreams. Under hypnosis it soon developed that
she had lived as a child in the Temple of Sacrifice, apart
from the mother who bore her, dedicated to the will of
the state. Her simple wants were all taken care of—food,
clothing, and shelter. Love was spoken of, but it was a
love instilled by a system that thought of love as something impersonal, desirable only because of the objective.

As she spoke, the Virginia matron disappeared. She
was twelve years old, one of a group of young girls, clad
in virginal white, preparing the sacrificial maidens. Her
voice became airy, almost childish, wondering, as though
recalling something long forgotten that had once de-

lighted and entranced her. It was so true, so natural, yet so low-keyed, I could almost visualize the scene myself.

"I see a priest on the altar, with another person. I seem to be running around bringing things, like flowers. There's a bowl of water with a mist. I see a young woman, of great beauty, with the priest. She's lying down on a raised platform. Her skin is fair, but her eyebrows and hair are dark.

"She is older but still barely twenty. There's no fear or horror about the sacrifice. It's not a negative thing. I feel comfortable with it. The sacrifice is not a blood sacrifice. The girl seems to be embracing a new philosophy and a new life. The priest is performing some sort of ritual and is making some signs with his hands, much like a Catholic priest would today. He's holding the bowl, and I'm standing beside him. I approach the platform with him. The water is creating a slight mist, but it doesn't appear to be hot. I'm holding my hand to the woman. She sits up on the platform, puts her legs to the side. She is in white and has flowers in her hair in a wreath around her head. I'm leading her now, holding her hand. She looks happy and serene. There are six or seven others, dressed the same way, waiting to go through the same ceremony. In this ritual the priest is sprinkling her with the water, which is still misty."

As Ann paused, seeming to come to the end of this recollection, I advanced her to the age of twenty, the age of the young woman who had been the central figure of the ceremony not quite completed. She was now in the place of that woman, taking a similar posture on the altar of the Temple of Sacrifice in ancient Egypt. She spoke in the same wondering voice, as though astonished at something of the enchanting past coming back to her.

"I had grown now," she said, "to the time when I was up on the altar and was one of the novitiates. I had been a water carrier before, and I notice other younger girls doing that now. We are all there to be of service, to go through an apprenticeship and become one of this group, first taking care of the sick and assisting the priests in the healings . . . and then moving on from there to what we were trained ultimately to do."

"Do you have any contact with Ra?"

"We all do."

She seemed to be mulling it over quietly. And then cried out in almost ecstatic surprise.

"Oh, my goodness. He is the father of these perfect children."

"Not all of them?"

"No, there are others. I take care of some of the children. They are not any one woman's children. It's as if they're all everybody's. But each mother knows which child she gave birth to; there is nothing impersonal about that."

"And the priests who are the fathers of all these children? Are they chosen to be the best there is? And who chooses them?"

"Ra. He picks the fathers and performs the cleansing ceremony with the bowl of water."

I was curious about a state of affairs where women gladly gave themselves for the good of the nation, without any emotional involvement. It seemed to me to be contrary to nature, though I suppose anything was natural if you were told long enough that it was.

"After the woman has a child, does she ever have sex again and produce any more perfect children?"

"She just has the child. It's physical; it has to be. But it's really done for a greater cause, regardless of what others may think."

"Doesn't anybody think it wrong to have sex without loving one another?"

"Well, they do love each other, as they consider what they're sharing and why. But the primary idea is not to make love; it's to make a child who will add to the nation."

"And do the fathers have any interest in their offspring?"

"They have an interest. And they have opportunities to have more and more children, to increase the numbers of perfected children, while it's more difficult for women by their very nature."

It seemed a rather one-sided equation, with the propagating men having all the better of it.

"And the women have to do this, whether they want to or not?"

She shook her head.

"This is what they were trained to do. There is nothing

to discuss. There are no negatives. This is what they were born for."

Many images were flashing across Ann's consciousness, with such rapidity she couldn't fully express them until I took her out of a period she seemed to be struggling with.

She sat up and rubbed her eyes. She was in a bit of a daze, in that curious dichotomy of regression hypnosis, half-conscious of the present while still sorting out the subconscious impressions of that ancient past.

She finally seemed to come out of it.

"I had many impressions I didn't respond with," she said, "for I didn't want to make any hasty judgments. These were very human, physical people. They were dealing in physical values; that was the experience they were in. I wouldn't discount the human element. No matter what the ideals were, what the purpose or the goals. . . . People aren't machines, not when thrown together as they were."

I was a little surprised at her vehemence.

"All this was passing through your mind during the regression?"

"I didn't seem to be able to verbalize it. Maybe it was because I was so much a part of it. But we weren't dealing with robots. We weren't dealing with misty spirits but human beings who went through a certain amount of soul-searching to do what they had to do, one with the other."

Ann was a little more spirited and defensive than any objective observer would have been. But then in her subconscious she was very much involved, first as an altar girl, then again as a young woman engaged in an exalted mission in the name of the fatherland. It was as though she were a spokeswoman for the people of her past.

"It's very human," she repeated, "and that doesn't mean it's wrong. God put us here in human, physical form. The leaders, the priests, said this is how it's done. This is how we can reproduce a better race. God could have chosen a different path and just allotted reproduction to the soul. But we do need physical bodies to house the souls. And these people had souls, great souls. And they reproduced souls, which is how so many souls came into being."

Not since Taylor Caldwell emerged as the mother of Mary Magdalene under attack in a Jerusalem square had any regression moved me as this experience of Ann Wagner Tynes. There was little doubt that the images charging through her mind were very real to her. In their actuality, the events she described were as vivid as any I had ever witnessed as a reporter. But now it was over, and with some regret I bid the Ellington family a fond farewell. Helen Ellington walked me to the door. On the threshold, we stood and looked at each other for a long moment.

"You know," she said, "you never got into my soul consciousness."

I nodded and waited.

She gave me a piercing glance.

"Do you know what a soul is?"

I thought of an Edgar Cayce definition. "Is it that part of us that relates to our Creator?"

She shook her head. "No," she said, "you are a soul. And that is all you are—a living, breathing soul that never dies." She smiled and looked deeply into my eyes. "And know that you are never alone—for the companions you knew best are still your companions."

There was no doubt in my mind who that might be as I looked back into her eyes and saw the light that was there. We had just renewed an old friendship.

CHAPTER 16

Thanks for the Memories

They would just look at each other, these companions from the past, across a crowded room or a Laundromat and feel a closeness that went back a number of lifetimes. They were people, quite often, who didn't make friends easily. Yet, to their own astonishment, they would find themselves hobnobbing with strangers they ordinarily would no more than nod to.

"It really amazed me," said Mignon Helms, "the way I became friendly with the Ellingtons. For normally I kept very much to myself. But as Margaret Ellington [Wilkins] and I were waiting for our children to finish their dancing lessons, our eyes met. We started talking, as mothers will, about their children, then went on to talking about ourselves and our husbands. She was so easy to be with that I found myself wishing we could see more of each other. She must have read my mind, for she invited me over to her home to help sew the children's costumes."

And there, of course, she met Helen Ellington.

"I was enchanted. We had no more than said hello than Mrs. Ellington began talking to me about Edgar Cayce. I had never heard anything like it. She would talk for hours about Cayce, and I never got tired of listening. I couldn't get enough of the man. I went to the Ellington house regularly for a year after that, boning up on Cayce. I was fascinated. And I soon discovered why. The Ellingtons urged me to have a reading. I really didn't need any urging. Yet, as I look back, I think I was a little apprehensive that I might be disappointed, let down, after the big buildup."

There was no danger of that. When she walked into Cayce's study, she only had to look at him once to know that he, like Margaret, was an old friend.

"I couldn't take my eyes off him. And it wasn't like a man and woman caring for each other, more like a pupil looking up to her teacher. His eyes looked right through me, and I remembered hearing how he could tell what kind of person you were by looking at your aura. Helen Ellington had told me how the whole Ellington family had been in ancient Egypt with Cayce, and I didn't know what to make of that. They all seemed so very sure about it. But I saw no proof, not then, and wondered whether some of this might not be wishful thinking to dress up their lives a little."

And then, lo and behold, in her reading she found herself in Egypt with Cayce and in Palestine. Without knowing how true it all was, she got to thinking that it explained why she felt so close to this man she had known for only a few minutes, closer than to people she had known all her life.

She was the kind of person who had to know the reason for everything that happened to her. It was nice to be told you were once the intimate of a high priest and a prime minister of a great country, but where was the proof? She remembered that Christ, seeking acceptance, had performed miracles of healing. And now, in like fashion, Cayce told her something that made a believer of her. She had been having a digestive problem, not being able to hold any food. Cayce told her to stop cooking in aluminum. She changed her method of cooking, and her problem ended.

Cayce had his favorites among his companions, and Mignon was high on his list. She was not surprised. For in the Egyptian period, of which much was made, the sedate Mignon had a child by him when he was a not-so-sedate high priest.

Coming from the lips of this very proper, very Christian lady, this little revelation threw me for a while.

"By Edgar Cayce?" I said with a raised eyebrow and the proper intonation of shock.

"Oh, yes," she replied matter-of-factly. "That was in Egypt many, many years ago when he was Ra-Ta the high priest and I was part of the program to produce a superior race of people."

I was not really dumbfounded, for I knew by now that

Edgar Cayce was no angel in his past lives any more than any other creative man of normal vitality.

As one of the Cayce old guard, Mignon was considered aloof and distant by the newer generations of Cayce devotees who had never known the old master.

"She's a very private person," a fresh-faced member of the A.R.E. staff advised me. "I doubt whether she'll be regressed in time or even speak to you of her memories."

"Oh, I anticipate no trouble," I said. "Any friend of the Ellingtons will be a friend of mine."

In all my years of tracking down readings at the Cayce center, I had never said more than a brief hello to this sturdy lady of obvious independence. However, I did recall her as a close friend of my dear friend Gladys Davis and well remembered the nostalgia with which Gladys spoke of her.

"She was one of Mister Cayce's favorites," she told me, "the kind who can be depended on whenever there was a need for anything." She laughed. "I guess she was just picking up where she left off."

"You knew her way back?"

"Oh, yes, but that wasn't the chord. It was how you were connected. That was what counted."

Gladys's eyes twinkled, reflecting the memories of old, not quite forgotten, places.

"She is hard to get to know," I had said.

She smiled. "Not when you know her."

Mignon was pleasant when I phoned. But I would hardly call it a warm reception.

"You know," I said, "that I was close to Gladys."

She knew why I had called. For there was a very active grapevine among these old companions.

"Oh, yes," she said, "Gladys trusted you. That's good enough for me. But I really don't know how helpful I can be. Nobody can hypnotize me."

"That may not be necessary. You have so much to remember. It must be brimming over."

There was a pause, and she started to say something and then changed her mind.

"I will see you as you like," was all she said.

Without really knowing Mignon, I knew her to be a devout churchgoer, a widow of scrupulous morality, a

devoted mother, and a doer of good works. She was of
the old school, a person of substance who could be relied
on in a crisis, known for her straightforward manner and
her plain common sense. I had known of more than one
unbeliever who said, "If Mignon believes in reincarnation, maybe I should look into it." She was a no-
nonsense person, and yet when the Cayce readings gave
her the same daughter in three different lifetimes, she
did not question it. In all the years she had known Cayce,
like so many old companions, she had never known him
to be wrong about anything. There was a strong feeling
between them, one she never quite understood until she
learned she had shared at least one life and one child
with him.

This was something, she felt, that Cayce had known
and kept to himself until he thought she had progressed
enough to understand the drawing together of people
from the past.

Since he rarely suggested a reading to any of the "regu-
lars" in his study groups, when he did make the suggestion one day, she knew it was for a very good reason.

"Oh, yes," she said, as we sipped our late afternoon
tea in her tidy little Virginia Beach home, "we were all
sitting around the table in Mister Cayce's Bible class
when he turned to me and said, 'Mignon, don't you want
to get a reading?'

"I was surprised because I knew at that time they were
booked far in advance, but I thought a moment and said,
'Yes, I would like my Palestine period.' He had touched
on this in an earlier reading, provoking my curiosity by
saying there was much more to be said.

"But he replied, 'I want the Egyptian period.' That's
all he said. And I said, 'Well, I'll get the Egyptian
period.' "

I regarded this stalwart, stiff-backed octogenarian with
a smile.

"Did you always do what Mister Cayce said?"

She smiled back. "When he was talking about readings
I did."

"And you really believed you lived before?"

"Oh, yes, we all have. We just remember in different
ways, as I remembered this one daughter very well in
three lives."

"Isn't that a bit unusual?"

She shrugged. "The unusual is only what we think unusual."

I had always been intrigued by the Egyptian period, for the mystery of Egypt and its pyramids stood as a symbol today of how little we know about our past.

It is astounding, as one thinks of it, that our planet, as the scientists tell us, is millions of years old, and yet we can retrace our civilization no more than ten or fifteen thousand years at most. It was no wonder old Cayce companions like Mignon and the Ellingtons put so much stock in Cayce's description of an advanced civilization in prehistoric Atlantis.

"I don't know how anybody can question it," said a feisty Mignon, ready to do battle for her beliefs. "The scientists said there was no proof that ancient Troy existed outside the ballads of Homer, and then explorers found not only one Troy buried under the sands of time but seven Troys, one heaped over the other."

It was pretty much the same with ancient Egypt, where an advanced civilization, according to Cayce, had been put together by displaced Atlanteans who in the end, through the genius of the great Ra, imposed their advanced culture on a reluctant land.

The problem at this time was more than one of producing a better species. For as Cayce explained, there was the binding of several different and often conflicting peoples to form one positive race in mind and body. In his exile, traveling the known world, learning how other peoples were advancing themselves with metaphysical powers, the priest had concluded that the blending of the races into a single improved breed would end the dissension and bring Egypt to the forefront. So this was the cause, in the eyes of the high priest and of certain handpicked women, that justified the sacrifice of their innocence. It reminded one of the Romans, and the Spartans before them, in their sacrifice for the benefit of the state and made the process understandable in the twentieth century.

The sacrifice was somewhat blunted by a sense of improving the common lot, comparable to the surge of feeling that commits a modern nation to war, and it was a mark of support for the returning high priest, as the highest power in the land.

How much of this was understood by the people with readings from the Egyptian experience? I had often listened with a secret smile to the vyings of this Egyptian posterity for position or acclaim by virtue of their rank in the land of the pyramids. It was something Cayce had warned against, and it was something that Mignon, in her simplicity, would never have dreamed of, although it was all very real to her. For she was soon describing to me how the people of that place and time had evolved, just as though she had been there and experienced it all.

Mignon's name was Tekleon then. She was given up to the state by a mother who had herself been given up. "In the early experience when the body was first presented by the mother to the priest, the entity was among the first individuals to be offered in the Temple of Sacrifice, as one who might be dedicated to the activities of a perfect type of individual."

Her mother had gone through the temple before her, and she, the child, was selected because she was considered a brighter prospect because of that. Cayce was to explain the law of attraction, which led to men and women getting together after a series of operations, which raised them to a higher standard of beauty and health.

"As to that which causes the attractions or detractions when individual entities meet in any experience," said Cayce, "it is because, as in body and mind and spirit, like begets like. There has been an attraction in a given experience that was creative in nature to bring the entities closer in understanding of the Creative Forces; these are attractions, seeking relationships in either body or mind.

"Thus, as indicated in the relationships in that experience with the priest, there comes to the entity the periods of close attraction, others when there is almost a revulsion in that particular period of the entity's unfoldment."

One phrase had struck me.

"How did you feel about Mister Cayce?" I asked. "Attracted or detracted?"

"Oh, I was very much drawn to him but not in any physical way, though I was a young woman at the time.

I just felt, like so many others did, that he was our teacher. We had all come together to learn from him and know that we would not fade into the dust but be rejoined one day with the people we had known before to work things out on the level we found them. For Mister Cayce always stressed it was the human condition that counted, not the personality. You could be a princess in one life and a scullery maid the next, but it was how you handled things on that plane, working out your karma, that determined your balance and happiness. He stressed that all the time—that the condition, not celebrity or lack of it, was the test and the way of karma. The significant lives were not necessarily the ones with the greatest glory but those that provided the greatest testing ground."

"And you were tested?"

She answered as any woman of substance would.

"Anybody compelled to leave their mother as a small child, as happened in Egypt, would certainly not find life a bed of roses, at least not until they reached an age of understanding, with some sense of knowing they were participating in a common cause. But it would still be difficult."

There had not been much in her first reading about the Egyptian experience. Yet there was something that must have whetted Cayce's interest. For even before the reading for Phyllis, Mignon's younger child, disclosing the Egyptian connection, he had looked at the child and laughed, "That's my baby."

"It was the first time," said Mignon, "that I had carried Phyllis down to the A.R.E. I set her down on the sofa, and Mister Cayce walked in, and he took that one look and seemed to recognize her out of the past. And that was before she got her reading.

"I thought at the time that he had been joking, as with the song, 'Yes Sir, That's My Baby.' But then when Phyllis had a reading, it became clear that back in Egypt she had also been my child, with Ra-Ta, the first perfect child born of this generating program."

She had some memory of that time of sacrifice. Cayce had said there would be shadowy fragments of incidents from the past that she put down to imagination, as something distilled in her mind by the readings themselves.

"Those activities during that sojourn, while materially

not easy, were such as to awaken the entity mentally and spiritually to those possibilities (of perfection). So that the entity even now catches the glimpse of that way, all in keeping with the tenets of him who was and is the way."

But wasn't this a form of loveless love? Hardly the love that Jesus spoke of, hardly the joining of two people together out of a feeling of unity.

"It was a form of dedication as I see it," said a staunch Mignon, "the making of a people that would do so much for civilization, regardless of their own feelings. And that was why it was called the Temple of Sacrifice."

Mignon had never known Cayce to suggest a particular reading in a particular time frame before.

"He wanted to know more about our connection," she said, "and that was the best way he knew how, going into trance. I guess he knew somehow that he was involved. Maybe he wanted to know why he felt so close."

"How did you know that?"

"Oh, the way he would talk to me and sometimes pick me out of a crowd. A woman knows. But it was the closeness of family, not of a man and a woman, nothing like that."

I marveled at Cayce's detail. He was not only the observer but the observed, though as Ra, the "father of his nation," he modestly kept in the shade.

"Tekleon," he said, "was purified in the Temple of Sacrifice for the propagation of a new race. Also that she might understand the sources of attraction to individuals with whom there has been a connection in this material plane from her experience in the spiritual."

Mignon had no copy of the reading, so I had read this part to her aloud from my own copy.

"This," she said, "could account for my friendships with the Ellingtons, Gladys Davis, and the rest."

As I read on, I had to laugh, for if it were not for plastic surgery in the Temple of Sacrifice, she would never have been deemed beautiful enough to mother a child by the high priest.

"The entity, Tekleon, was among the offspring of those having blemishes in the body that kept them from their (intimate) associations with those of the race represented by the priest in that experience."

I looked across the table at this normally distant woman I was beginning to think of as an old friend.

"I wonder how you looked with feathers and all those other appendages."

She laughed.

"I like myself the way I am now."

"Well, the Ra can take credit for that," I said. "He got an awful lot of people looking good, one way or the other."

It had been a combination of things in Tekleon's case: surgery, then the breeding process with a superior Atlantean male. "The projection of spirit into matter," so Cayce said, "had not brought about the change in a gland still existent in the body. So there would not be such blemishes in the offspring, this gland was removed by the operators with the priest. Then were brought about those connections, and associations, until there was the reproduction that was perfect in body."

And that, of course, was Mignon's child by the Ra—the first perfect baby in the land of Egypt.

As a neophyte in the Temple of Sacrifice, Tekleon had been rated an almost perfect specimen. In the mating with the highest of the high, the high priest from advanced Atlantis, she had reached the fulfillment of nearly every neophyte's dream.

And what was Isis, the partner of Ra, doing while all this was going on?

"That, I imagine," said a wise Mignon, "must have been her sacrifice."

The high priest, in his zeal to help in the perfection process, relaxed his ties with the lady Isis long enough to contribute to the regeneration program. And from time to time he withdrew from the public eye for a rejuvenating program of his own.

This regeneration took place in the Temple Beautiful and was a reward for services performed as well as perpetuating the concept of the survival of the fittest. The priest, of course, had to keep himself youthful if he was to continue in the perfecting process.

"I imagine," said Mignon with a straight face, "that no sacrifice was too great for one so advanced."

The consummation had taken place in the Temple of Sacrifice. "My mother had given me there into the temple as a baby to be used, experimented with, along the lines the priests were doing because they were trying to eliminate the blemishes and vestiges of appendages in the people. Their purpose was to bring about a well-balanced and proportioned person. The mind and soul were also affected by the changes, for when they operated on certain glands this helped to produce the form that we have today some twelve thousand years later."

"So why did they not call it the Temple Beautiful, rather than the Temple of Sacrifice?"

"The mothers sacrificed the children for the common good. They were brought up in the temple, and though the parents could visit, their children were considered the nation's."

As she spoke of the child that she bore the high priest in Egypt, I felt a vague jogging of my own memory bank.

I had the uneasy feeling that I was missing something, some connection that would not have eluded an initiate, one more versed in past lives than myself, one like Hugh Lynn Cayce who could write so graphically about lives shared in Persia and Egypt.

Something Gladys Davis had said kept rolling over in my head. "It was *how* you were connected." That was it, the nature of the connection.

The temple connection was not of the heart, not with Cayce, not when he was, as they believed, the high priest and the progenitor of so many perfect children. There was an almost machinelike response to the life-giving process, not anything to stir the emotions, however pleasurable the experience at some point.

I kept thinking about it. And then it came to me as I heard Mignon saying, "It was something to be proud of, bearing the first perfect child, and that the Ra's, whom everybody looked up to."

It was a competition, in a sense, to please the leader who had opened broad new vistas of life to so many.

There had been another child, one not bred in the temple, one whose mother was even closer to Cayce in this life. That child was left behind as its father and mother—the priest Ra and the lady Isis (Gertrude)—were banished from Egypt.

It did not require a genealogist to summarize the connection. By the reckoning of old companions in this sojourn, Mignon's perfect baby and the Egyptian child of Edgar and Gertrude were sisters, half-sisters, if you choose.

I looked across the table at Mignon coolly sipping her tea. She could have pieced it together much faster than I, for she had her memory to expedite what a slumbering Cayce had said of this old association from the land of the pyramids.

"I knew many of us were connected from the Egyptian period because of our closeness to Ra," Mignon said. "But I had no way of knowing how we were connected, because none of our present names was given for reasons of privacy."

"Did you have any idea," I said, "that Gladys Davis and your daughter Phyllis were sisters in the Egyptian excursion?"

She had an excellent sense of humor. "Some people might think of it as an excursion. But I regarded it as an experiment, to produce a better race."

There was a light in her eye as she added, "God gives us the tools, and we do the rest. My daughter was the youngest of the Ra's children. Gladys would have been before that. But very few of us sat around and gossiped of the past. We lived it in our own way."

I recalled the Ellingtons' granddaughter, Ann Lynne Tynes, relating under hypnosis how Ra had fathered so many of the perfect children.

There was a glimmer of a smile on the rugged face. "I always surmised that. But why not? He was the perfect man from Atlantis. That adds up, as you think about it, to the perfect child."

It was all very interesting, and there was no doubt in my mind that all of these companions believed every word of what they were saying. They were buttressed by the belief, particularly when regressed, that anything said under hypnosis is true; more subtly, as true as that person thinks it is.

Still, where was the proof? That was the question I asked time and time again.

Mignon's smile broadened.

"I see it every day in how we old companions react in our closeness, even when angry or upset. We still hang together."

I found myself nodding.

"In your readings you visited hospitals and were always interested in the sick and the poor. That's what you're doing now—at the age of eighty and more. Do you think the readings were self-fulfilling?"

She shook her head.

"I have this feeling that I want to do these things. I had done so much of it before." She laughed. "And lived to be 298 years, which was part of the regeneration program they had there. I was sold on the idea of the breeding program because I lived long enough to see the results, not only with my daughter, but with thousands of other children as well. It gave Egypt a culture superior to that of any other land."

Twice now regeneration had been mentioned, coupled with Mignon's claim of an incredible longevity.

"How," I asked, "do you get to be 298 years old, or even 198?"

"You went into the Temple Beautiful, once it was considered that prolonging your life would be for the benefit of the country. It was the high priest who made the decision, and he alone."

"Obviously you did something to deserve it."

She had the grace to blush.

I still didn't have the answer I wanted.

"How do they rejuvenate you? That is something everybody would like to know."

She wasn't sure. "The only things you remember are the things you experience emotionally, only this seems to flood your mind with all kinds of recollections. But my age was in a reading, and I believe the readings. It wasn't Edgar Cayce the man saying it. He made that distinction. He'd always say, 'I'm not saying this. The reading says it.' If somebody wanted the truth, he'd say, 'Well, let's see what the reading's got to say, not me.' "

We sat for a moment, staring at each other.

"I'm trying to figure out," I said, "what would be going through a woman's mind if she got a psychic reading that said the man giving that reading had fathered her child."

Mignon was not in the least embarrassed. She had thought of the reading long enough to work it out to her own satisfaction.

"The way I look at it, I was like a guinea pig. There was no true love there. As I said, it was an experiment. And I thank the Lord I was that far developed at the time to understand it that well. That's the reason I took it as I did. I thought it was right."

A question slipped out.

"Right in what way?"

"When my daughter was born perfect at that time I could see where they were right. I never regarded it as a sexual thing. In this life my marriage was always a beautiful experience to me and a reflection of love."

"But there was no talk of love in Egypt?"

"No, it was for a cause. I realized what a wonderful mother I had. She thought enough of the goal to give up her baby. Look how many years I had to live in the temple, going through all those operations, not having a family of my own."

The readings had said that her daughter, Phyllis, born in 1937, was a reincarnation of that perfect child born not only in Egypt of Ra but again in colonial Virginia of a different father—and, of course, in the present by Mignon's late husband.

"You mentioned," I said, "that you had a special affinity for Phyllis from the moment she was born."

"Yes, before I knew anything of her past lives. It was an overwhelming feeling. When they handed her to me in the hospital, something just turned over in me. Ellen had been my firstborn, and I had wanted a baby so badly. I couldn't have been more pleased. But it wasn't the same. When they wanted to bring Ellen in to me, it was late and I was tired, and I said, 'Oh, that's all right, bring her in the morning,' my being that fatigued."

"And the feeling between you and the two girls was different?"

She laughed. "I don't want you getting me in the doghouse. But when you love somebody special, you're conscious of that different feeling. You can't explain it, but it's there. Mister Cayce described love at first sight between a man and a woman as a recognition of their past. I suppose you could apply the same idea to a mother and daughter. If they had known each other before like that, naturally there would be an added dimension. And with us it was the third time."

Every now and then Phyllis would say or do something that brought her up with a start.

"One time she was doing a lot for me at Thanksgiving and I said, 'I don't want you to do all that much for me.' And she laughed and said, 'Well you've done for people all your *lives*. It's about time somebody did for you.' "

Little Phyllis had her Cayce reading at the age of three. Even at that age she had some idea of a great event taking place in her life. She was so excited she caught hold of her mother's hand and cried, "Oh, Mommy, I wonder who I'm going to be."

The daughter was given a life in the Holy Land in which she knew Christ and was known as one of the holy women. And this, too, helped endear her to Mignon, with remembrances of her own of the Master she worshiped.

"Before this," said Cayce, "the entity [Phyllis] was in the Roman and the Palestine land. For the entity was among those in authority in Palestine when there were the beliefs being presented by the Prince of Peace. The entity was a companion of those in authority, knowing the holy women, knowing the Master himself. For the entity was that companion that brought the periods of activity for the great dinner for the Master, his disciples, and his followers. This was the greater occasion of the dinner given in honor of the Master during his early ministry. It was from the entity's desire to see all groups that were not only the followers but the listeners, to know the character of the apostles, or disciples, as they were called at that time. The entity will ask questions of those times, as 'What did Jesus say?' Never refrain from taking advantage of such opportunities to fully explain this questioning to the entity. For, as it did then, the entity will gather much missed by many in practical application of the principles of his teachings. The name then was Nannoi."

The name Nannoi meant nothing to Mignon. But she did recall the dinner, mentioned in Luke and Matthew, that Levi, the tax collector, later the Apostle Matthew, gave for Jesus and his followers. It was known as the great supper, as distinguished from the Last Supper. It was a time of celebration, and many publicans and sinners came to dine with Jesus and his disciples. And when

Jesus heard that the Pharisees complained that a holy man would eat with sinners, he said, "They that be whole need not a physician, but they that are sick."

Mignon finally got the reading to clarify thoughts of the Holy Land that came unbidden into her mind. There was no figure she identified more closely with in her spiritual life than the man who carried the cross to Calvary. She had a name then, Moro, and a kindred feeling for the man she thought of as the Son of God.

"The entity was in the teenage years when first becoming acquainted with the teachings of the Master, as an acquaintance of Peter, Andrew, James, and John. Because of the entity's parent, the father associated with those upon the sea, the entity was acquainted with Peter's mother-in-law and was healed in the early ministry of the Master. In Bethesda, when the Master preached by the seashore, as well as when he rested, the entity was acquainted personally with the Master. Oft the entity sought to make the conditions more comfortable for the Master. And thus it may be said that the entity became so closely associated as to call him by his name, Jesus, not Master, until after his Crucifixion.

"Thus the entity became so imbued with these teachings that so great grew the love of the entity for those ideas, and great became the desire, the purpose of the entity, in telling the stories, encouraging others, by those direct experiences she had with the Master.

"In the present analyze these and aid as a helper for those of the young who seek to apply such in their experience. Even to learn how to interpret to children as to how an individual may pass the collection plate in church on Sunday and swear like a sailor on Monday."

In two paragraphs Cayce had explained Mignon's strong atavistic feeling for the Christ and the men and women who had served with him to the last full measure of devotion.

And with Cayce, as Lucius of Cyrene, this became spiritually more binding than the bond of parenthood with the Egyptian Ra.

I sought to lighten the moment.

"And did you explain the Sunday Christian to your children?"

"I have tried," she said, with a formidable look.

I saw now why she had wanted the Palestine reading. All her life she had recurring impressions of Christ and the disciples, but she was never sure where they were coming from or how valid they were.

"But in moments of deep meditation and prayer," said Cayce, "there comes oft that vision as of seeing his face, worn at times, other times that smile, that expression that brings the hope so necessary in the heart of the human, that there's a better way. There's safety in his presence. And a consciousness of the abiding faith in him."

I looked up and saw a tear in this strong woman's eye.

"Does this have a special meaning for you?"

She nodded, unable to speak, then quickly collected herself. Her remembrance of the Christ she served long ago was impressed on a secret chamber of her mind not for reporters like myself to probe but for her to manage her life by, with her companions of old.

I had developed an affection for this sturdy woman who faced life—and death—with a fearless eye. We had met perhaps five or six times, and by this time I was an old friend.

As I was leaving after a final visit, she brought out a thick bound volume and without ceremony said, "This is for you."

It was her own preciously held collection of the Cayce work readings that guided the A. R. E. down to the present day. In it I saw a transcribed report of Cayce's trial in New York on trumped-up charges.

"This must mean something to you," I said.

She nodded her head, and there was the ghost of a smile. "That's why I am giving it to you."

I was too touched to know how to thank her.

"It would make Gladys very happy," was all I could say.

She took my hand and squeezed it.

"Yes," she said, with an even look, "and it pleases me as well."

I remembered how she had hesitated when I first called on the telephone.

"You were thinking of not seeing me?"

She shook her head. "Not for a moment. It was something else."

"Something in Egypt?" I said half in jest.

There was a twinkle in her eye.

"You were one of us, you know."

I had to laugh. "As a newspaperman, I had many opportunities to visit Egypt. I shunned it like the plague."

"There was a reason. We don't like or dislike anything we don't know about without a reason, however buried in our consciousness."

Where had I heard that before? From the old master, of course, in many a reading on the shadowy but not forgotten past.

She gave me a curious look.

"It was no accident that you wrote *The Sleeping Prophet*." There were no accidents, that I knew. But I had been an observer so long, looking on from the sidelines, that I found it hard to think of myself as a participant.

"Think back," she said, "how did it come about?"

I didn't have to think very hard. I would always remember that midnight call from Madame Bathsheba. But was it Bathsheba or was it Cayce? And why had I been chosen and then plunged in so eagerly, later writing about the young Edgar Cayce and now this book?

When I looked up, I could see she was smiling.

"Why do you think we have all been working with you?"

I had felt this familiarity and taken advantage of it but had not related it to my writing or what lay behind it. Sometimes we don't see what stares us in the face. It is much too obvious.

We parted as old friends do, without regret, not thinking of the past but only of the morrow. And there was no doubt in my mind what that day would be like. As Cayce said, it was the condition, the quality of life, that determined the life course. And that condition was the same wherever I turned among these old companions of Cayce's—one of love and giving for one of their own.

CHAPTER 17

Beyond the Divide

Almost as though he had done all he had come back for, Edgar Cayce began to fade as he said he would. His own readings had said he would disintegrate if he did more than two readings a day. And toward the close of the war, reading as often as he did for people with sons overseas, he soon wasted away. But there was a light in his eye as he calmly faced the God he had faced so many times before. Gertrude could see him failing, losing his grip on life. But knowing they would not be long parted, she was able to accept the inevitable.

Death had no fears for either of these soulmates. These twin souls died as they lived, believing unquestionably they were to be together always. Each had a smile as they cheerfully faced not the unknown but, for them, the known.

On New Year's Day, 1945, a dying Cayce impishly told visitors, "It is all arranged. I am to be healed on Friday, the fifth of January."

They looked at him in wonder, for his body had dwindled away to less than seventy pounds, though there was a gleam in his eye and his spirit was high.

They understood what he meant when they arrived that Friday for the funeral service at the Cayce home.

The night before his death, as his wife reached across the bed to kiss him goodnight, Cayce's face lit up in a smile, and he said, "You know I have always loved you, don't you?"

A lump came into the throat of the woman who had made him her whole life on this plane, molding her life to his as she had done before.

She nodded, and he asked, "How do you know?"

"Oh, I just know," she said with a little smile.

"I don't see how you can tell. For when you love some-one, you sacrifice for them. And what have I ever sacrificed because I love you?"

Standing by the bedside, the tears came to Gladys Davis's eyes as she saw the curtain coming down on a life that had redeemed and enhanced so much of what had gone before.

After Cayce's death, Gertrude had no wish to live. She told friends she felt as though her heart had been bodily removed and her soul was leaving her. She had two sons at war to live for, but she felt her husband gently pulling her to his side, as he had done before. On a Sunday, April 1, 1945, the day marking Christ's Resurrection, Gertrude Evans Cayce followed her husband beyond the divide. Only the day before, on March 31, Hugh Lynn had written from his Army post in Germany, releasing her as only the father's son could.

"It makes me deeply happy," he wrote, "to know how happy you are to pass through that other door. There is so much beauty in your living that I cannot be sad at the thought of your joining Dad. You held up his right hand—sometimes both hands—so it does not surprise me that he may need you now.

"It is important for you to realize how much fun it has been being your son. So many times I have seen you faced with problems, conditions that I have known to crumple up so many people, and you have risen above them and carried others with you. It makes me proud to think of you."

And the son, designated by the father to spread the work, showed his readiness for the task. His message was a salute to his mother's undying love, bound, as he believed, for the ages.

"We have come, Mother, to an understanding of karma in a way that we have been a long time explaining to others. And I find that your life represents so much that is fine and beautiful that I cannot allow my selfish desires to mar this period of waiting and wondering."

And so he released her with love, just as she had re-leased her twin flame, the only soulmate she had ever known.

After Cayce's death Gladys married and was twice

widowed. She was the last to go. Believing as she did, she had no fear of death. "I will be back with both of them again one day, for there is still much to do and work out." She smiled that sweet smile that so many knew so well. "And with Hugh Lynn, as well, for in the end I understood his anguish. And I found it easy to forgive that time long ago in Egypt when I was a child and he the Pharaoh. For in forgiving, we find forgiveness, which keeps the slate clean for the next time around."

My heart went out to these remarkable people who gave so much to so many and took so little of life's comforts and pleasures for themselves. Yet they had the satisfaction of having done this time around what they came back for, with a greater message than ever before. For as Cayce said, "It is not what we know that counts but what we do about what we know, in our dealings with our fellow man. 'For as ye do it unto the least ye do it unto thy Maker.' The Lord hath not willed that any soul should perish but with every temptation, with every failure, with every fault, hath prepared a way, a means, a manner of escape, that all may know the beauty of his love."

There was a mist in Jeanette Thomas's eye as we read together this last requiem of a great soul. For she cared, as I did, for what he was to each and everyone he knew and for what he meant to a troubled world.

"He has shown us all that there is no death," she said, "only a resting place, a stopover, where we come back stronger than ever one day, remembering our companions of old as the leaves remember to bud and the flowers to bloom."

And so I, too, remembered the Harold Reillys and the Ellingtons, Mignon Helms and Ruth Burks and dear Anne Gray Holbein, who passed away only recently with a smile on her lips. The whole group of them and others as well were all linked to Cayce. There was not only total acceptance and trust but a community of interest, with Edgar Cayce and past lives the focus of that interest. I was very aware of what Cayce had said about people coming back in groups, yet with no obvious plan, so they could accomplish more together out of the head start they had out of the past. And over a period of years I saw it happening—with me and others.

It was all very natural. None of these people were the kind that lived their lives on their sleeves. They were very private people. They lived pretty much within themselves, outside of their interest in Edgar Cayce and his work. Not knowing why at the time, they had all been drawn to Cayce's little enclave in Virginia Beach, and many had settled there so they could live under the umbrella of the man who had guided them in other places and other times.

On a more intimate level, it also explained my own interest in Cayce, which kept pulling me back to Virginia Beach until I finally bought a home there so I could spend more time with the people I found myself so much at home with. This was the one place in the world where I never felt alone.

It also explained my diverse friendships with such men as Harold Reilly, my physical mentor, who was like a father to me, and Alan Jay Lerner, the world-famed composer of *Gigi, Brigadoon,* and *My Fair Lady,* who moved in a glamour world entirely apart from my own. Yet on meeting, we formed an instant friendship, and the first thing we talked about was Edgar Cayce.

I had always marveled at Cayce giving life readings to children a few days or years old, telling of their pasts—and of their futures. And here I was, at a small gathering in New York, having just met the famed songwriter, listening wide-eyed as he eagerly related the Cayce reading he had when he was about four or five, requested, he said, by a curious father.

At the time I did not understand the depth of Lerner's interest in reincarnation, or sense the lasting nature of the friendship we were to form with this as a beginning. On the surface, he seemed more the bon vivant, a regular in the café society world of New York and London, with a cocktail-party interest in the psychic. But appearances in this instance proved deceiving.

I have to laugh now as I remember how lightly I responded at the time. "And what did Cayce say about you?" I asked rather glibly, reaching for an hors d'oeuvre.

Alan Jay Lerner smiled. "He said I should go into music."

And, of course, he had. A host of other musicals had

rolled off his versatile pen. And now he was telling me of the musical he had always wanted to do, about reincarnation. It was to be called *On a Clear Day You Can See Forever*.

"I'm getting into your area," he said, with a smile. "And I find it exciting."

Months later, *On a Clear Day* came to Broadway. Alan had done the lyrics, and just about everybody was singing them. Any time I turned on the radio, or caught a singer on television, the magic music of Burton Lane and Alan's lyrics burst on my consciousness. The title song was totally inspired, and the words came from the composer's soul:

> On a clear day, rise and look around you
> And you'll see who you are.
> On a clear day how it will astound you
> That the glow of your being outshines every star.
> You feel part of every mountain, sea, and shore.
> You can hear from far and near,
> A world you've never heard before.
> And on a clear day
> You can see forever and ever more.

I found myself humming the song along with millions of other Americans, but I had been on the move and hadn't stopped in New York long enough to catch the show. And then one day I got a call from Alan.

I was not at all surprised. For though I saw him infrequently, we had by now established a strong bond. It was rooted in a mutual interest in the mystical and Edgar Cayce's espousal of reincarnation, but at this time it had not occurred to me there was anything more.

Alan was never a man to waste words, onstage or off.

"Have you seen my show?" he asked.

"Not yet," I said.

"Well, you better hurry. It may close before you get there."

I couldn't believe it.

"Not your show?"

"Listen," he said. "I'll leave a couple of tickets for you any night you can make it. Something isn't quite right, and I'd like your opinion." He laughed. "Not on the music. But on reincarnation. The public isn't buying it."

Anything short of a blockbuster was a disaster for the author of *My Fair Lady*. I thought it was possibly too early in the day for reincarnation. But then Alan had touched on this theme before, notably in the Broadway hit *Brigadoon*, preceding *On a Clear Day* by nearly two decades. How well I remembered the movie, with Gene Kelly and Van Johnson, about a village in Scotland that came to life for one day every one hundred years. It stirred the soul with such love songs as "Come to Me, Bend to Me" and the unforgettably haunting title song:

> Brigadoon, Brigadoon
> There my heart forever lies
> Let the world grow cold around us
> Let the heavens cry above
> There my heart forever lies
> Brigadoon.

The word *forever* struck a responsive chord. I hadn't caught it at first, but this was long ago, and like Alan, I was a young man, an unsentimental newspaper reporter in New York City. Reincarnation was only a word to me at that time, and it was years before I took a serious look at it.

Anybody who knew anything about reincarnation could tell that Alan was reaching out. *Brigadoon,* had I known it then, was a lyrical ode to soulmates, that timeless partner out of the dim and wondrous past:

> Though I'll live *forty* lives
> Till the day arrives
> I'll not ever grieve
> For my hopes will be high
> That he'll come strollin' by:
> For ye see, I believe
> That there's a laddie weary
> An' wandering free, who's
> waiting
> For his dearie: Me.

Alan had married several times in his search, and I had an idea his music reflected his yearning for the perfect twin soul out of the past, an idyll easier dreamed than attained. The line about forty lifetimes, I could well imagine, may have been written with a sigh.

I didn't discuss any of this with him, for he was completely engrossed with *On a Clear Day*.

"I never wanted acceptance more for anything I wrote," he said, "and this is the only show I've done in years they haven't stood in the rain for."

I thought to hearten him by mentioning *The Ladder*, a play about reincarnation that had a good run on Broadway because the producers gave tickets away to anyone who wanted to see it.

He laughed.

"That's hardly my idea of acceptance."

In a way, I felt he was looking for public assurance to shore up his own uncertainty about the reality of reincarnation. For without remembrance, even a moment of it, reincarnation could be a midsummer night's dream.

I wasn't sure what was stirring inside Alan. I was having my own problems with reincarnation. It seemed plausible, for it gave meaning to a life that all too often seemed to lack meaning or direction. Perhaps it was an accident, as so many thought—a couple of vast planets exploding with a big bang to throw off a pesky little planet whose inhabitants were formed by the heat and came out of the slime. But, of course, I didn't believe this. I had seen too much of a divine order in the seasons and the stars, in the prophecies of the Bible, and in mystics like Cayce, who followed in the steps of Christ. These prophecies, validated, showed a design in our life. And where there was a design, there was surely a Designer, whether you knew him as God or the Divine Intelligence. I could see this design in the insect life, the ants and the bees, even the termites, and the caterpillars who came back as butterflies. They all lived and died, in an orderly manner, and procreated as the Lord had planned, and none thought this process odd but humans.

Of course, like others, like Alan, I needed validation. I needed proof, not to just write a book, for the writing was just a step in the searching and the wondering, trying to understand the Resurrection, and the being reborn in heaven to be born again on earth, but to comprehend Christ and, in this instance, to analyze the reality of Cayce's readings.

It was not like validating the clairvoyant gift, for I could check the predictions of any psychic, including those of Cayce, and find the proof of extrasensory perception, of clairvoyance, in their fulfillment. But nobody had ever convinced me—not yet—that he had died and come back to earth in a different body. Yet more and more, in the remembrances of Cayce and others, I was filled with a growing sense that death and life were both parts of the same thing, and this, the continuity of the soul.

I had mentioned some of this to Alan and found him responsive. His mind had traveled the same road, and he had come to the same dead end, except for the glimmerings into the soul that came through in his haunting verse.

He was important to me, not because of his celebrity—I had been a newspaperman in New York too long for that—but because of an easy familiarity between us apparent the moment we met. It was a feeling ever constant, despite the long lapses between meetings.

I had arranged to take in the show later that week, then sit down with him right after that. Since we made a date, I was rather surprised to hear from him the next day. He seemed a bit hesitant over the phone. He had been asked by the show's producers to help with publicity and to go on a popular all-night radio talk show featuring the esoteric and the psychic. He had never done anything like this before and felt somewhat awkward about it.

"Would you go on with me?" he asked.

I smiled to myself, knowing how shy he was about putting himself forward.

"We'll be discussing reincarnation for the most part," he said half-apologetically.

I said I would be delighted. I don't remember now how the show went. But it was somewhat curtailed—no longer, I think, than a couple of hours.

I saw his show, and while there were things in it I liked, it didn't grip me as *Brigadoon* had. It didn't have the same haunting air, the same mystique, and was not nearly as intriguing and soul-stirring as the undying love of a people who came back for a day every one hundred years.

The setting was rather comic and didn't seem to go well with anything as provocative as reincarnation. The story was amusing: a Greek shipping magnate had made a lot of money and, believing in reincarnation, wanted to know who he would be in his next life so he could will the money to himself after he died and came back. There was a whole jumble of things—hypnotic regressions into past lives, demonstrations of the power of the mind on plants, clairvoyance, and telepathy. Altogether quite a potpourri.

After my evening at the theater I tried to lighten his mood.

"The house was pretty well filled," I reported, "and the audience seemed to like it."

"We were sold out six months in advance," he said, "so that's meaningless in view of the dwindling response."

Any other composer would have loved the attention his musical was getting, but he didn't want to hear that. His instinct told him this play wasn't working like the others, and he wanted to know why. I respected his talent too much to beat around the bush.

"May I say what I think?"

He nodded grimly.

"I think you have too much going on. It's too busy. You should have focused on one thing—reincarnation."

He half-groaned and made a face.

"That's what everybody tells me."

I laughed. "And everybody is wrong?"

"Anything else?"

"In *Brigadoon*, reincarnation was only hinted at, a pure fantasy. People may not be ready for the reality, not on stage."

His eyes snapped, "You're ready for it. And it didn't get to you.

The story line hadn't touched a responsive chord. "Where did the plot come from? It's rather unusual."

He didn't reply for a moment.

"It was basically a true story," he said. "I dressed it up a little."

I couldn't remember anything like it.

"Oh, it was a long time ago." He seemed very offhand, and I didn't pursue it. He made no apologies for his light-handed treatment of the subject matter.

"People keep asking me if it's a fantasy because it

deals with reincarnation, and I tell them, it's not a fantasy to hundreds of millions of Indians and Chinese."

"It should do well in China," I said with a straight face.

He was rather defensive. This often happened with sensitive people in promulgating a concept generally considered ridiculous by others. Alan didn't find it strange that he should have gotten into reincarnation. Neither did I, once I recalled his having a life reading with Cayce.

Ever since he could summon a thought, he must have been sure of his destiny and the portent of the Cayce reading. After getting out of Harvard, he did three musicals, and they were all flops. His father, who had founded the Lerner Stores, told him he'd have to get in the family business or he'd get no more help. Alan pleaded for one more chance.

"If this one doesn't make it," he said, "I'll go into the business and work hard at it."

The next thing he did, with composer Frederick Loewe, was *Paint Your Wagon*. And it was a smash Broadway hit. The clothing industry lost an indifferent salesman.

I didn't believe in chance, any more than Alan did, so I knew his meeting with Loewe had been intended to give the world the gift of his talent—and the benefit of his thinking.

I didn't wonder how or why he had come to reincarnation. It was very obvious to someone in the same bind himself. There was a constant, gnawing feeling that there had to be more in life. The lessons gained in hard, arduous experience, with toil and tears, could not be so carelessly lost. The God that made humans in his image could not be that frivolous and wasteful. So I told myself, and Alan echoed my thought.

"Shall I tell you," he said, "why I decided on this musical?"

It was a rhetorical question, and I waved him on.

"It seems to me," he said, "that it offers an explanation for the way we all behave, for our aptitudes and inclinations, our likes and dislikes, for poverty and riches. No other concept or philosophy makes it so clear. The psychiatrists have an explanation for everything, but they explain nothing. For they do not consider the human spirit, the innate hunger of man, the déjà vu that brings a lingering familiarity with people and places. They know little of intuition, of extrasensory perception, and nothing of the soul and its infinity."

How amazing, I thought, that this man, considered a dilettante and confirmed party-goer, should have such penetrating insight into the nature of Edgar Cayce's search for the meaning of life and death. He was truly an apostle of the New Age, and I saluted him as such.

"You said it all, musically."

His tone was challenging.

"That was what I was trying to say, for only on a clear day can you see forever. I was visualizing a world with no barriers to truth, no boundaries but the human spirit."

He loved to roam the gloaming of the psychic world. One evening, with Jean Kennedy Smith, the late President Kennedy's sister, we hunted up a psychic, the late Mary Talley, who confounded Alan with the accuracy of her psychic perceptions, to the point where he suspected me of having clued her in.

In the course of the evening, Alan mentioned that the slain President's brother Bobby had invited him on a little trip to ride the rapids in Wyoming.

"You can get killed doing that," Alan had responded.

And Bobby had shrugged, "What difference does it make? There's a curse on this family."

It was to be as prophetic as anything Mary Talley had said that evening.

Alan claimed only one psychic experience himself and that with *Brigadoon*, though I myself felt his lyrics were often psychically generated.

In *Brigadoon*, for a necessary scenic effect, the wedding of two principals in this eighteenth-century Scottish fantasy was staged outside a church. Alan had to figure out why the wedding should occur, not indoors, but in the heather and the hills, and he described the wedding in an imaginative way.

Years later, in London, he came across a book, *Everyday Life in Old Scotland*. And there was the wedding ceremony, word for word as he had it with the outdoor ceremony properly sanctioned:

When there is no minister present it is perfectly proper according to the laws of Scotland for two people to be wed by sincerely mutual consent. There need be nothing in writing. All that's necessary is the promise of love as long as ye both are on earth.

> I shall love ye till I die
> An' I'll make all effort
> to be a good husband to ye.
> An' so much will
> I try . . . to be a
> fine . . . an' lovin' wife.

Before *On a Clear Day* closed, I saw Alan a number of times. His spirits had lifted, and he was looking forward to a movie version of his play. "You might do better," I said, "if you throw in a few more songs about reincarnation. It would provide a sugarcoating of fantasy for a doubting public."

He demurred with a wave of his hand. "But it isn't a fantasy."

He was already plotting the movie he would be doing on his Broadway play. *On a Clear Day* was by no means a bust. It had a good run. It just wasn't up to what Alan Jay Lerner and his former partner, Fritz Loewe, were accustomed to. But Hollywood wanted it, and Barbra Streisand was slated to star. So the end of the world was not at hand.

On a Clear Day brought more interesting mail than any Broadway production in years. There were letters from Dr. Joseph Rhine, who had a study grant at Duke University for the unknown, and from Hugh Lynn Cayce, Edgar Cayce's son. But it was popular support Alan wanted for what he was saying in music.

He told the *New York Times,* "To me there are several explanations for reincarnation—or, as they say—the survival of human personality. Either there is such a thing as genetic memory or there is a thing of being able to tune in on sounds of a bygone age, or something related to that."

He fell short of acknowledging a belief in reincarnation. And I can hardly blame him. For this was 1966, and anyone who believed in reincarnation was considered a kook. But the hypnotic regressions into past lives, featured in his production, mirrored his beliefs.

I was curious about Alan's reading and looked through the A.R.E. files for it. It was nowhere to be found. At the time of his reading, in 1925 or 1926, the readings were filed episodically, and some even from the landmark Lammers' readings were never located.

There was nothing like creative work to keep a man from brooding. Between his marriages and his revisions of *On a Clear Day* for Hollywood, Alan had his hands full. He gave me a call in California, wanting me to meet his new bride. Ever in search of a perfect mate, his twin soul, he had taken a fifth wife, the former Karen Gunderson. The romance could have come out of one of his musicals. The two had met while Karen was interviewing him for *Newsweek* magazine. There was an instant rapport. Karen was young and beautiful and searching herself. It looked like a perfect match. Alan was struggling with the movie script, and she was very supportive, interested like himself in the pursuit of an idea that gave greater purpose to an existence so often without purpose. In *Brigadoon*, there was always another chance, every one hundred years or so—another chance to learn and to grow, to carry over a gift, and to develop it.

In *On a Clear Day*, perhaps drawing on a distant past, Alan was able to say,

And who would not be stunned to see you prove
There's more to us than surgeons can remove?
So much more than we ever knew
So much more were we born to do.
Should you draw back the curtain,
This I am certain,
You'll be impressed with you.

The Cayce connection was perpetuating. "In my opinion," Hugh Lynn wrote Alan, "you did a magnificent job in presenting in a thorough, sympathetic fashion many of the ideas which have been involved in the Edgar Cayce psychic readings for many years.

"You indicated a thorough knowledge and background of the whole field of extrasensory perception, as well as the challenging concept of reincarnation."

Alan had browsed through the Cayce readings, and no other mystic or psychic had the same appeal for him. I had been researching *Edgar Cayce—The Sleeping Prophet* in Virginia Beach, making an occasional trip to New York, but was not far enough along to know what of Alan's came from Cayce and what came from his own head.

Not until recently did I come across a 1937 reading that gave me a clue to the central event in *On a Clear Day.* The germ of the idea was contained in a newspaper story, the subject of a Cayce reading, that Alan had stumbled upon twenty years later, adding a few twists of his own. The story told of one Arthur M. Hanks who had made a fortune peddling flowers in the Los Angeles financial district. When he died, Hanks had left no will because he believed he would return through reincarnation and claim his life's savings. According to the news report, on November 23, 1937—seven months after Hanks's death—Judge Joseph P. Sproul had opened the way for relatives to divide the flower peddler's $100,000 estate.

Alan didn't have to do very much to it. Hanks became the Greek shipping magnate Kriakos who offers a past-life regressionist a fortune to tell him who he will be in his next life so that he can will his millions to himself in advance.

Two days after reading the article, Hugh Lynn Cayce and Tom Sugrue, Cayce's first biographer, asked the mystic to elaborate on the obvious implications of reincarnation in the news story.

Cayce, with a smile, went into trance. As he slept, they asked him to explain the universal laws governing a person's selection of time, place, race and color, sex, and parents as well. And then they inquired, casually, how Cayce—or anybody else—could establish some proof of memory by leaving a record of time and place, or money as in this case, that could be hunted up in the next appearance.

I had to smile at the last request, it was so human.

But Cayce didn't seem comfortable, even asleep, dealing with spirituality and materiality in the same breath. Proof could be established not by leaving a record of any kind, he replied, but by living one. The more spiritual the individual, the more advanced from his past, the more of that past he would remember and profit by.

"Think thou that the grain of corn has forgotten what manner of expression it has given? Only man forgets. Only when he manifests that expression of the divine may man begin to know who, where, what, and when he was—and why."

I could imagine anybody's disappointment in not learning when they were coming back, particularly if life appeared not to have given all it should. But not Alan Jay Lerner. There was no disappointment there. His life had been a happy medley of promise fulfilled. He lived what he remembered—in music and in rhyme.

"I am sure you come back when you are supposed to, in keeping with God's plan." So he told me. And so he believed.

Alan Jay Lerner passed away in June 1986, in London, one of his favorite haunts. He had lived his life to the hilt and had known fame and riches. He had powerful friends such as the Kennedys, having known John F. Kennedy from Choate and Harvard, and his *Camelot* became their theme. But with all these he was never tainted by the ghost of materialism. He was always questing, always searching, peering over the rainbow into what lay beyond. And as I see his face before me, the haunting strains of *Brigadoon* stir my whole being:

> The mist of May is in the gloamin'
> An' all the clouds are holdin' still
> So take my hand and we'll go roamin'
> through the heather on the hill.

I sigh as I write this, regretting that I had never fully explored this close but distant companionship, as dear in a way as was Edgar Cayce's, who had brought us together in his own fashion as he had so many companions of old. "You are not alone. You are never alone," Edgar Cayce had said.

And you never were, as long as the human soul, undying, could reach back into the past, as Alan had—and Cayce did so often—to tell a story of life eternal and the sojourn of the soul.

Afterword

In death, there has been no deification of Edgar Cayce at Virginia Beach. Cayce deemphasized the cult of the personality. The supreme law for companions everywhere was, "Thou must love the Lord thy God with all they strength, and love thy neighbor as thyself." The A.R.E., Cayce's Association for Research and Enlightenment, is still run by a voice from the dead—Cayce's. More than sixty years ago, when there was no widespread acknowledgment of extrasensory perception in any form, the sleeping Cayce plotted the growth of the work. "For such work must of necessity first appeal to the individual and through individuals, groups, classes, and then the masses, as it gains credence necessary for recognition by the general public."

In 1956, through an unexpected gift of the sort that the sleeping Cayce would have understood, the A.R.E. was able to buy back Cayce's old hospital in Virginia Beach—known as the "white elephant"—reopen the vaults, and begin the analysis of some fifteen thousand readings, which apply more than ever today in their broad understanding of the nature of the universe. Today at the A.R.E., in a spacious new library, the files have been laboriously classified by categories—cancer, arthritis, homosexuality, reincarnation, Atlantis, etc., as recommended by the sleeping psychic. Doctors, archeologists, scientists, oceanographers, and cultists have all found their task made easier—for Cayce stressed simplicity. "Be able at a glance, from whatever phase of human experience, to have the information in the setting it was presented to that individual. Whether it pertain to marital relations, separating the silt from the gold, or adding to a body that vibration necessary to alter the very fires of nature within the individual itself."

Inherently, the value of Cayce seems to rest in the recognition that his glimpse into the divine purpose of the universe can be shared by all ready to count themselves an infinite part of an infinite universe. Cayce dealt with the mundane and the bizarre, the trivial and the universal. In his prophecies, he stressed a lesson of courage and resolution in adversity, so that to humanity at one with nature, even disaster was a manifestation of God's superior, if often veiled, purpose of everlasting life.

There was nothing accidental, nothing left to chance in the Creator's grand design; so Cayce believed, as he pictured reincarnation as an instrument, not an end in itself. "Each and every individual," he said once, "follows out that line of development in the present earth plane as it has received from the preceding conditions, and each grain of thought or condition is a consequence of other conditions created by self."